AF581038

HOT SEAT ★ HOT CITY

STEVE ADLER

HOT SEAT ★ HOT CITY

THE AUSTIN MAYOR'S STORY

This book is a memoir reflecting the author's present recollections of experiences over time. Its story and its words are the author's alone. Some details and characteristics may be changed, some events may be compressed, and some dialogue may be recreated. Some names and identifying characteristics of persons referenced in this book, as well as identifying places, have been changed to protect the privacy of the individuals and their families.

Published by Greenleaf Book Group Press
Austin, Texas
www.gbgpress.com

Distributed by Greenleaf Book Group

For ordering information or special discounts for bulk purchases, please contact Greenleaf Book Group at PO Box 91869, Austin, TX 78709, 512.891.6100.

Design and composition by Greenleaf Book Group and Mimi Bark
Cover design by George Stevens

Publisher's Cataloging-in-Publication data is available.

Print ISBN: 979-8-88645-545-8

eBook ISBN: 979-8-88645-546-5

To offset the number of trees consumed in the printing of our books, Greenleaf donates a portion of the proceeds from each printing to the Arbor Day Foundation. Greenleaf Book Group has replaced over 50,000 trees since 2007.

Printed in the United States of America on acid-free paper

26 27 28 29 30 10 9 8 7 6 5 4 3 2 1

First Edition

To the women who center my life—
Diane, Karen, Susan, and Sarah—and
to the magical city of Austin, Texas.

Praise from America's Mayors

(both sitting and former)

"Mayors occupy the rare nexus between democracy and accountability—fixing problems and managing crises alongside their neighbors. At their best, mayors lead as Steve Adler has—with intelligence, heart, and guts—taking us through our worst moments toward our best possibilities. A powerful memoir from one of America's greatest mayors, showing us where democracy still lives and thrives—in the local communities where our hopes and urgent work reside."

Mayor of Los Angeles

Eric Garcetti

Former U.S. Ambassador to India

"This is the book I wish I'd had when I became mayor. Steve Adler has written something rare—a political memoir that's actually useful. Every chapter teaches something new about crisis management, coalition building, or the art of making impossible decisions under brutal pressure. I recommend it to every mayor. You should read it twice."

Mayor of Columbia

Steve Benjamin

President, U.S. Conference of Mayors (2018–2019)

"Steve and I both know what it's like when a crisis doesn't wait for a committee meeting. This book shows the real work of city leadership—fast decisions, imperfect information, and the weight of knowing your call will shape thousands of lives. Required reading for anyone who thinks governing is easy."

Mayor of Chicago

Rahm Emanuel

Former U.S. Ambassador to Japan

(excerpted and condensed)

Mayor of San Jose

Sam Liccardo

"Adler was a 'mayor's mayor'—nobody is better equipped to show what it takes to solve the problems that Washington won't touch."

Mayor of Pittsburgh

Bill Peduto

"Adler's book reminds us that governing is both a science and an art."

Mayor of Baltimore
Stephanie Rawlings-Blake
"No backup. No playbook. No time for consensus. Just you and impossible choices. Adler delivers the leadership blueprint they don't teach anywhere else."

Mayor of New York City
Bill de Blasio
"Democracy doesn't die in Washington. It survives or fails in our cities. I watched Mayor Adler deliver where it mattered most."

Mayor of Chicago
Lori Lightfoot
"Raw and candid in ways few elected officials ever are. A must read for people who care about our democracy."

Mayor of New Orleans
Mitch Landrieu
"Steve's account [is written with] unflinching honesty. This is what it actually feels like to carry a city through the impossible."

Mayor of Kansas City, Missouri
Sly James
"This book pulls back the curtain on what it really means to lead a city—where decisions are immediate, consequences are personal, and there's nowhere to hide."

Mayor of Houston
Annise Parker
"Being a mayor is walking a high wire without a net—if you slip, people's lives will be irrevocably altered. Adler gets it."

Mayor of Portland, Oregon
Ted Wheeler
"I've been in that meeting. I've made that call. I've carried that same weight. Steve's account rings true."

Mayor of Corpus Christi
Nelda Martinez
"Mayors solve problems or people suffer. No excuses, no delays. Steve's book is honest about what that means."

Mayor of Richmond
Levar Stoney
"Steve's account captures the challenge of moving fast enough to matter but slow enough to bring people along."

Mayor of Louisville
Greg Fischer
"Great mayors need the head of a CEO and the heart of a social worker. Adler takes readers inside the mayor's office for a gripping, behind-the-scenes look."

Mayor of Mesa
John Giles
"This book should be on the desk of every mayor and elected official in America."

Mayor of Oklahoma City
David Holt
"Mayors are America's most effective leaders—optimistic, inclusive visionaries who are serious, pragmatic, and get things done. That is Mayor Adler."

Mayor of Nashville
John Cooper
"Mayor Adler provides a masterclass in the management of a modern American city. Great mayors deliver!"

Mayor of Lincoln
Leirion Gaylor Baird
"It's not easy, but important, to revisit what cities faced during Adler's tenure. His book offers a candid account."

Mayor of Boston
Marty Walsh
"Governing isn't about grand visions—it's about potholes, whether people can afford rent, if the bus shows up. Steve gets this."

Mayor of Oakland

Libby Schaaf

"With rare vulnerability and humor, Adler renews our hope that faith in democracy can be rebuilt where it matters most—on the ground, in our cities."

Mayor of Rochester Hills, Michigan

Bryan Barnett

"Steve's account captures what every mayor experienced: impossible decisions with incomplete information and no time to wait for the perfect guidance that never came."

Mayor of Reno

Hillary Schieve

"Adler's book is about building a great American city by bringing people together, rather than pulling them apart."

Mayor of Minneapolis

Betsy Hodges

"Not every mayor has to lead from inside the crucible of police violence and racial reckoning. This is an honest account from someone who had to make those decisions in real time."

Mayor of Miami

Francis Suarez

"Steve and I don't agree on everything politically, but we agree that mayors have to get things done regardless of party. His book shows what bipartisan leadership actually looks like."

Mayor of Shreveport

Adrian Perkins

"Adler writes with an earned clarity, forged not in perfection, but in effort, ingenuity, and a deep compassion for the people he serves. This is leadership."

Mayor of Denver

Michael Hancock

"Steve Adler offers an intimate look at how mayors stepped up to lead—with humility, leadership, and courage—often while a disorganized federal government failed to step in."

Mayor of Cleveland

Justin Bibb

"I saw Steve's leadership up close—how he handled tough challenges, stayed steady, and kept people at the center. This is the kind of leadership our cities need right now."

Mayor of Atlanta

Keisha Lance Bottoms

"Steve captures the tension and the creativity it takes to lead when others won't."

Mayor of Phoenix

Kate Gallego

"Among mayors, Steve was a leader we turned to for wisdom and partnership. This book shows why."

Mayor of Augusta, Georgia

Hardie Davis

"Steve Adler led Austin through extraordinary challenges. This book captures that reality with openness and candor. It's about governing in the moment—where decisions matter and cities shape people's lives every day."

Mayor of Orlando

Buddy Dyer

"I recognize every crisis Steve describes—the calls at all hours, the moments that test a city's resilience."

Mayor of San Antonio

Ron Nirenberg

"A mayor's heart pulses with every triumph and trauma of the people they serve. Steve brings the reader into the middle of Austin City Hall with clarity, humor, and a hard-earned perspective."

Mayor of Plano

Harry Larosiliere

"A fiercely honest and deeply human story about leadership, responsibility, and the communities where we live."

Mayor of Dayton

Nan Whaley

"The Midwest doesn't do hype. We show up, do the work, take the heat or the praise, and show up again. Steve governed the same way. This book won't make you love politics. It might make you respect what cities demand from the people who lead them."

Mayor of Oklahoma City

Mick Cornett

"Governing isn't about ideology. This book is honest about what it takes to deliver."

Mayor of Anaheim

Tom Tait

"Steve Adler brings a candid and personal perspective, offering a clear and engaging look at the realities of the role of mayors."

Mayor of Dallas

Mike Rawlings

"Steve's account is both a window into Austin's transformation and a mirror for anyone who's led a Texas city through explosive change."

Mayor of Atlanta

Shirley Franklin

"While Washington deadlocks, mayors solve problems. Steve Adler shows how cities become America's real laboratories of democracy."

Mayor of West Sacramento

Christopher Cabaldon

"Mayors govern in the real world while legislatures debate. Steve's book captures the gap between policymaking and problem-solving."

Mayor of Providence

Jorge Elorza

"Adler's book shares those lessons with the candor I remember. This is the experience of being mayor."

Mayor of Seattle

Jenny Durkan

"Mayors are on the front lines fighting for our future. Mayor Adler shows what it takes to govern when results and accountability are immediate."

Mayor of San Diego

Todd Gloria

"Steve's book cuts through the noise and takes on the real challenges mayors face when national dysfunction shows up locally."

Mayor of Salt Lake City

Ralph Becker

"Steve Adler has captured his life, and the life of a mayor, with unparalleled revelation and depth."

Mayor of Cincinnati

John Cranley

"Steve is a friend who taught me much when we served as mayor during the same years. The most important lesson: lead with compassion."

Mayor of Columbus

Andrew Ginther

"Steve's book shows how to honor the tension in moving a city forward without leaving anyone behind."

Mayor of El Paso

Ray Caballero

"A frank and compelling insight into the challenges Adler faced and the paths he chose."

Mayor of Chattanooga

Andy Berke

"Buy this book. Then run for office."

CONTENTS

FOREWORD

One of the most striking things about becoming a mayor is how lonely it can be. Of course, you are surrounded by others constantly, your days rich in community and teamwork. Yet you are also, by definition, the only person at a time to wear your title in your city—which often means fielding calls, facing decisions, and shouldering pressure that no one else can share.

For that very reason, one of the best sources of encouragement and insight for a mayor is the fellowship of others in the same role in other cities, men and women from around the country facing some version of the same civic and personal challenges that make your work so rewarding and demanding. While the job naturally calls on a mayor to spend nearly all of his or her time and attention close to home, many of the best find ways to engage their counterparts elsewhere and are better off for doing so. The community of American mayors is a group of leaders and doers that transcends geography, generation, and identity. Uniquely among groupings of high-profile American elected officials, it generally transcends ideology and party.

When I first got to know Steve Adler, we were mayors of very different cities—my Indiana hometown of South Bend and his Texas metropolis, Austin. Steve's state capital was booming, wrestling with growth and equity. My Midwestern community was fighting for its survival after decades of industrial loss. But as different as our communities might seem, they faced many of the same kinds of challenges, and we bonded over the values that guided our respective approaches to leading. We compared notes often, each seeing in our own work the stakes of meeting the challenges of the moment—on infrastructure, on public safety, on how to keep people safe in the streets while protecting their right to speak out.

A well-run city empowers its residents to thrive, making everyday life more livable by delivering basic services and creating the conditions for everyone to be better off. For mayors like us seeking to deliver on that vision, the day-to-day work entailed early morning meetings on housing or transportation mobility, late-night phone calls about floods or protests, public meetings that featured passionate and often heated speech, and a broad sense that whatever was animating national political debates and media coverage, at home we just had to deliver.

With today's political and policy landscape in a state of upheaval at best, toxicity at worst, I am convinced that our salvation will come from the local—from the style as well as the specifics of problem-solving that America's mayors bring to the challenges they face. That makes this a particularly important time to understand the lessons that cities and mayors have learned about what works.

In these pages, through Steve's faithful retelling and thoughtful analysis of his own experience, you will benefit from a rich account of one mayor's experience. This book will help you to sense what it's like to carry the responsibility of leading a city: the exhilaration of decisive wins in making a city better off, the anxiety of knowing that every decision will disappoint somebody, and the pain that you sometimes take on board as the living embodiment of your community in its most difficult times.

Steve's stories illustrate the nature of governing at the level closest to the people—far from the way it might look in *The Wire*, *The West Wing*, *Veep*, or *Parks and Recreation*, yet with flickers of resemblance to each of those more popular portrayals of power and public service.

This book is a timely contribution: a mayor's-eye view of civic leadership in a time of polarization and disruption, arriving at a moment when we would all benefit from the lessons that have been learned, sometimes the hard way, in the spaces where democratic ideals meet street-corner realities.

In my own work, I've argued that we can't fix what's broken in Washington unless we also strengthen the civic muscles that are built close to home: trust in neighbors, respect for facts, a willingness to listen before shouting. I hear those same lessons echoing through Steve's accounts of crises faced and choices made—from transportation policy fights to public safety dilemmas to the unglamorous but high-stakes details of city budgeting.

Steve's account is not just a chronicle of one mayor's time in office but an invitation to look differently at your own community—to see the hard choices behind a zoning map or a transit line, to appreciate the people who show up at town halls, and maybe to better envision how you yourself can approach important problems as a local leader.

Municipal government can't solve every problem, but it may represent the best venue for public policy problem-solving in America today. That's why it matters to understand what it really takes to manage that kind of office: the sleepless nights, the quiet satisfactions, the unshakable immediacy of facts that come with everyone's knowledge of how things are going on their own street.

If this book leaves you with a deeper respect for the work of city halls everywhere—for the mayors, council members, planners, police officers, fire fighters, transit workers, and neighbors who together shape the daily life of a community—then Steve's effort will have been a contribution not just to the story of his own city but to the civic spirit that fuels progress in our democracy.

PETE BUTTIGIEG,
former U.S. Secretary of Transportation
and Mayor of South Bend, Indiana

1

THE HOT SEAT

On March 2, 2018, Austin resident Anthony Stephan House picked up a package delivery on his porch. The package exploded, killing him instantly. He was thirty-nine and had an eight-year-old daughter. An African American man, House had graduated from Texas State University in 2017 with a degree in finance. He had been working as a project manager for Texas Quarries. He was going to be part of a mentoring program for young Black children in the summer. It's hard to understand why anyone would have wanted to harm him, never mind kill him.

Homicides were—and are—relatively rare in Austin. The police believed this one was an isolated incident—and a deeply strange one at that.

"We have no reason to believe this is anything beyond an isolated incident that took place at this residence," said Austin Police Chief

Brian Manley. "And no reason to believe this is in any way linked to a terrorist act."

He assured the public that the Austin Police were conducting a thorough investigation.

If homicides were rare, bombings were unheard of. A rumor circulated in the city that the explosive device might have been intended for a known drug dealer who lived in the area and who had been raided earlier that week. It wasn't a very good theory, but then, neither were any others.

A high-ranking police officer spoke to the press and walked them through what he saw as the possible explanations, including that Mr. House had accidentally blown himself up while building a bomb for his own purposes. That officer is a good man and someone I valued working with as mayor, and his theory was, in the most technical sense, a possibility. But many heard the suggestion as victim-blaming, and it fit the unfortunately familiar narrative of the police besmirching the reputation of a dead Black man. The police investigated the victim's finances.

His grief-stricken family understandably found this appalling.

The police continued their investigation, including into Mr. House, but it didn't turn up anything to help explain what had happened. The FBI, which is regularly consulted whenever someone dies in a bombing because of the possibility of terrorism or organized crime, concurred with the APD that this appeared to have been an isolated incident.

As mayor, I didn't hear much more about it, and our attention was on the following week when four hundred thousand people from all over the world would be descending upon Austin for the annual South by Southwest Music Festival & Conference (SXSW), which transforms our city into one big party town.

Then in the early hours of March 12, Draylen Mason, a seventeen-year-old high school student and promising musician, opened a package in his home that he had also found on his porch. It exploded, killing him and injuring his mother. Mason and his mother, like House, were African American.

Five hours later, seventy-five-year-old Esperanza Herrera was injured when she picked up a package on her mother's porch and it too exploded. It would take her several months and multiple surgeries to recover.

We—city leadership, law enforcement, the whole city—reached a terrifying conclusion: this was the work of a serial bomber.

There was an even darker possibility to consider. All the packages had exploded on Austin's East Side, which, because of past segregationist policies, has been historically the home to the largest concentration of residents of color in Austin.

The first man killed by the bomber was the stepson of one of Austin's most revered Black Baptist preachers, a strong indication for the police to conclude that he had not accidentally blown himself up.

Draylen Mason, the second young man to die, was the grandson of one of Austin's most respected and successful Black dentists. Both elders were friends and members of the same prominent African American fraternity. Both victims attended that preacher's church. Mr. Mason's grandmother was a founder of the Austin Area Urban League.

The Black community was reeling with the immediate and offhand suggestion by the police that Mr. House, the first victim, was himself a criminal. These bombings were bringing back memories of bombings by the Ku Klux Klan in Birmingham, Alabama.

The third victim, Ms. Herrera, was a Latina, a fact that broke the potential pattern of the victims all being Black, but it did not refute the possibility that the serial bomber was some kind of white supremacist terrorist.

More than five hundred agents of the FBI and the ATF (Bureau of Alcohol, Tobacco, Firearms and Explosives) swarmed into Austin to assist local police in the investigation. It was billed as the biggest investigation nationwide since the Boston marathon bombing in April 2013.

On the afternoon of March 12, because I was mayor, I found myself standing off to the side in a crowded command trailer belonging to the FBI and the ATF, just down the street from where the explosive package had injured Ms. Herrera.

The public and the media had been cordoned off several blocks away. The few federal agents who had been with us over the prior week were now joined in force by other agents, technicians, and specialists of all sorts. The street buzzed with activity.

The agents were focused and businesslike from the moment they arrived. It was clear that this was not their first rodeo, nor even the first time that they had worked together. Many of the agents were part of the team that handled the immediate aftermath of the Boston marathon bombing. This was our country's highest level of expertise on crimes related to explosives.

In the trailer, Austin Police Chief Brian Manley went through what we knew about the three bombs—two that day—that had exploded over the prior ten days. I had heard stories about jurisdictional battles when different law enforcement agencies arrive on a crisis scene at the same time and fight for control of the investigation. I saw none of this that afternoon in the trailer. It was a brief meeting. Austin's police chief and his staff commanded respect in that space. If there had been any question of the APD being superseded by the feds, it passed. The Austin Police would remain in charge, supported by the FBI and ATF.

The trailer emptied, and we all began to walk the two blocks toward the assembled phalanx of cameras, all kinds of media, and gathering members of the interested public.

In my three years as mayor up to that point, I had faced the media many times, but never when the city was in the midst of such a terrifying emergency in which the greater public was potentially at lethal risk. We had no remembered precedent.

The mayoral position doesn't come with an instruction book.

And even if there were an instruction book, I doubt there would be a section on how to deal with an anonymous serial bomber. As I walked, I wondered whether I should say something to the media and to the public. And if I did say something in such an obviously critical moment, what would be my best use of that opportunity?

I was still shaken from the two explosions in the recent hours and yet another death, but I knew I had to gather my thoughts. I had to figure out my appropriate role. At a moment like this, I thought, *What exactly is a mayor for?*

As I walked, Chris Combs, the FBI agent in charge, waited for me to catch up to him. He had fallen back from the lead group to walk beside me. We turned the corner and faced hundreds of cameras. Looking straight ahead as we walked, Agent Combs told me how much he liked Austin and enjoyed visiting our city. He congratulated me on being the mayor of such a special place.

Before I could think of how to respond, he said, in a casual manner, "You know, you're the mayor of Austin, and you can say anything you want, and I wouldn't presume to tell you what to say." He paused.

"In fact," he said, "you don't have to say anything if you don't want to."

He let that sink in.

"Your community is looking to you to figure out how they should be feeling and reacting right now. If you look scared and uncertain, then they will be scared and uncertain. If you show concern and determination, then that's what they'll feel, too. You should tell your city what you'd want to know . . .

"And by the way," he reminded me, "there's not a lot you can say about the actual investigation because there's not a lot you do know. And you don't know what you should and shouldn't say about anything you might think you know. Some things we choose to keep quiet about because that might help us identify the killer later on."

I stood at the podium confused and very conflicted about what I should say or if I should be saying anything at all. In that moment, I wasn't sure what to do with Agent Combs's advice. There were so many cameras and microphones. The lights were very bright and shining directly into my eyes. Because the bombings had attracted national media attention, out-of-town reporters were arriving. This was in addition to the dozens and dozens of media who had come to Austin because of SXSW.

I had to think quickly about what I needed to say.

I told my community of my shared concern for the victims and their families and of my anxiety and alarm, which they too had to be feeling. To help put them at some greater ease because it was helpful for me, I let them know of the increasing number of federal law enforcement agents and technicians arriving on the scene to work together with our own police force—like the cavalry coming over the hill.

I really didn't have the time to be very calculating. I talked about being reassured by how well and seamlessly everyone was working together, the determination and professionalism that all the first responders were exhibiting, and the confidence they instilled that they would solve these crimes and solve them quickly.

I promised that I would share with the community all the information I could, just as soon as I could.

If I sounded confident, it was because I *was* strangely confident. Hell, I was more than confident. I was mightily impressed with the expertise I had watched in the command center. I couldn't imagine there was anything else that could be done that wasn't happening, and that was what I wanted the public to know.

The community was on alert but stayed calm. Some wanted to know what they could be doing to help, while others wanted to know what they needed to do to better keep themselves and their families safe.

"If you see something suspicious, report it," I said. "If you see something odd or out of place, report it. If you're wondering if what you're seeing is worth reporting or not, report it.

"We should all ask ourselves to be attentive to what is going on around us and to really know our neighbors.

"If someone around us appears to need help or support, let's work to get them the help they might need," I said.

Anxiety continued to grow in the African American community about whether the bomber was targeting them. Our police department indicated they were no longer investigating the victims and were keeping open the possibility that we were dealing with hate crimes.

In the ensuing days, I was out in the community as much as possible to answer questions as best I could and to make clear that I shared the community's fear and anxiety but also to share with them that the law enforcement response was without limit and impressive.

The combined agencies collected and fed a massive amount of data into a large computer in hopes of finding patterns and paths. They found hardware store receipts and watched parking lot videos along with Ring videos of cars that passed near the incidents.

Despite the collected evidence, there seemed to be little progress in apprehending a suspect. In many of these kinds of cases, I learned, a serial killer just stops and disappears. In these cases, the community never has the closure or the sense of certainty that the killings might not start up again.

That would be horrible, I thought.

I didn't want the bomber to get away. A part of me was hoping that our serial bomber would act again in a way that didn't hurt additional people but would provide clues leading to capture.

We were trying everything to catch him. On the morning of March 18, our police chief and the FBI agent in charge held a press conference to ask the serial killer to contact us.

Later that evening, he did, but not in the way we wanted. Two men, ages twenty-two and twenty-three, detonated a tripwire while walking their bikes down a sidewalk and suffered serious but not life-threatening injuries. This occurred in the more prosperous southwest residential area of Austin. The victims were random, and they were white. The bomb was left under a sign that read "Drive Like Your Kids Live Here."

This new attack was concerning because the authorities weren't positive that it was planted by the bomber we were chasing. It could have been the work of a copycat. If it was the same bomber, this new attack suggested that he was growing more sophisticated.

Because of the type of device and its location, the police and FBI began to see the bomber as someone most likely acting randomly.

The tension in the city was growing. It's one thing to avoid package bombs—just don't pick up packages. But a tripwire bomb is a different matter. No longer did parents think they could protect their children by prohibiting them from touching strange boxes delivered in the mail. How do you protect your children from a nearly invisible tripwire stretched across the sidewalk on the way to school?

Our community was beginning to fray, and I could feel it. We had moved past general concern about something that seemed to be happening far away, because now it felt like everyone's child was at risk.

The bomber then, finally, made a mistake. The materials used in this last explosion, including the sign the bomber had placed to conceal the weapon, provided clues about the store or stores where he had bought the materials to produce the bombs. Law enforcement reviewed thousands of receipts from businesses in the greater Austin area, looking for suspicious or consistent purchases—and began finding some.

We were in a race. Could the community hold it together long enough to catch the bomber? I thought we would. I certainly hoped we would. There were now almost one thousand public safety agents, officers, and professionals on the ground working this case. They were collecting evidence and shipping it to the national command center in Washington, D.C. The pieces to the puzzle were coming together.

I addressed the media in the immediate aftermath of the tripwire explosion. I told them that I was feeling confident and that we would catch the bomber.

The next morning, I saw both the thirst for and the power of words from a mayor. The banner headline in the *Austin American-Statesman* read, with quotation marks, "We Are Going To Stop It." Those were my words, now captured in bold, four-inch type plastered across the front page of the newspaper. I couldn't get out of my head the image of President George W. Bush standing on the aircraft carrier with the premature banner "Mission Accomplished" as his backdrop. Not only had I conveyed my confidence in the assembled army of law enforcement investigators, but I was personally guaranteeing their success.

I had made a promise, and I didn't know if I would be able to keep it.

The big break in the case happened on March 20, just a couple of days following the tripwire explosion, when a bomb went off in a FedEx facility in Schertz, Texas, between Austin and San Antonio, injuring an employee. The package had been marked for an address in Austin.

FedEx in the area went on alert, and it worked with law enforcement to discover and defuse another explosive, this one at a FedEx sorting facility in southeast Austin. Tracing both packages, agents found that the bomber had sent them from the same FedEx storefront in Sunset Valley, immediately south of Austin.

And they had him on video, wearing a disguise.

Law enforcement also had footage of the bomber's vehicle, a 2002 Ford Ranger with no license plate. Because investigators obtained a sketch of the suspect from a witness, they knew who they were looking for. They reviewed surveillance footage from area stores where they found suspicious purchases, and they got a match at a Home Depot in Round Rock, just north of Austin, where video showed the suspected bomber buying the sign he'd used to cover the tripwire as well as materials that could make another explosive.

The police identified the suspect as a certain twenty-three-year-old Caucasian, who lived in Pflugerville, Texas, outside of Austin.

The coordinated task force obtained a search warrant for his home and his IP address. They executed the latter immediately and found that he had used Google to search for local shipping information.

The police, acting on the side of safety, declined to execute the warrant on the bomber's home that night. It was dark, and there were no guarantees that the suspect hadn't booby-trapped the approach and entrance to his home. The hope was that he would leave his home on his own, making his capture a little less risky for the officers and the bomber's neighbors. Law enforcement personnel took positions around his home, and we all settled in to wait.

When serving warrants at a potentially booby-trapped home, it is common practice to have an ambulance standing by. Because the suspect's home was in the nearby city of Pflugerville and not in Austin's Travis County, the emergency medical services team with the Travis County EMS didn't have jurisdiction in this area, so the call went out to the emergency service provider in Pflugerville to position an emergency vehicle a couple of blocks away from the residence.

Unfortunately, the request was either miscommunicated or misunderstood. The EMTs didn't park their ambulance two blocks away. Because they thought they were responding to an emergency call at the suspect's home, they parked the ambulance right in front of it. The officers surveilling the home watched with trepidation as the ambulance drove right up to the house and an EMT got out and walked up the sidewalk to the front door.

He was very lucky. Nothing exploded. The EMT knocked on the front door and asked for the suspect by name and whether the suspect needed help. The suspect's roommate answered and told the unspeakably lucky tech that the bomber wasn't home.

Police had obtained a warrant to track the bomber's cell phone, and soon he made a call. He and his truck were located in a hotel parking lot not too far away. Law enforcement descended on the parking lot, but the command center directed them not to approach the truck but rather to hold position—and for a very good reason. Among the bomber's purchases at the Home Depot in Round Rock was a large quantity of nails. It seemed he was planning to build a shrapnel bomb; he might already have built it. The officers on the scene were ordered to wait until the protective armor arrived from Austin, about twenty minutes away.

Before the armor arrived, however, the bomber started his truck, left the hotel parking lot, and headed for the entrance ramp to the nearby highway. The assembled officers wanted to stop him from getting onto the highway, where the danger to the public would have been intolerable. The officers on the scene asked permission to stop him en route, within the first few blocks, and the command center agreed. The officers drove their van into action without the protective armor, which had not yet arrived.

Officers drove a police van in front of the bomber's truck, and other law enforcement vehicles lined up behind him. When the front van stopped at a traffic light, the suspect stopped behind it, and the trailing police car rammed the suspect's vehicle.

Despite knowing of the risk of an explosion, the officers of the Austin Police force charged the suspect's vehicle. The plan was for an officer to reach the driver's side window first, so that he might disable the bomber and prevent him from detonating any bomb.

In the scramble to reach the truck, the plan went awry. The first officer to reach the bomber's truck was on the passenger side.

The police concerns proved correct. The bomber did have a bomb in the truck.

And he detonated it.

It was sheer luck that the officer who first arrived at the passenger door wasn't badly hurt, never mind killed. The blast knocked the officer back from the truck as the shrapnel flew around him. Most of the force of the blast exploded out of the driver's side window. An officer getting to the driver's side first, as planned, would have been killed or severely injured. Instead, the officers who had charged without armor at a vehicle were shaken but unhurt.

The bomber was dead. Several officers fired a round of bullets into the vehicle so there'd be no doubt and no second explosion.

In the press conference held along the highway a few blocks away, the public safety officer leadership, exhausted and proud, reported to the community. I earnestly and thankfully cheered them on. As mayor, a big part of my job was just to stay out of their way. The credit was theirs for the rapid end to our communal nightmare. Mine had been the eyes and ears for the residents of Austin who couldn't be in the command trailers or listening on the phone while reports were being made. It fell to me to share widely what I knew that could be shared. We all had cause to be very proud of Austin and Central Texas for pulling together and for keeping it together.

I went to sleep in the very wee hours after the bomber had been stopped and the press conference questions had been handled. I slept for a very long time.

The following morning, again with a four-inch, bold type, banner headline on the front page, the *Austin American-Statesman* quoted me from the press conference: "We Got It Done."

I remain incredibly appreciative that law enforcement protected our community and made good on my unintended guarantee. The Austin Police did their job. They also deserved medals.

It's probably true that a lot of the time, the job of mayor is technocratic and not very exciting. The mayor goes to council meetings and does the small and mundane tasks that keep a city running, even if most people don't know what they are. The mayor often sits at a desk talking to constituents about their problems and attends neighborhood meetings, parties, and store openings.

Being mayor is also a 24/7 job one loses sleep over. If you are the mayor, as I was in Austin, Texas, from 2015 until 2023, you must be prepared for whatever comes your way. You find yourself thrust into critical situations that are hard and frequently have no clear, correct answer. As the person who has to make decisions that impact an entire city, you hope and believe you make the right calls, and you fear making the wrong ones.

A little over two years after the bomber, as you'll read in Chapter 13, I would overrule that same police chief and not impose a citywide evening curfew during the George Floyd demonstrations. This was among the very hard decisions I had to make during my two terms as mayor. I chose not to order a curfew because I didn't think the risk of unrest warranted it. The greater risk, I thought, was creating a situation that would invite more conflict by imposing restrictions that assumed significant crowd violence would occur otherwise. Most importantly, I saw the decision not to impose such a measure as a clear and important affirmation to the community of our values and identity as residents of Austin. In our city, your right to protest is celebrated and protected under the First Amendment. Government will only impose limits when a clear and present danger presents itself.

Was Austin in a precarious place as those demonstrations were first happening? Yes. Was I worried and concerned about violence breaking out on our streets? Yes. Were we safe?

That was the question we all had, but I had to answer it.

Just like with the bomber, I knew that many would be watching what I was doing and would use that as a sign indicating how they should be feeling.

I was very fortunate that my decision not to impose a curfew proved correct.

There was no headline that said "Mayor's Decision on Curfew Was Correct!" But I knew that I had dodged the headline that might otherwise have run: "Mayor Ignores Warning to Impose Curfew That Might Have Kept Us Safe."

Being mayor means living a life in which every decision you make will be hated by some people, many of whom will broadcast their displeasure very publicly. In a progressive city like Austin in a very conservative state like Texas, it means fighting on the front lines of the political and partisan divide that has gripped our country in recent times.

Of the many decisions I had to make during my years in office, most worked out. There's nothing more gratifying than the appreciation of your neighbors. But not all decisions proved correct; a few left me the recipient of well-founded criticism, and others centered me as the target of partisan right-wing attacks.

There were many difficult situations and policy dilemmas to navigate. Some were high octane and concerned immediate threats to public safety—like responding to the bomber and deciding on the curfew. Others involved the near impossible balancing of competing needs—such as building more housing supply at the risk of preserving the unique character of beloved neighborhoods (Chapter 8); employing COVID masks, vaccines, and stay-at-home orders that threatened the economy (Chapter 9); addressing homelessness, with the anxiety that arises from increased visibility (Chapters 10 and 11); allowing new economic innovation without abdicating government's responsibility to keep us safe (Chapter 12); wrestling with what kind of policing culture would keep us both safe and true to our values (Chapter 13); understanding the role of race, racism, and DEI in the context of ensuring access and opportunity for all people (Chapter 14); and caring for our immigrant neighbors when they were being demonized (Chapter 15).

And dealing with each in a time of uncertain, disputed, and manipulated truth and the political use of the immense power of fear (Chapters 16 and 17).

These moments and others are what made being mayor of a magical city with incredible residents, a progressive city in a predominantly right-wing state, so challenging, fulfilling, and fascinating. There is much to be proud of, and in Chapter 7, I lay out some of what we accomplished during my time in office.

I had a long journey to public office, growing up on the east coast (Chapter 2); becoming a first-generation college student at Princeton University (Chapter 3); beginning my career as an attorney and finding a home in Austin (Chapter 5); and ending up surprising everyone, including myself, by successfully running for mayor (Chapter 6).

Throughout, I carried with me a reverence for the preciousness of time that came from becoming responsible for myself at an early age (Chapter 4).

This book presents a behind-the-curtain look at and sheds light on the lessons, experiences, policy discussions, anecdotes, and controversies that were my path and my much-scrutinized life as mayor of one of the top-performing U.S. cities.

As you will see.

Let's begin as the journey began.

2

GROWING UP ON THE EAST COAST

When you grow up in the two-hundred-mile stretch between Washington, D.C., and New York City, like I did, you feel like you're in the center of the world. The local news is also the national and international news. Everybody and everything seem close, and no person and no outcome seem out of reach. I grew up thinking anything was possible and accessible, way beyond what I know is realistic. I pretty much still feel that way.

I was born in Washington, D.C., in 1956, and I grew up in the metro area. Dwight Eisenhower was president. Elvis made his national debut. "In God We Trust" became our national motto. When I was three, we moved a couple of minutes north of the D.C. line to Kensington, Maryland, and I went to school there in Montgomery County.

I was raised with much love, enjoyed a pretty happy childhood, and had a lot of fun growing up.

D.C. felt like the focus of not only national but global politics. And so maybe it isn't surprising I caught the political bug early. My political career began when I was elected president of my fourth-grade class on a platform in which I called for the school lunches to be bigger and for the school year to be shorter. These were my campaign promises.

I tried to make these changes. I *really* tried.

I petitioned (wrote a letter to) the school superintendent outlining my demands. The school district had over 100,000 kids in it. What was the chance that he would get it and respond?

But I had a mandate and the confidence of a newly elected official.

One day, the elementary school principal called me down to his office. I wasn't sure why. When I got there, he was holding the letter I had sent to his boss. He gave me a stern lecture about following the chain of command.

"If you ever have a problem with the school, you can always bring it to me," he said.

He handed me a reply letter from the superintendent. *Yes!* The letter said that a lot of food gets thrown away, and if I was still hungry after I ate my meal, I should reach out to the principal and the school lunch personnel. *No!*

"You can always get a little bit more," he wrote.

I was angry because the superintendent made it sound like I was asking for myself and not my class. He then explained that he couldn't shorten the school year because that was set by the state legislature.

My first attempt at politics turned out to be a failure.

When I was in sixth grade, I was elected to the school's highest elected office: captain of the school safety patrol. I ran home and excitedly told my parents about my electoral success. A party was about to start—I was surprised that my parents had found out about my news so quickly. But then, I learned the party was to announce to my brother, my sister, and me that we were leaving Washington, D.C., and moving to New York City.

My father, Lee, was a film editor for CBS in Washington, D.C., and during my childhood, I remember sitting on the CBS newsroom floor watching Walter Cronkite, Eric Sevareid, Dan Rather, Roger Mudd, and the Kalb brothers. I grew up idolizing these network news giants. My father passed his interest in journalism on to me and my daughter Sarah.

My father had been asked to help launch *60 Minutes*, a brand-new CBS show. It was a huge achievement for him. I, of course, immediately melted down at the prospect of having to leave my friends and abandon my new electoral safety patrol responsibilities.

My father did not take the job. I'll never know for sure whether he stayed in Kensington because he decided that moving would unsettle the lives of us kids growing up, but I've always felt sad and responsible for my father not taking the chance to help create the new show.

I also saw firsthand how a child's self-perception, something their parents can help instill, can have a huge impact on how their life ends up. I grew up in my home thinking I was a leader.

For six years, I played Little League Baseball for the Falcons. At age sixteen, I got a letter from one of the chief scouts with the Pittsburgh Pirates inviting me to a free-agent tryout camp in the D.C. area. Wearing my Little League purple T-shirt, I stood out like a sore thumb among the uniformed high school, college, and semi-pro recruits. They looked like real baseball players.

The scouts and coaches debated whether I was too young to participate when they saw me. They decided to let me try out. I became the event's mascot.

I got one at-bat, and my quarter swing popped a single over first base. The coach signaled me to steal second. I was thrown out when I slid and came to rest a comically short two feet from the bag. And that pretty much ended my professional baseball career at sixteen.

In high school, I played football and baseball without distinction. And I began wrestling because it was a sport where most of us tenth graders were beginners together.

In the first match, the coach moved me up to varsity to face Kelly Ward—a future NCAA wrestling champion and Hall of Famer—not because I knew what I was doing but because he wanted to sit our team captain and avoid a loss on his record that early in the season.

Ward knew of my lack of experience, and he was determined to set the state record for fastest pin. Before the opening whistle had finished sounding, I was on my back. He tried to work too fast, and in his rush, I managed to fight him off. I lost badly, but I avoided the record pin.

Afterward, my father was the only one left in the stands.

"It's exciting for you to be wrestling in a varsity match," he said. "It's good to see you learning a new sport."

He made me feel proud. And then he said, "But you went into that match trying hard not to get pinned. I will always wonder what might have happened if at the starting whistle, you had been thinking you were going to pin him."

That stuck with me. I always ask myself that question. A criticism I received as mayor is that I and my council frequently tried to achieve what might realistically have been just beyond our grasp. You'll read about some of those efforts in later chapters. Sometimes my council and I got pinned, and sometimes we were able to surprise. Other times we opened doors that councils behind us have walked through. But I have never wondered "what if?"

I wrestled each year of high school and earned the coveted reverse letter—red, not blue—to wear on my jacket for lettering in the sport all three years.

I held leadership positions in high school: president of the local

Montgomery County Region of student councils and leadership council of the Maryland Association of Student Councils.

When Gerald Ford became president, he wanted to show how different he was from Richard Nixon, who, in his imperial presidency, had not made himself available to many. President Ford spent his first one hundred days meeting with every special interest group he could think of. He met with farmers, business leaders, and many others, including student groups. I represented the National Association of Student Councils in a meeting with President Ford, and I made my first entrance into the White House, a building I had driven by my entire life.

I walked up to the black wrought iron gate and ceremoniously announced that I had an appointment with the president. The guard at the White House checked the list.

"You're early," he said. "You'll have to wait."

I stood waiting in line with the tourists, wanting them to know that I was about to meet with the president.

Finally, I went into the White House. A group of student leaders and I were first briefed in the Roosevelt Room. Then the president's aides ushered us into the Cabinet Room, where we sat around the large conference table. I exchanged excited glances with the likes of the highest-ranking Boy and Girl Scouts in the country and the national presidents of the Future Homemakers of America, the Future Farmers of America, and the 4-H clubs.

I felt very sophisticated wearing a brand-new sports coat my mother had purchased just for the occasion. If you look at the photo of me, you'll see that the patterned jacket was kind of garish, something I wasn't aware of at the time. I didn't own a suit. I didn't appreciate the difference between a suit and a sports coat. To me, wearing either meant you were dressing up.

When President Ford came in, we all stood up. He walked in from the nearly adjoining Oval Office, looked at us for a second, and grimaced because he had left his notes on his desk. Immediately, I thought of Chevy Chase on *Saturday Night Live*, the way he impersonated President Ford when he stumbled. I almost started laughing, which would not have been the right response to meeting with the president in the Cabinet Room of the White House.

We all sat down.

"I'm going to do this the way I do this at home with [my children] Susan and Steve," Ford said. "I'm going to go around the table and have an individual conversation with each of you."

What surprised me was how conservative most of the students in that room were. Many of the students suggested to him that he speak more about religion.

"The students have lost their way and need more moral grounding," one of them said.

When it was my turn, I talked to him about the need for increased internships, summer jobs, and apprentice programs for kids, and I urged him to legalize marijuana.

The room became silent, almost to the point of becoming uncomfortable.

Ford's laughter broke the silence.

"When I'm at the dinner table with my kids," the president said, "that is actually something that often comes up."

In that short meeting, I found him to be warm and engaging, sharp, and well-informed.

Walking into the White House that first time was surreal. Once inside, I saw real people at all levels trying their best to do their jobs well. I returned to the White House about a dozen times while mayor, mostly to meet with staff while advocating for my community. My wife Diane and I were invited to the holiday parties. Visiting never became less of an honor, and with each successive visit, the experience became more familiar. Our national leadership and their teams, sometimes especially smart and skilled and sometimes incredibly lucky, are no more or less than regular people wrestling with issues—just as we do at city hall.

Growing out of my student council work in high school, I taught leadership skills to high school kids at summer camp workshops. A school district in San Antonio invited me to speak and flew me down to Texas, my first foray into that state.

My family expected I would go to the University of Maryland after high school. My father never earned more than $17,000 a year working for CBS. It was a middle-class wage back then, but he let me know he wasn't in a position to pay for college beyond the in-state resident cost of Maryland's public university.

My brother Reid, who was two years ahead of me, was already attending Maryland. He was the first in our family to go to college. He is really smart and scored an eight hundred on his math college entrance exam, the SATs, an incredibly rare thing to do, especially at that time. I'm sure he could have gotten into higher-ranked colleges, but with that in-state residency status, he went to the University of Maryland down the road because it was all my father said he could afford.

I didn't score an eight hundred on my SATs, but I still did very well. My brother put his arm around my shoulder.

"I'm sorry," he joked, "for not helping you get better prepared." He said it in a competitive brotherly way. "There's a whole world out there . . . You should apply to other schools than just Maryland."

Which I did. When I got the letter of admission that I had been accepted into Princeton University, I was elated but also frustrated and sad, because the partial scholarship Princeton offered wasn't nearly enough to get the cost down to what my father said we could afford.

I was also admitted to both the Naval Academy and West Point. That was a huge honor. Those schools were free, and I was close to enrolling in one when Princeton called to say that I had been awarded an additional scholarship.

The Beinecke Scholarship was funded by the Sperry Fund. The Sperry & Hutchinson Company made the green stamps that you licked and pasted into a redemption book after getting them at the supermarket checkout. You could then exchange a completed book for gifts from the Sperry & Hutchinson catalogue. They also apparently gave out college scholarships, and I was lucky enough to get one. My financial aid package now was big enough for me to attend Princeton. Little did I know that those years of my mother licking and pasting green stamps into redemption books would result in me earning the biggest prize of all.

When I reflect on my admission to Princeton, I recognize that I was lucky. Sure, I was smart and worked hard, but there were lots of people not at Princeton who were smarter and worked harder than me. My family didn't have the money for me to go without help, and even the thought of going to an Ivy League school was such an unreal and unfamiliar scenario that I barely knew how to apply. In Chapter 14, you'll read my thoughts on access and opportunity. While we would like to think our society rewards merit, I'll show you why being successful is often more about being given a chance.

3

IN THE IVY LEAGUE

These are the things that change your life, and getting into Princeton changed mine in more ways than one. The scholarship I was awarded required that I work part-time, which I had intended to do anyway, and that I participate in a varsity sport.

The last part would be tricky. I had played baseball, football, and wrestled in high school. Wrestling might have been the best choice, but I had injured my knee in my senior year, so it didn't seem like my best option.

Early in the fall of my freshman year at Princeton, I was sitting in the campus pub with five other semi-athletic-looking guys. There was an empty pitcher of beer on the table. We were each waiting for another of us to refill it when an elderly guy came walking over with four pitchers of beer, two in each hand. He asked if he could sit down.

Anyone arriving with free beer was more than welcome.

"Join us," we said.

His name was Stan Sieja. He was in his early seventies, and he was the coach of the Princeton fencing team. He obviously didn't have much of a budget for recruiting, thus his focus on incoming freshmen in the pub. After he sat down and visited a little, he asked us all to become members of his team.

"I guarantee that if you come out for the fencing team, you will win an AAU fencing medal by the time you graduate."

"I don't know fencing," I said. "I'm thinking of trying out for the baseball team and fall practice is about to start."

"Come work out with the fencing team," he said, "and I'll get your legs in shape, and when baseball starts, you'll be ahead of where you would have been otherwise."

That sounded like a reasonable idea to me, so I showed up at a fencing team practice. We did a lot of leg work, which meant a lot of lunging, and I was getting stronger.

I felt welcomed in the Jadwin gym fencing room, and the team spirit enveloped me. The sport was new and kind of exotic and romantic.

I'm having a lot of fun, I had to admit.

Still, I was going to try to walk on to the baseball team because at least I was familiar with that sport, and I needed to be on a varsity team to preserve my scholarship. The Friday before the first baseball practice was to be my last day attending Coach Sieja's fencing practice.

"Thanks for letting me work out with your team," I said before I left.

"I wish you luck playing baseball," he said.

He went back to training his fencers without missing a beat. As I was walking home, I was surprised and a little disappointed that he hadn't tried to convince me to stay.

At four o'clock very early the next morning, my dormitory room phone rang. It was Coach Sieja.

"I'm heading to a fencing tournament at the New York Athletic Club in Manhattan, an hour or two up the road," he said. "I was going to go with one of the seniors on the team who offered to help me carry the equipment, but he just called in sick. I want to know, will you help me? After all, I've let you work out with my team for the last couple months."

I couldn't very well say no. Thirty minutes later, he picked me up, and we headed off to New York City.

Coach Sieja was wonderful. He was an incredibly engaging storyteller, and he told me the histories of competitions and the stories of the men who had been involved in fencing at Princeton.

We arrived at the New York Athletic Club. The tournament, I was informed, was unclassified. Like a maiden horse race, you couldn't enter if you had won or placed in another AAU tournament. All the contestants would be relatively inexperienced.

The equipment I was carrying, as it turned out, was equipment intended for . . . me. I had been registered for the tournament a month earlier.

"You can be mad at me and just drive back to Princeton," Coach said. "But what the heck, since you are already here, wouldn't it be fun to see what you can do?"

I placed third in that tournament and won a bronze medal, which I still have. I didn't have to wait until I graduated to win a medal. Incredibly, I won one in my first tournament.

I drove back with Coach Sieja to Princeton that night from New York City, and during the entire ride back, we talked about a lot of things, but he never once mentioned the tournament, my medal, or his team.

When we pulled up to my dormitory, I was sure he was going to give me a speech about why I should join the fencing team, but he didn't do that.

I got out of the car.

"You know," he said, "I don't know how good a baseball player you are. For all I know, you're going to be one of those who will play for a year and then go on to professional ball, but if you work out with me for four years, by the time you graduate, you'll be a nationally competitive fencer. But maybe your prospects are better as a baseball player. I just don't know."

On Monday, I had a decision to make. It really wasn't that hard. I knew I'd make the fencing team and keep my scholarship. That afternoon, buoyed by the excitement that comes from taking risks and trying new things, I returned to fencing practice. Coach Sieja barely acknowledged my presence when I walked in. Somehow, he knew I would show up.

The highlight of my sophomore year was our match against Cornell. The year before, Princeton had lost to Cornell, its only Ivy League loss, a loss that cost us sole possession of the Ivy League championship. This year was to be payback.

We went up to Ithaca, and the night before the match, we went out to dinner. Everybody was nervous. No one discussed anything but the match at dinner. This team was excited but very uptight, and you want to be loose before a significant match.

After dinner, Coach Sieja didn't take us back to the motel where we were staying. Instead, he took us into downtown Ithaca to a discotheque called The Gazebo Lounge. This was 1976, and disco was at its peak.

We walked in, and we all ordered a drink. We sat there, and a few of the team members got up to ask girls to dance. Most of us were too shy and intimidated to do that in a strange place—or any place.

Coach Sieja walked across the dance floor straight to the most beautiful woman in the entire bar. He whispered something in her ear, and she smiled, and they began to dance. Our team erupted into laughter. We were dumbfounded and amazed that the prettiest girl in the place would be dancing with our short, bald, elderly coach.

He danced her over to our table and then stopped. He clutched his chest near his heart and said to her, "I really appreciate you dancing with me, but I can't keep going."

This feigned exhaustion came from a man who was actively fencing with his team several hours a day. He grabbed one of the team's weapon leaders and pulled him up, and he said, "But *he* can dance for me."

Just like that, the senior fencer found himself dancing with a very pretty girl.

Coach then told each of us that if we wanted to fence the next day, we had to ask someone to dance.

"The girl doesn't have to say yes," he said, "but you have to ask."

Coach gave the captain of the team enough money for all of us to have a second drink and money to buy a drink for the girl we were dancing with. He told the captain to have the team home by midnight, and then he left.

We stayed while everyone asked someone to dance so they could fence the next day.

We were a small army that had invaded this disco. Everyone was curious about us, and the girls were trying to figure out who we were. I'm not sure I would have gotten up and asked one to dance but for the assignment that came from the coach. I was young and shy and needed a little prodding. Most of the team members did.

I danced. I had my second drink.

The next morning as we stretched, getting ready to fence, we told stories about the night before. We were ribbing each other about how we looked and talking about our dancing abilities, the girls we were dancing with, and what they were like.

It was the most relaxed our team had ever been going into an important meet, and we killed Cornell.

Coach Sieja, I have to say, was a pretty darn good coach. A few months later, he would win the NCAA Fencing Coach of the Year award. Funny how most of what I learned from Coach, most of what made him so good, had nothing to do with fencing.

I never had the form that the more experienced fencers had. I was able to keep a match going until I could figure out the weakness of my opponent. Five points win a match, and in my last year fencing, about half of my matches went 4 to 4, which meant that I really wasn't any better than many of my opponents. But somehow, I just seemed to know what to do to win that fifth and match-winning point. I had a ridiculously high number of 4 to 4 matches, twenty to be exact, and I ended up winning all but two of them. That measure of patience, study, and strategy has stayed with me since. All too often, as mayor, as you'll read later, I was back in that "4 to 4" place angling to win what French fencers call that last point, *la belle touché.*

Just as Coach Sieja had promised, I became nationally competitive. My senior year record was thirty-seven wins and nine losses. I was named All-Ivy, and at the season's end, I was ranked fourteenth in the entire country.

I was the co-captain of the fencing team along with Bill McKee, who was an All-American foil fencer. My roommate Lee Shelley was on two United States Olympic épée teams and is enshrined in the U.S. Fencing Hall of Fame. My other roommate was Don Anthony, a sabre fencer like me and later a United States national team member and president of the International Fencing Federation. He is now the head fencing coach at Ohio State.

When I came to Princeton in the fall of 1974, there were several significant political issues swirling around the university. Students were taken with the issue of Apartheid in South Africa. Most joined in the boycotts of companies with garment factories there.

I wasn't involved with any of those issues. My freshman year, I was a rube, and my focus was on fencing, which meant that every day I would go to classes and would then head down to the gym. I couldn't stay away from student government completely, though, and I served as the student government parliamentarian. Grades were not my main focus.

I had to make money to pay the part of the tuition that was my responsibility. It turned out to be fun to work part-time at the campus pub making pizzas, but my most disciplined study time happened while at my job monitoring the library's reserve reading room.

My first year was full of pre-med courses because my father wanted me to be my own boss and thought being a doctor was the best way to become that. I didn't enjoy those classes much, and my grades were not all that stellar in science, but I was fascinated and energized, and I did very well in my history, economics, and political science classes. These were the subjects about how people interacted and communities were built. This was the core curriculum in Princeton's prestigious Woodrow Wilson School for Public and International Affairs. (Recently, that president's name was dropped because of his troublesome history with race.)

I was accepted into and graduated from that program.

At the end of my sophomore year, I joined Cottage—an all-male club where you eat your meals. It's one of Princeton's versions of a fraternity, but few members live in these houses. With house parties and activities, though, your eating club still becomes the center of your social life.

Many of the Cottage members had gone to private and often boarding high schools. I didn't know people who had gone to such private schools, so this was very different from anything I had ever experienced.

Part of my goal in going to Princeton was to put myself in a strange environment where I could learn new things. When I got to Princeton, the university was my vision of what a country club looked like, even though I had never been to a country club. Cottage presented that same challenge and opportunity. The club was a bastion of Southern aristocracy, as best as I could tell, and was part of a very different lifestyle than my family had known.

Cottage held a father–son dinner every year. My father planned to participate, and I became increasingly anxious about his coming as the date approached.

Sitting at each dining hall table for that dinner were four or five students, their fathers, and a couple members of the faculty. My father didn't have the business success or social standing of the other fathers, and he didn't have the education that they had. He also wasn't dressed as sharply as the other fathers, all of whom had tailored suits and starched white shirts. My father's suit didn't fit him that well, and he was wearing a blue shirt. Maybe I was the only one who noticed or cared. But I did.

I look at myself now with shame about how I was feeling. I doubted my father.

Night came, and we all sat down to dinner. At my table, the students were joined by Bill Bowen, the president of Princeton, and by the head of the Classics Department.

We were a table full of guys, and the talk turned toward current sports. It didn't take long before the fathers were talking about their childhood sports memories, and then the discussion worked even further back in time to the treatment of sports in ancient Greek and Roman literature. The only people learned enough to still be actively participating in the conversation were the senior faculty member of the Classics Department—and my father.

I felt such incredible pride. And I was ashamed that I had doubted him in this environment. I should have known better.

At Princeton, I got to see how the "other half" lived. Honestly, I came to Princeton and fantasized about and wanted to live that life, too. Princeton taught me a lot and exposed me to new situations and cultures. It demystified things I didn't know. I became part of a network that gave me advantages and further opportunities. Most importantly, seeing my father on campus and in my club also made me realize that it would never really be about the spaces, only what I brought to them.

I went to fencing tournaments in New York, and I would go as often as I could to the theater to see Broadway plays. After the first act, there was sometimes the opportunity to be let into the theater to fill the empty seats, and I took advantage of this access. I loved the theater.

I spent time in Times Square, which was a rough part of town back then. You had to be careful, but there on Broadway was the first arcade where I was able to play computer games. For hours, I played *Gun Fight*, *Sea Wolf*, and *Space Invaders*.

My senior year thesis was on nationalism. I was intrigued by the power and the dangers of a nationalistic political appeal.

In 1978, I interviewed Robert Bourassa for my thesis. He was the premier of Quebec from 1970 to 1976, and listening to him was fascinating. Bourassa lost his premiership to nationalistic forces calling for the separation of Quebec from the rest of Canada. My paper was about whether and how he could ever win reelection for premier in the face of such a populist, separatist movement. I wrote about trying to create the same emotional power and appeal behind a more institutionalist and pro-federalist position.

Bourassa thanked me for the work. In 1980, I saw some of what I had written in Bourassa's successful leadership in his winning "No" campaign in the Quebec sovereignty referendum and again in his 1985 successful run for reelection as premier.

I studied the power of nationalistic appeals and was fascinated and scared by the dangers and the promises they present. I shudder when I think back to that study and about what's happening in America and around the world today.

The path to my later law degree was not a direct one. In my senior year at Princeton, Procter & Gamble invited me to join their brand management teams in Cincinnati. Those positions usually went to business school graduates from Wharton or Harvard, but they held open a certain number of spots for undergraduates. The job offered a starting salary of about $22,000, pretty darn high for a new college grad. It was an enticing opportunity to be out in the real world with a job of great responsibility.

When I had talked to my father about what I might do after college, he had reservations about my working for a big company with a set career track.

My dad was a big proponent of working at a job where you're your own boss. He hadn't graduated from college. I'm not sure he even graduated from high school. He went into the military, and not too long afterward, he took the job at CBS. He became a film editor, but that was as far as he could go in that company without a college degree.

"If you take a job working for someone else, especially too early," he would caution, "you could get trapped there. Many people look up thirty years later, and they're still in that same place. You may regret getting tracked so quickly into a job that, over time, will become harder to leave."

It was a great piece of advice. Being who I am, I would find a way to try both the business world and law school, but I would end up following my father's advice, and it was a big part of why I would stay in Texas.

I wish my father and I had had more time together.

4

LEARNING ABOUT TIME

I have an uncommon sense of my mortality and the preciousness of time.

I have lived my adult life at every moment uncertain as to how much time I have left. None of us knows, of course. But when your parents die when you're young, you become a member of the next generation to die. A parent still alive is like a buffer between you and what will inevitably come. The end is there, it just seems further off.

I was early in my senior year at Princeton University when my fencing team buddies, Lee and Bill, found me on campus and brought me the news that my father had fallen gravely ill as a result of myasthenia gravis complications.

"You need to get the next train home," my friends told me.

My father had stopped breathing on his birthday, September 18. He was resuscitated and in a coma for nearly a month. During much of that time, I sat beside his bed, and we had hours of one-way conversations. He died on October 14, my younger sister Carolyn's birthday.

I joined a family group hug in the hospital hallway outside my father's room after he was gone. My mother Selma, my older brother Reid, my younger sister Carolyn, and I cried together and held each other, knowing that our world had profoundly changed. In that moment, I couldn't help but feel that the torch had passed to the next generation. I was twenty-one years old.

My mother would hold our immediate family together in the following years, but I know it was hard for her. She had been a homemaker for two decades and now had to return to the workforce as a saleswoman in a lampshade store. She would continue to push me to do my best, however that might end up, but her strength was in helping to make me more empathetic and attentive to others around me. I can close my eyes and still remember what it was like to share a hug with her. She was my biggest cheerleader and always a safe place for me. While she was living halfway across the country from me after I moved to Texas from the east coast, that last part of me that believed in a child's sense of immortality assumed she would be around for a long time. I didn't understand how sick she was.

My mother would pass away six years after my father from complications associated with primary amyloidosis, also an autoimmune disease. My brother, my sister, and I were alone. My siblings and I had very warm relations with our other relatives, but we weren't close, and we didn't see them very often. After our parents died, the three of us used to half-joke that we had become orphans.

I grew up feeling loved and supported—also pushed and challenged. My parents never went to college, and I never saw pictures or heard stories of a high school graduation, if there was one. Getting an education and living to your potential were driving forces in my home.

My parents did not seem happy with each other, and they poured all their being into their three children. From their example, I learned two things. First, how important and lucky I was to have parents who loved me without condition or reservation and expected me to be both responsible for and true to myself. Second, how important it is for parents to recognize that prioritizing their own relationship with each other, filling a home with that love and that example, is an important part of doing the best by your children. I've tried to live both of these lessons.

When my parents died, it was as if a starting gun went off, and the clock started ticking. My own mortality had become all too real. I've never been confident that I have a long enough runway to take my time. I've always pushed myself to try to do too much in too short a time.

My siblings, Reid and Carolyn, and I were all nervous about whether our gene pool would get us past fifty-three years of age. We celebrated mightily when Reid turned fifty-four. When he did, the three of us were very happy but in uncharted waters.

5

HEADING WEST TO PRACTICE LAW AND MAKE A NEW HOME

While at Princeton, it was clear I was headed to law school. I figured a law school degree could be a tool to do a lot of important but very different things, and I didn't need to know what I wanted to do. Many of the change makers we studied at the Woodrow Wilson School had a law degree and had applied it in different ways. Some had found paths to devote their lives to helping others, and my gut said there was no higher calling. Besides, I liked speaking in front of an audience.

Growing up, I had romanticized law, watching the attorney TV show *Perry Mason*. The rooms in my small Maryland house were such that if I lay on my bed and looked across the hall, I could see the television in my parents' room. There were many nights when I was supposed to be asleep but watched and listened to *Perry Mason* as best as I could. Wouldn't it be great to be him!

Every summer, Princeton has reunions for its alumni, and many graduates return to campus every five years to celebrate those reunions. Current students are hired to work during those reunions. The week-long job paid as much as what I could earn during the rest of the summer.

In the summer of 1977, I was hired to work the fifteenth reunion of the Class of 1962. Getting that gig directed the rest of my life, because the grad who chaired the reunion for the Class of 1962 was a man called Tiny, who not only was huge but a Texan through and through. (I don't think I ever knew his real name.)

Tiny could not stop talking about Texas. I found that to be typical for Texans. I spent four years on the Princeton campus, but I can't say that I ever saw a New Jersey flag. I knew what the Texas flag looked like, because it flew from so many dormitory rooms on Texas holidays. It seemed like students from Texas celebrated Texas holidays about every other week. Texas chauvinism was real and unlike anything I had grown up with in Maryland. I don't ever recall any Maryland chauvinism.

Texans loved being Texans.

Tiny told stories about the University of Texas and what was going on in the state. He was quite the cheerleader, and after listening to him, I'd have to say that living in Texas and going to UT sounded like a whole lot of fun.

I applied to law schools other than the University of Texas, but I never seriously considered them, in large part because the tuition of the University of Texas Law School was so much less than anywhere else. When the University of Texas Law School offered me a $100 scholarship, it automatically came with in-state residency status and a tuition rate of $8 a semester hour. A fifteen-hour semester at law school cost $120. And they were giving me a $100 scholarship.

This meant all I needed to earn money for was to pay for room and board.

I arrived in Austin for law school two weeks before my graduation ceremony at Princeton. This was the summer of 1978, which was incredibly hot.

Flying into Texas felt like arriving in foreign territory. I got off the plane in the Dallas-Fort Worth airport to connect with the Austin flight with a feeling of paranoia. I was a rabid Washington Redskins fan, and Washington and the Dallas Cowboys were heated rivals. Their fans hated each other. Now, I was behind enemy lines. When I walked through the airport, I was afraid someone was going to point at me the way the zombies in movies point at the living.

I had planned to meet two friends from my high school days when I arrived at the Austin airport. They both had gone into the Navy, and they had ended up in Austin. I hadn't seen them in five years, but they had offered to give me a place to live until I could get settled at the law school. I hadn't had much time to prepare for law school since I was beginning in the summer and had just completed my classes at Princeton. I didn't know when the dorms would be opening, and I hadn't even gone to the law school bookstore, where first-year law students got their first assignments and their course books.

I got off the plane and stood at the gate at the airport. My friends were supposed to be there. This was back when people could come to the gate, before 9/11. I waited. Nearly everybody had cleared out.

The last two people waiting with me had hair down to their waists. At first, I didn't recognize them. I then realized they were, in fact, my friends. They welcomed me to Texas. I got into their old car, and as we pulled out of the airport, one of them rolled up a joint as big as a circus cigar.

"Everything is big in Texas," he said.

A police car pulled up beside us at the first stoplight. The police officer was looking over at us, and my friend was blowing smoke at the closed window right at the officer. I was dying. I figured my law career would end even before it began. When they saw my reaction, they laughed and explained that this was Austin.

"You don't get in trouble for this kind of thing," one of them told me.

On the way back to their house, they took me to Barton Springs pool, which is a municipal swimming hole in Austin fed by a natural spring. It's the heart of the city, culturally valued as representing Austin's history and its commitment to environmental stewardship. It's where the area's early Coahuiltecan and Tonkawa residents lived hundreds of years ago. It's also topless optional. What's not to love?

The water temperature is a constant, year-round sixty-eight to seventy degrees, clear and crisp, and I was in that water within minutes of arriving in Austin for the first time.

This is a place where I could spend the rest of my life, I was already thinking.

We went back to my friends' house. All night, people dropped by.

My friends have a lot of friends, I thought.

Turns out most people were coming by for marijuana.

My friends put a mattress down on the floor for me. I had to go to sleep. The next day was my first day of law school. I disappeared into the mattress with six inches of smoke that hung low over the floor of their house.

I went to class the next day, and I was still high. My first class was contract law.

I sat down at my desk. I hadn't bought my textbooks. Everyone else had. They had taken notes and were prepared. I was not. Because my last name began with an A, I was very high up on the seating chart.

The professor started the class and called on me. He cited the name of a case in the textbook and asked me for the facts of the *Case of the Hairy Hand*.

"I am not prepared," I said.

I started laughing inside because I was living the opening scene of the *Paper Chase* movie, in which the professor gives a brand-new and also unprepared student a quarter so he could call his mother and tell her he would be coming home shortly.

I was waiting for my professor to tell me the same thing.

My professor was much kinder than that, and he just went on to the next person.

I went back to my friends' house after my first day of classes. I was incredibly hungry, and I went to the fridge. There was old ketchup, old mustard, and a container of cheese spread. I found bread that wasn't moldy. I put the spread on the bread and ate it all. It was great.

My friends came home. I told them how much I enjoyed the sandwich I had made.

Alarmed, they ran to the fridge.

"You have just eaten our entire stash of psilocybin mushrooms," one said. "We put them in the cheese spread to cut the bad taste of the mushrooms. You're not supposed to eat that much."

For hours, I hallucinated wildly. I missed the second day of law school. At least I think that's all I missed. I can't remember exactly. My friends were kind and supportive, and they took very good care of me.

The next day, I moved into the law school dormitory.

It was a matter of survival.

My mother's words, always with me, were in my ears when I arrived at the University of Texas to begin my law studies. My mother used to tell me that all she ever expected of me was that I would do my best. And it was understood that if I did my best, I would do well in life. It's a privilege to be born with that understanding. It drives the sense of confidence, even overconfidence, that I've always had and that you'll see as you read on.

I really liked the University of Texas campus. There was a high energy and exciting spirit, and I found I really loved Mexican food. I discovered that what they served as Mexican food in Washington, D.C., wasn't Mexican food at all.

I also really liked law school. The cases that we read to learn the law and how to think as a lawyer were like finding clues in a mystery novel.

Because I had started during the summer, I completed my first year of law school later that year, in December.

And then, as per my plan, I left law school to try working at that job with Procter & Gamble in Cincinnati for a year or two. It was the compromise I had made with Procter & Gamble, the Texas law school, and my father's memory.

Working at Procter & Gamble would provide exposure to what could be a future in a very attractive world I knew nothing about. It would also help me pay to finish law school if I returned. By first starting law school, I was less likely to choose a life working for someone else solely because of the inertia of having started a corporate job.

It was a wonderful year and a half, and I learned so much from the smart, motivated, and competitive people who worked there. It was my first exposure to and where I learned about entrepreneurship and running a business.

The pull to Texas and the law was strong, so I returned to finish law school, and I'm glad I did.

I helped put myself through law school by working part-time as a law clerk for the firm of Womack and Barron, a small firm that did eminent domain work. The firm represented property owners whose land the government was taking for public projects. The disputes were over fair compensation. The government rarely offered the landowners what the property was worth. I tried cases as a law student with the equivalent of a learner's permit.

It was great to be in a courtroom so early in my career—trying cases for real, talking to juries, and coming up with my own strategies. It was exciting, and I was good at it.

Two of my earliest cases stand out. We represented a rancher and his family just outside of Lubbock. The state was putting a highway through his ranch, and the trial was over how much compensation the rancher was due.

The senior partner, Danny Womack, with whom I was trying the case, sent me to Lubbock in advance to meet with the client, his wife, and some of the neighbors who were potential witnesses.

When I arrived at the client's home, he and his wife had planned a small barbecue for the neighbors and me. Getting invited to a real country barbecue was new to me, and it was so good. At the end of the meal, we gathered in the living room of the ranch house, where I explained to the client and his neighbors what would happen at the trial, what the issues were, and what everybody's involvement would be.

Five minutes into my talk, which I thought was an eloquent presentation, my client's wife raised her hand. I called on her.

"Steve, I'm sure what you're saying is beautiful," she said in a slow, thick West Texas drawl. "But if you would slow down, I'm sure we could understand what you're saying."

I slowed down, and as I spoke, I even picked up the slightest hint of that West Texas sound and cadence, which I continued to adopt when I spoke to the judge and jury in the coming days.

At the end of the evening when I was leaving their home, the client's wife gave me a hug and thanked me for helping her family, then she looked down at my penny loafers and said, "I'm sure you have a pair of boots to wear in court."

I didn't have any boots, but on the way home, I stopped at the general store and bought the pair that I wore at the trial.

We won that case, and I won another case in which a utility company was putting in an electric line across a homeowner's property in Lockhart, Texas, just outside of Austin.

I tried much of that case. The senior partner let me take the lead on it. The issue once again was how much compensation my client should get from the power company.

The attorney on the other side was Ed Small, one of the most experienced attorneys representing condemning entities in Central Texas. Ed was the main partner in one of the large Austin law firms.

It was a thrill trying a case against him, because he was really good and had such a large and wonderful reputation as an outstanding litigator. He was a very big man in many ways.

Throughout the trial of several days, Mr. Small taught me how to do better, even though he was on the opposite side. At one point in the trial, a legal issue had to be argued, and the judge asked the attorneys to meet him in chamber out of the presence of the jury.

The judge asked me to state my position, and I delivered it to the judge. It was Ed Small's turn to respond, and he began to talk and stopped. He looked at me, and he said, "Steve, that was not your best argument."

I thought for a second about what he was trying to tell me, and I realized that I had not made the best case for my client. I asked the amused judge to give me permission to start over and try again. I ended up winning the argument in the judge's chamber, and I won the trial, mostly because the facts were on my side.

I have always considered Ed Small one of my heroes because of the graciousness with which he treated me then and through the years. I promised myself to try to be the kind of lawyer he was to me.

After I graduated from law school, I had the opportunity to begin practicing law and making a lot of money by returning to Washington, D.C., or going to one of Texas's big cities, like Houston. Or I could become an associate lawyer with the Austin firm where I had been clerking.

When I first arrived in Texas, I thought that after law school I would return to Washington, where I grew up, to practice. Or I would return to the New York metropolitan area, where I went to college.

But a funny thing happened.

Austin became home.

I was twenty-four years old. The live music was great. I could live on breakfast tacos, and the Texas women were beautiful. In law school, I treasured and grew in a few wonderful relationships, one of which was with a woman who is still a close friend almost fifty years later. Austin always felt like home. It was a forward-looking city, taking risks was rewarded, and there was a sense that Austin was coming into its own and that there were a lot of future opportunities. There was such a feeling of optimism in Austin.

Back then, it was an inexpensive city, much less expensive than living in Houston, Fort Worth, Dallas, or even San Antonio. In Austin, there were a lot of free spirits: artists, musicians, and even hippies and former hippies. We had Stevie Ray Vaughan, Ray Benson's Asleep at the Wheel, and Uncle Walt's Band, among many other incredible talents to go see. I learned to like country and western music, especially Willie Nelson, who I used to go see at small clubs back in the late 1970s.

So I stayed in Austin and became an associate attorney at the firm I clerked for as a law student.

The firm, Womack and Barron, was going through a transition, splitting up and forming two separate firms. So I asked Mike Barron if I could join his firm as an associate, but he was cautious.

"I can't do that," he said. "I don't think I'll have enough business for us both."

I began my law practice with Womack and McClish.

The new firm couldn't pay me what I was being offered by the bigger firms in Washington, D.C., and Houston, so they sweetened their salary offer with a very small percentage of the firm's gross fees. In my first year, we hit a jackpot. I bought a shiny, brand-new Porsche 944 with my share of the fee.

At the end of that first year of practice, I got a phone call from a partner of another firm in Austin that handled eminent domain cases. He told me that he and his partner were thinking of retiring and they were looking for a succession plan.

"We're certainly not going to give our cases to an attorney with your firm," he said, "because our firms have been competitors for so long. It's a shame there isn't anybody young and independent out there to take over our book of business."

I was stunned and confused by what I was hearing. I wasn't exactly sure what he was telling me, and I was too overwhelmed to respond.

Did he just offer me their practice? I wondered.

I thanked him, wished him and his partner well in retirement, and hung up the phone.

A couple of days later while I was still thinking about the call, I was invited to sit down and talk with the two senior partners of my firm.

"We're very pleased with your work," Danny told me. "You've done a fine job, and though we paid you the percentage of that big case that was settled, we think it was too big a windfall. Beginning next year, we're going to raise your salary, but you will no longer get a profit participation in the firm's revenue. It's not personal, it's just the best business decision for us to make."

"I appreciate all you have done for me," I said.

I then resigned.

I went back to my office, and I nervously called back the partner from the firm across town.

"I have quit my firm," I said, "and if I understood what your call was all about, I want you to know I am a young eminent domain attorney who is not connected to your longtime competitor. I will gladly take on your cases."

I then held my breath because this eminent domain attorney was also unemployed.

We cut a deal, they gave me their large book of untried and pending cases, and I started my own law firm.

I called Mike Barron back.

"I'd still like to work with you, and working with me no longer is the same risk," I said. "I now have more cases than you do. Maybe now we can work together, but I no longer want to be your associate. How would you like a new partner?"

It took a year, but eventually he accepted.

I was twenty-seven years old when my partnership with Mike Barron began, and we continued as partners for thirty-five years. Mike is a great lawyer and was a great partner. I trusted him absolutely. We were very successful in court. We never lost a jury trial.

Mike and I are different in a lot of ways. He is politically very conservative, and I'm pretty progressive. But because we ran in different circles, we knew a lot of different people, and between us, we were invited to many of the parties and events around town. Our combined reach was impressive, and that helped to build the practice.

Our firm became the leading eminent domain firm in Texas, and I chaired the condemnation committee for the American Bar Association. I became a continuing author of the eminent domain section in one of the annual treatises on Texas property law, and we were the convenors of the annual eminent domain seminar in Texas. For years running, I made the list of Texas's Best Lawyers. When I walked away from the firm and my practice, I was making a seven figure annual income and just hitting what should have been my most lucrative years as a lawyer.

The firm survives today, though I'm no longer a part of it. I had to leave the firm when I was elected mayor because it represented a lot of people who were in lawsuits with the city, and I would have had a conflict. After I was no longer mayor, I couldn't go back to the firm because those conflicts still existed, and I didn't want a headline suggesting I was making money off infrastructure projects I had initiated as mayor by representing landowners whose property was needed for those projects.

I really enjoyed and felt good about my years practicing law. In addition to eminent domain law, which paid my bills and allowed for my family to travel, I also spent a lot of time in my early career handling federal civil rights cases. Most were employment discrimination cases and workplace sexual harassment claims. It was my opportunity to help people who most needed help and were least able to get it. It was the reason I had wanted to be a lawyer.

I brought lawsuits for all sorts of workplace discrimination—employment, sexual, race, and ethnicity. Most of these cases involved an administrative process for the Equal Employment Opportunity Commission that began at the city level. The Austin Civil Rights Commission had jurisdiction to hear these complaints. After such a case was filed, an administrative officer held a hearing and rendered a decision.

Very few attorneys take on this work because it doesn't pay very well. I was starting a new career with very few personal responsibilities, and I didn't need much money, so I had the freedom to take on as many of these cases as I could handle, representing claimants who didn't have much. I was able to help a lot of people, and it was great practice. Right away, I was getting experience in contested hearings, and doing civil rights work put me on track to someday become that civil law Perry Mason that I had once fantasized about.

I must have done a hundred of those hearings, and I was also in court. I won for Black workers who drove for a beer distributor and for Hispanic workers in federal court who were discriminated against at construction sites. The way to get promoted in the construction industry is to move from smaller pieces of equipment to heavier pieces and then to a supervisory position. But the company would not give the Hispanic workers the chance to work on the heavier pieces, so they rarely got promoted.

I also represented women who were claiming sexual harassment. I recall one woman in her early seventies who came into my office and told me she was fired because she "wouldn't put out for [her] boss." I was incredulous when she told me that, maybe in the same way that children don't think of their parents as sexual beings, and I was young and naïve. What I didn't know then was that these cases are generally not about sexual attraction anyhow but rather about power in relationships.

I asked her what happened, and she told me how the boss had chased her around a desk, grabbed her, and kissed her against her will.

"Are there any witnesses?" I wanted to know.

There were no witnesses. No one had seen it.

"This is a tough case to prove if this comes down to a swearing match between you and your boss," I told her. "But sometimes people who do this to one person do it to other people, too. Maybe you can find others with a similar experience to establish a track record. If you find anything, let me know."

I never thought I'd see her again, but a couple of weeks later, she came back with a notebook full of statements, including one signed by a member of the board of directors of her New York company who said that her complaint had reached them, only to have the president and CEO tell the board, "Boys will be boys. Let's move on."

I took her case and filed it. I sent the CEO a deposition notice ordering him to fly down to Austin from New York. He fought that, but I won, and he had to come and testify. When he walked into his deposition, he reminded me of Bob Guccione, the founder of *Penthouse* magazine. His shirt was unbuttoned down to his navel, and he wore gold chains.

The morning portion of the deposition went horribly for him. At the break, the company's attorney suggested I meet him for lunch.

"We need to talk," he said.

We settled the case over lunch, and my client won a lot of money because it was going to be difficult for her to find another job. The opposing counsel was Kirk Watson, later the mayor of Austin from 1997 to 2001 and again when he succeeded me in 2023.

I had a case in federal court that I tried with Tom Kolker, representing a woman who claimed the police had violated her constitutional rights when they stopped her car, frisked her, and then roughed her up. These cases are hard to win because the accused police officer explains that he beat up the victim in response to the accused resisting arrest, and there are usually no witnesses.

Our client denied she had acted in any way to suggest she was resisting arrest.

This was the first use-of-force jury trial in Austin history that found an officer had violated someone's constitutional rights. The jury awarded her only one dollar in actual damages. Still, it was a significant victory, and the police department had to pay her legal fees. Most importantly, the verdict validated our client's claim that she had done nothing wrong and that there could be meaningful community oversight.

This work on civil rights and discrimination cases was among the most fulfilling experiences I have had practicing law. I have been able to address some of the injustices I remembered seeing while growing up in the Washington, D.C., area and to be in court helping to bring justice to people who deserve it. It was also frustrating work because the need for justice for so many is great, and my client list, compared to the magnitude of the challenge and while still having an important impact, seemed insufficient. I later got involved more broadly in the community and even as mayor, to satisfy a need that was growing inside me to have an impact at a greater scale.

My need to be socially active was channeled into joining boards of nonprofit organizations and doing occasional pro bono legal work. I wanted to contribute to organizations and people doing good. The most impactful and efficient way I found to do this was by helping empower the best nonprofit executive directors and future public servants that I knew.

Somebody I had always wanted to work with and help was Eliot Shapleigh. He and I were in the same law school section when we started in the summer of 1978, and he became one of my closest friends throughout law school. I had hoped that after graduation, he would remain in Austin and we would find a way to work together, but I hadn't realized just how much he loved El Paso, where he was fifth generation, and that he'd never leave.

It was Eliot who introduced me to the mystery of Marfa, Texas, and showed me the majesty of Big Bend National Park. He took me quail hunting.

I was never a hunter—I didn't grow up around hunting and hunters. But Eliot lent me a shotgun, and we went out to quail hunt with some other folks. I had no intention of shooting the birds, but I went for the camaraderie and the beer.

As I walked forward holding my shotgun, I scared up a quail that was a little slow in making its escape. It flew into the end of my gun, causing it to go off. The shot took off the bird's wing. It immediately fell to the ground, but it was still alive. I dropped down and held it. The bird was in shock, breathing heavily and looking at me. I felt terrible.

"You know what you have to do?" Eliot said to me. "You know what has to happen now?"

I told him I did.

"We have to find a vet just as quickly as possible because this bird is hurt," I said.

"That's *not* the right answer," Eliot said. "Would you like me to kill it for you?"

I declined. It was my responsibility.

"I'm sorry," I said to the bird for the last time before I beheaded him.

I've lived in Texas for almost fifty years, but it's not quite like I was born here.

In 1996, about twenty years after we graduated from law school, Eliot called me up to tell me he was running for the state senate from El Paso. I assumed that he was looking for a contribution, which I was happy to make, but that wasn't his request. He was coming into the race late. It was an open seat, and an announced candidate was already running, and she was acknowledged as the favorite to get the nomination. Eliot was concerned that the lobby in Austin soon would start giving her campaign contributions, effectively closing out his chances.

"I need you to figure out how we can stop the lobby from doing that," he said. "I need them to see that I'm the candidate most likely to win. I need the Austin lobby to keep its powder dry long enough for me to demonstrate that they should be giving their money to me and not her."

Though I lived in Austin, I didn't know a thing about the Texas legislature or how the lobby worked or even who they were, but having been given this charge and responsibility, I began to learn. I made the case for Eliot to the right people, and the Austin lobby agreed to wait to see how the race would develop. By doing that, I met a lot of players in Austin and around the Texas legislature. I made connections and developed a network that proved to be important to me when I ran for mayor.

Eliot won the election and became one of the leading progressive state senators in Texas history. The Texas legislature meets in regular session for five months every other year, so for those five months in his initial sessions, Eliot came to Austin, where the legislature was meeting, and he stayed at my house. I served as his chief of staff and general counsel to help him set up his office and his systems as he was learning the ropes and functioning as a state senator. During those months, I'd do my law work at night.

I learned a lot, and I loved it.

I also got involved in another aspect of politics that turned out to be of great benefit to my later mayoral campaign. I was an advisory member of President Barack Obama's finance committee when he first ran for president. The experience taught me more about how campaigns work, and it further connected me with a donor and organizer network that I would turn to when I later launched my campaign for mayor.

But future politics was not something I thought about. I was focused on the practice of law and enjoying my friends.

When I was in my thirties, I was retained on one lawsuit that changed my life. I was representing the Trammell Crow Company in an eminent domain matter. I was in my conference room with two smart, accomplished, and attractive women getting ready for trial.

One woman was my client's representative, Diane Land. The other was Melany Maddux, my expert appraisal witness.

As I sat there with them on either side of me, it was as though God or some higher power was whispering to me, "The woman you need to marry is in this room."

Diane was married and pregnant, so I figured it wasn't her. I married Melany. Together, she and I have a wonderful daughter, who is now CEO at *The Texas Tribune*. The marriage, however, didn't last, and five years later it was over.

Eight years after that first meeting, I found Diane again. By then, she was also divorced. I had scored a couple of tickets to the Rolling Stones in San Antonio just a few days before the concert, and at the last minute, I called her.

"It's Steve Adler. I don't know if you remember who I am, but I have two tickets to the Rolling Stones this weekend. What do you say? Do you want to go?"

"Can't," she said, "but if the Stones come back into town, give me a rain check."

When I hung up the phone, I wondered what she meant by that, because it could be ten years before the Rolling Stones played around Austin again. It turned out that she remembered me and very much wanted to go, but she was dating someone else at the time.

She needed to break up with the guy she was dating before she would go out with me, which she did, and we ended up getting married.

Diane brought two daughters, Karen and Susan, into the marriage, and I came with Sarah. The three girls are incredibly close, and we are one family. I love these four women without limit. They are my closest and most favorite people, except for my grandkids. I love my sons-in-law, too. Together, we have traveled the world. We've always been there for one another. I am unbelievably proud of who they have become and what they are able to do. I am beyond appreciative of how they have supported and encouraged what I do, including my service as mayor. The children of elected officials often pay a price for their parents' service. I love them very much.

Diane and I have been married since 1998. We're lucky and blessed and have done very well. We've both served on the boards of a lot of nonprofits. Diane is a trustee of Huston-Tillotson University, a historically Black college and the oldest university in Austin. She has served on the boards of the local PBS station, SAFE (the shelter for victims of domestic violence), The Contemporary Austin (Austin's contemporary art museum), and the Girls Empowerment Network, among others.

We both served on the Austin board of the Anti-Defamation League. I was on its national advisory council. We worked with Regional Director Karen Gross to create the Austin Hate Crimes Task Force, and we launched the local No Place for Hate program that, at one point, was in over four hundred area schools.

I'm proud to have been on the founding board and later the chair of *The Texas Tribune,* working with publisher Evan Smith and founder John Thornton to successfully establish a national model for sustainable, nonprofit, stellar, and unbiased journalism.

I also chaired the board of Ballet Austin, and I worked with Cookie Ruiz and Stephen Mills, the executive and creative directors, to use that art form to further community conversations on tough issues like bullying and anti-Semitism with works like *Light: The Holocaust & Humanity Project.* I was on the first board for the Long Center for Performing Arts and on the board of Breakthrough, working with the Executive Director Michael Griffith to support first-generation college attendees like me.

In each of these roles, Diane and I worked together. We support each other. It's among the best and most enjoyable of what we do. Becoming mayor seemed like it would be the natural extension of this work together.

6

RUNNING FOR MAYOR

My law practice had become very successful, but by the 2010s, I was getting restless. If you appear in enough trials, you no longer get nervous walking into court, and the fear of being surprised is gone. I missed those feelings. And quite frankly, I regretted that I had stopped working on civil rights cases. I felt guilty about that.

In late 2013, a group of us were looking for someone new to run for mayor of Austin. After decades of serving on various nonprofit boards, Diane and I were more frequently seeing the impact local government decision-making had, good and bad, on the important work these organizations were doing. Did funding for the arts reach the greatest number of people, or was there a special focus on those with political connections? Were the interests of most being served, as with housing policy that expanded opportunities, or were legacy institutions and neighborhoods, more powerful over time, able to protect the status quo? Would our city recognize it was no longer a small college town and make the necessary infrastructure investments to ensure a great quality of life for everyone in a rapidly growing city? I found I was becoming increasingly invested in who would be running city hall.

Austin's form of government was about to change. It had been an "at large" council, which meant that every council member was elected by the entire city, as was the mayor. Beginning with the 2015 election, the city was divided into ten districts, and each district elected its own representative. Only the mayor would be elected at large.

With an "at large" council, parts of the town with the greatest election turnout had a disproportionate representation on the council because those parts of town had greater voting power. With the new system, each of the ten districts had a representative with an equal number of residents. That way, the less-advantaged parts of Austin, which voted in lower numbers, had as much sway as the richer parts of the city. The new system changed the demographic balance on the council racially, ethnically, and economically, better reflecting the makeup of the community.

When a city makes such a transition, it usually faces significant challenges for the first four to eight years because the new government quickly devolves into ward politics. Suddenly, a part of town that never seemed to get what it wanted now had a representative promising to deliver on that thing, whether that thing was in the best interest of the city as a whole or not. Sometimes it was the right thing to get done. Regardless, if that representative could get five more council members to vote for what they wanted and if the other five council members could get those same others to vote for what they wanted, they could get all their wants passed.

But who was looking out for the best interests of the city as a whole? And who could get everyone working together?

The mayor.

What the council now needed was a strong leader. There were several Austin residents who would have made very good mayors, and we talked to them, and they all said no. It wasn't what they wanted to do, or it wasn't the right time for them to do it. Two current city council members were running, and their significant name recognition kept many potential challengers out of the race.

With the change in the rules, it was apparent that almost all the council members would be new. A lot of us thought we needed a mayor who had *not* sat on the council previously, so that no one at the council table would begin a sentence, "Let me tell you how we've always done this."

With no one else stepping up, it became apparent that someone from our group would need to stop what they were doing and run.

My name came up.

The first to urge me to run was Melba Whatley, a successful businesswoman and one of Austin's most prolific civic activists. Through the power of her personality, she gets large projects done. She was persistent.

My wife Diane and I started talking about whether I should consider running. She was supportive. Diane recognized that I was getting restless in my law practice. She said she would help. Diane is more of an extrovert than I am. She has run her own company. She has greater ease walking into a room of strangers than I do. She is loved and respected by so many members of the community. She's comfortable in her own space. If she had had any interest at all in running herself, I think she would have done well. She pointed her finger at me.

"You can do this," she said. "Running for mayor will be like us doing the nonprofit work we've already been doing, only at a bigger scale and with greater opportunity."

We had no idea how different it would really be.

"And no one else is stepping up," she added. "Besides," she looked at me very seriously, "if you don't run, I don't want to hear you complaining about city hall ever again."

It was true; I did that more than she did.

People approached her and asked her to talk me into running. We knew a lot of people because of all those nonprofit boards and the considerable reach of both our companies. Even though we underestimated how much was involved, we were ready for the major time commitment that being mayor would require. My background involving local government, my patience with and ability to get people working together in a common direction, and our strong and cooperative work ethic were attributes we could uniquely offer to Austin voters. About thirty days after our initial conversation, in December 2013, we decided I would run.

As I said, several candidates had already announced they were running. Two were incumbent council members, Sheryl Cole and Mike Martinez.

A third announced candidate was an entrepreneur, had led successful community organizations, and was running as a political outsider. I knew if I didn't announce early that I, too, was running for mayor, her candidacy would pick up steam and she might well go on to win. She had a stellar track record, was well qualified and well liked, and there would be appeal in having a woman serve as mayor.

She called me up, angry. She didn't understand why I would enter the race when she was already running.

"Did you enter the race because you didn't feel I could do a good job?" she asked.

I told her nothing could be further from the truth.

"I've never heard anything but wonderful things about you," I said.

I wasn't running because of her or to stop her. I was running because I had something unique to offer.

She and I arranged to meet for coffee, and as soon as we sat down, she urged me to get out of the race.

"I will do whatever I need to do to win this race," she said. "You don't stand a chance." And in that latter sentiment, she wasn't alone.

She ended the conversation by saying, "I'm going to beat you, and I will spend whatever it takes to win."

"I won't get out of the race," I told her.

She got up and left me sitting there. As I walked out of the coffee shop, I thought to myself, *Wow, so this is politics!*

This was the moment my life in politics became real.

There were five serious candidates running for mayor at the start of January. By the end of the month, two had withdrawn—the two non-incumbent candidates in the race most similar to me. Longtime local civic champion Bill McClellan left the race and endorsed me. The candidate with whom I met to have coffee also withdrew, saying she didn't like the campaign process. She didn't endorse me.

I started calling people in my network, lots of people: clients who worked with my law firm, other volunteers with the various organizations Diane and I supported, and others who had also supported President Obama's campaign.

In January 2014, I made the announcement, but despite all my phone calls, I didn't have much name recognition, so I knew I had to run a serious campaign. An early poll tested how many people knew me, and my name recognition registered between 2 and 3 percent. And I knew that most of the people who thought they knew my name were mistaken. I had a lot of work to do.

To run a campaign, I had to build a staff. I knew I needed to find someone to help me run. Jim Wick, a very colorful guy, had been a seasoned campaign manager who had helped other local candidates win many races. He was a free spirit who had been in the Peace

Corps in Korea and had worked on President Obama's campaign in Nebraska.

I called him in January.

"I'm going to be running for mayor," I told him. "I need help, and I want you to be my campaign manager."

He turned me down because he was running Andy Brown's first campaign for county judge.

"I'm in the middle of the race," Wick said. "The primary election is in March. I'm not going to talk about anything else while I'm in this race."

Because my election for mayor was nonpartisan, there would be no primary election. Everyone running for the mayor's office would be on the general election ballot in November. If no one got 50 percent of the vote, the top two vote-getters would be in a run-off a month later—in mid-December.

I told Wick I would get back to him after his March primary race was over. But I knew I couldn't wait. If I did nothing, the mayor's race could be over by then, too.

I didn't know anyone else locally to call, so I reached out to Robert Gibbs, who had been the press secretary for President Obama. I had met him (barely) while serving on President Obama's advisory finance committee in 2008.

Gibbs was a big deal, and I knew it was a long shot for me to get him to help a guy who was just getting into politics on the local level. It was like asking Mickey Mantle if he would help coach your son's Little League team.

Surprisingly, Gibbs said yes, and he brought in Ben LaBolt, who had worked on special projects for the Obama campaign and later became the communications director for President Joe Biden. Now I had Mickey Mantle and Sandy Koufax as my interim campaign leads.

Gibbs and LaBolt got my campaign off the ground, albeit mostly by telephone. They found a campaign worker by the name of Quinn

Stout, who had done field work for campaigns around the country. Quinn was willing to come to Austin and brought all the confidence I needed with him.

I was self-funding at this point. Under the campaign laws for the city of Austin, I wasn't allowed to solicit contributions until the first week in May. But if I waited until May to get the money to run, I knew the race would be over for me before it started.

These men helped me identify and focus on what needed to be done to launch a campaign. They gave me excellent feedback on how to think like a candidate. We came up with a campaign slogan: NEW WAY FORWARD. Kamala Harris used that when she ran for president, but I came up with it first and had better luck with it.

I was on the phone a lot.

I continued to pursue Jim Wick to finish running my campaign when Gibbs and LaBolt would need to step aside, and I wanted to hire Laura Hernandez as my chief fundraiser and deputy campaign manager. Laura was a seasoned, successful campaign organizer.

As my campaign treasurer, I chose Eugene Sepulveda, a smart, strategic, and colorful guy. Campaign treasurer is usually an honorific position only required to sign documents recorded publicly. But that's not Eugene, who was one of the most involved in my campaign.

As a young banker in Austin, Eugene was one of the earliest professionals to come out as gay. He was very opinionated and very connected with thousands of followers on social media. He is very much an influencer and a connector. Tom Terkel, another spirited, popular guy and friend, a real estate developer in the town, was among the first to encourage me to run, and he and Eugene became my kitchen cabinet.

They both had spent a lot of time around city hall and city politics. I had never even been to a city council meeting. There was a lot I didn't know.

Though Tom had encouraged me to run, just before the launch of the campaign, he came to my home and we sat in my kitchen while he shared his concern that the campaign might affect me and my life in ways I would not welcome.

"Your life is going to change in ways you don't know," he said. "If you get elected, the relationships you have with everybody are going to change. You will never be treated the same way again. You'll lose your anonymity. You'll piss off a lot of people."

I didn't understand it at the time, but everything he said turned out to be true.

In the last week of March 2014, Jim Wick's primary candidate lost, one of the few races ever that Wick hasn't won. I took him to lunch at a Mexican restaurant in South Austin, and finally, he agreed to run my campaign.

"Okay," he said. "I will be your campaign manager, but you have to promise me one thing: You won't read the comments in the newspapers and on social media."

I wasn't sure what he meant.

He repeated himself.

"What I mean is, I don't want you reading the comments in newspaper articles, and I don't want you going online and reading comments on social media. If you do, you're going to get lost."

It's an easy promise, I thought. "Yeah, sure."

"Now I want you to repeat the whole sentence," he said.

"I promise I won't read the comments," I said.

He reached across the table and shook my hand.

"Okay," Wick said. "I'm your campaign manager, and as your campaign manager, the first thing I want to talk to you about is what I want you thinking about when you read those comments, because I know you're lying to me. Because it's irresistible. I want you to keep in mind that when it looks like there are fifty people commenting, it's really just one person, who doesn't even live in Austin. He lives in Omaha,

Nebraska, and he's eighty years old, and he lives in a barren efficiency apartment, except for a card table and a folding metal chair. He works alone on his computer at the table, illuminated only by a bare bulb hanging down from the ceiling. He's in his underwear on that computer, and he's commenting on elections all over the country, just riling stuff up. This guy will criticize you. He will call you names. He's going to challenge everything you do. He's going to build alliances against you as best he can, and you get to decide whether to engage with him. I want you to understand that what he wants is for you to engage with him. He will take from you as much energy as you choose to give to him. You get to decide how much energy you're going to give to him."

While I was mayor, I was told one weekend after a decision I made regarding Austin's homeless population that there were 18,000 reacting social media posts. Most were critical of me. As Jim had warned, most of those did not come from people in Austin. Jim helped me keep perspective. I wonder how I would have felt if Jim hadn't warned me about that. Whenever I read the criticisms or the accusations against me, it often brought a smile to my face because I couldn't help but think of the old guy in Omaha sitting at his card table typing away on his computer.

Elected officials receive very emotional communications and messaging because they deal with issues that are often hard-fought, many of which cannot or should not be resolved by finding a middle ground, so often there are concerned and invested people who will lose. Many times, these are the loud voices that elected officials most often hear. Frequently, the city council chamber is filled with such engaged people. It's important, however, to consistently remind yourself, as an elected official, that the people you most see and hear from may not represent at all the sentiments of most of your constituents. And they might not even be your constituents. Good and effective elected officials hear and consider those voices and also put them in their proper perspective.

I continued to make calls. It was April, and I still wasn't allowed to solicit money.

I had come from a law firm that represented property owners and tenants against the government in eminent domain cases. People in the real estate industry were supportive because they knew me, but with that base, I was attacked as being too conservative and in the pocket of real estate developers—not a good label in a progressive city like Austin.

I knew I had to define myself before other people did, so three times over that summer we sent out a citywide mailer. I did this three months before any other candidate reached out to voters. We mailed large cards that showed my values. One had a picture of me and President Obama. Another had a picture of me and the very popular Democrat Wendy Davis, a state senator who was running for governor. She had tried to stop the Texas abortion bill with a very impactful and dramatic filibuster.

I sought to establish my progressive, Austin bona fides. I talked to as many groups as I could. Little by little, I was gaining support. My team and I set up a phone tree system to raise money, which we would launch on May 1.

I figured correctly that I would have to raise a million dollars to win the mayoral race. We needed to fund a lot of messaging to win against my more widely known opponents.

Eight candidates ended up running for mayor, and because we were switching to a district system, we were also electing almost all new council members. There were ten districts, with seven or eight people running for each district seat. It was tough for any candidate to be heard.

It felt like there were about seventy different debates just among the mayoral candidates in the race. Every special interest group in town and every organization seemed like they were hosting a debate.

My most challenging opponent, Mike Martinez, an incumbent council member, tried to convince the community that I had represented the very conservative Koch brothers, which is something the electorate in Austin wouldn't appreciate. It wasn't true. I dealt with that. He did a forceful job trying to convince people I was a Republican. I had to deal with that too.

I had the most votes in the November general election, but I didn't get the over 50 percent of votes necessary to win the job. I had 64,416 votes to Martinez's 51,892, my 37 percent versus his 30 percent.

A month later, I won the run-off. I had 52,159 votes to 25,639 for Martinez. Mike was a good Democrat, and he and I split the Democratic vote. I won the race in large measure because I had 80 percent support among registered Republicans. Mike had convinced many Republicans that I was one of them.

And just like that, I was the mayor of Austin, Texas.

7

LEADING THE HOT CITY

What sets Austin apart from almost every other city in the world is its high tolerance for taking risks. In most cities across the world, if someone tries something and fails, that person gets punished financially or socially. He no longer has access to the same capital; he's not invited back into the same rooms. He had his chance, and it didn't work out.

Austin's culture is different. In this city, the real civic heroes are those who try new ideas, and if at first they aren't successful, they learn, innovate, adapt, and try again.

There's a reason why iconic legend Willie Nelson came to Austin in the 1970s to reinvent not only country music but also who listens to it. Twitter was effectively launched in Austin at SXSW. Computers for consumers started up in Michael Dell's UT Dobie Center dorm room (#2713). The first time a member of the public took a ride in a fully autonomous car was in a Waymo down an Austin street. Austin company Alamo Drafthouse reinvented the concept of a dinner and movie date, and Whole Foods began a healthy food grocery store revolution in Austin.

That culture of risk-taking is a reason why Austin has become an international tech center and why SXSW takes place in Austin, showcasing technologies, platforms, and startups. While only the fifth-largest city in Texas, Austin is where one-third of Texas's patents originate and half the state's venture capital gets invested. That culture is why Austin's local government continues to drive cutting-edge and progressive policy initiatives, despite the opposition of the state's Republican Party and especially the extreme right-wing leadership of Governor Greg Abbott, Lieutenant Governor Dan Patrick, and Attorney General Ken Paxton.

Austin is a very blue city in a very red state. There has not been a Texas statewide Democratic officeholder in thirty years. So those Republican leaders, who need an adversary or foil to organize their base and raise dollars, focus on criticizing and attacking their cities, especially Austin, where local government is controlled by Democrats.

It would be reasonable for statewide leadership to celebrate and try to learn from Austin's unique culture and values, but unfortunately, that isn't the case. Instead, they fight our progressive bent at every turn and try to turn us into and make us look like the rest of the state.

My argument to Governor Abbott and our statewide leadership was always that our state's economic position is stronger when we have a diversified portfolio of cities, each with its own individual strengths and cultures. Austin attracts businesses that wouldn't come to other cities in Texas, just as some businesses choose to be in Dallas or Houston rather than in Austin. If Austin becomes like the rest of the state, I argue, we will lose this economic development to other more progressive cities, like Denver, Portland, Nashville, Raleigh, and Seattle.

My argument has fallen on deaf ears. New state laws continue to be put into effect that preempt local control and the will of Austin voters, seeking to make Austin look like the Republican ideal of the rest of Texas.

I wonder whether Texas state lawmakers realize that those decisions make Texas less competitive in the marketplace for businesses that would choose to be in Austin precisely because of its unique culture and character or if the perceived statewide political advantage of beating up on "Austin values" is worth the overall economic harm to the state.

Against this backdrop, Austin nevertheless continues to innovate, create, and stay true to the values of our community's residents. The city expects that of itself, and it expects its leaders, and especially its mayor, to make that happen.

I served eight years as mayor of Austin from 2015 to 2023. In each of those years, Austin was the fastest-growing large metropolitan area in the country. This duration of continuous and consistent growth is very rare, and there are only a few other metropolitan areas in U.S. history that have been able to maintain that standing for a similar successive year run.

During this period, Austin was the nation's "hot" city and dominated across media, tech, music, and lifestyle coverage. It was the cultural capital with SXSW and Austin City Limits (ACL) festivals, live music density, food trucks, and a distinctive civic identity. It enjoyed economic momentum with explosive tech growth. Austin was at the top of "lifestyle signaling," with residents using where they live to signal their values—informal, creative, tolerant, and outdoors-oriented. The strong demographic pull to Austin fostered a great immigration of young professionals, creatives, and founders.

Austin was doing exceptionally well as measured by almost every metric used to compare cities. And when I left office, Austin was among the top five best big American cities to live in, according to the *U.S. News & World Report* annual rating, as well as one of the healthiest.

Austin ranked number one in wage growth and number two in job growth. We had one of the lowest unemployment rates among large U.S. cities. Our city budget was balanced and had projected surpluses for each of the next four years.

Austin was the best big city for job seekers and the best place for entrepreneurs to launch a startup. Equally important, Austin was in the top ten of the most fun American cities to live in, and it was rated the most fun city in Texas. And of course, we were in the top four best U.S. music cities and ranked first as the best city for live music fans.

Austin celebrated being the "Live Music Capital of the World."

You would think that the Republican leadership in the state would want to copy and expand on what made Austin so special and such an economic driver. Not so.

A lot of people working hard together, myself included, got these results. For the eight years I was mayor, the job took up virtually every minute of my life. I almost never had a minute to myself. I lost the close contact I had with most of my friends. But time was of the essence. I had never had a job before where I knew exactly how much time I had left in that job. When I was sworn in as mayor and every morning I woke up thereafter, I knew exactly how many days, how many hours, and how many minutes I had left to be mayor.

I wanted to get big things done, and I always felt there wasn't enough time because big changes take time. My time was limited, and I didn't want to waste any of it.

But being mayor is to not be in control of your time. An endless stream of residents wanted to talk to me or my staff. Everyone expected access. Those who needed a job, a home, or a meal always moved me. My staff and I always tried to be receptive to anyone reaching out, and most of the time, we were successful to some degree. I could have spent 100 percent of my time responding to constituent requests.

As mayor, sad to say, you can't do that.

We would hold a council meeting every week or two. On the agenda, the council decided issues, policies, or disputes between people. Twenty new controversial matters landed on our desks every week. Few were decided easily. Many involved two or more members of council working together to achieve acceptable solutions.

I spent more time with the council members than I did with my wife and family. Some will be good friends forever. I could have spent all my time on council meeting matters, but I couldn't do that either.

What I wanted to do as mayor was to focus my time and that of my staff on the large, significant, and thorny issues that would have the greatest impact on our city. I knew the best use of my time and resources was to help develop and gain support for the mass public transportation we so desperately needed. The most strategic place for me would be rallying voters to approve the infrastructure spending required of a growing city. Successfully addressing systemic inequities and issues of basic justice and access would itself require a very directed and real-time commitment. I also had to invest my efforts in housing affordability and homelessness.

For a public official, especially a mayor, the most precious commodity is time.

Even with all the time constraints, I wanted to achieve the big goals that would help make Austin a better place for all those who lived here. In my two terms, I focused on three broad goals: mobility, social justice and equity, and housing affordability and homelessness.

When I came into office, Austin was well behind on the infrastructure needed for such a growing city. Prior city councils had seemingly adopted the practice, if not an informal policy, of not investing in the necessary infrastructure in the hopes that fewer people would move to Austin. It was the "if you don't build it, they won't come" approach.

That strategy doesn't and didn't work. People come anyhow because Austin is a magical place. And yet, as you will see, we still don't have the infrastructure—the mass transit or the housing—that we need.

In the twenty years prior to my first term, Austin voters approved, cumulatively, around $750 million in mobility infrastructure. During the years I was mayor, our council and citizens passed a series of over twenty bond propositions, voter initiatives, and other programs. When I left office, Austin was moving forward with about $25 billion in mobility infrastructure projects, including our first serious effort at mass public transit. We started doubling the size of our airport, and we built and repaired almost four hundred miles of new sidewalks and safe routes to schools. We also invested in one of the fastest-expanding bicycle networks in the country.

In those eight years, our council and I delivered, defended, and preserved justice for those for whom it had been too long denied. In this regard, my greatest partner was Council Member Greg Casar, a young organizer who brought a clear and forward vision, constructive and keen political instincts, and a singular focus on improving the quality of life for all residents:

- We doubled our city's investment in public health.
- We created and institutionalized an equity office and equity tools to inform all that city government did.
- We prioritized homelessness and affordable housing.
- We committed to paid sick leave.
- We passed guarantees of Fair (or second) Chance hiring.
- We piloted guaranteed income to find more efficient, just, and cost-effective ways to keep families in their homes.
- We increased the city's minimum wage by over 80 percent to twenty dollars per hour.
- We ended prosecution of truancy and personal use of marijuana, which had been used to disproportionately incarcerate and bring

people of color into the justice system. By doing that, we helped cut by 40 percent the number of people in our local jail.

We did as much as or more than any city in the country to reimagine the concept of public safety. We didn't just talk about it. We initiated changes to the culture of our police force, moving from a warrior mentality to one focused on the police being guardians. We enacted new ways of training police cadets, including mandatory community-engagement and anti-racism training. We advanced the rules guiding when and how the police use force, and we increased funding and training for and embedded mental health clinicians in mental health-related 911 calls.

When I came into office, just over 30 percent of our general budget was devoted to social services, public health, parks, and our quality of life. When I left office, that number had climbed to almost 40 percent.

We opened a city Equity Office and a Civil Rights Office; we adopted an equity tool that would thereafter be used citywide to ensure that justice was centered in everything we did. We honored and supported the rights of LGBTQIA+ residents and, to the best of our ability, provided a safe place for transgender children. We acted to do all we could for those living in Texas to protect women making their own choices concerning their bodies and their health care.

This wasn't easy. For the eight years I was mayor, as you will see, I was the target of the Republican Texas legislature and its far-right leadership of Abbott, Patrick, and Paxton. Because we tried to make big and strategic changes, especially in a period of increasing national partisanship, those efforts brought out both strong support and fierce, adamant Republican opposition. Austin was becoming a more polarized and divided city. Pushing the envelope on issues like homelessness and policing provided fodder for those more powerful politicians with polarizing MAGA doctrines and bigger megaphones than I had.

As you travel alongside me as I worked to improve the lives of Austin's residents, you will get to see just how difficult the job can be.

I am very proud of our magical city and of what that city accomplished in my two terms as mayor. Even today, I continue to be invited to speak around the country and the world on our achievements. During the period I was mayor, Austin stood as one of if not the most successful city in the country.

Not everything my colleagues and I tried to do worked out as we had planned. You'll read about some of those moments, too. I try to lay out for you what happened in both the victories and the defeats, what I was thinking and what I learned. In many instances, you'll be able to see what I might have done differently with the hindsight I have now.

I may be most proud of all the hard things we tried to do, of all the difficult challenges we chose to confront, of where we succeeded and even where we just opened doors so that the city was better positioned to move forward after our time in office was over.

8

THE HIGH COST OF HOUSING

Transportation and congestion were the issues polling with the greatest popular concern when I entered office, but it was becoming increasingly apparent that we were entering into a crisis of housing affordability and supply.

More and more people were leaving Austin because they no longer could afford to live here.

With their exit, we were losing the diversity that was one of our greatest assets.

As mayor, I knew I had to do something about Austin's exploding cost of housing. It became my number one priority. This was true all over America, but it was particularly true in Austin because so many people wanted to move here. My fear was that if I and the council didn't do something, our housing prices would match or exceed those of the big cities like San Francisco, Los Angeles, and New York.

If that were to happen, I knew, only the wealthy would be able to afford to live here, ending the diversity of income, race, background, and vocation that has been the backbone of Austin's identity.

The question of housing, I was certain, was a matter of the city's survival. If we failed, Austin would be a city lacking its special spirit and soul, an outcome I couldn't bear to consider.

To that end, the council and I proposed significant and comprehensive zoning changes. On its face, zoning is a topic so dry that it's hard to imagine anyone wanting to discuss it. But zoning laws determine a lot of what it's like to live in a city by controlling the size and character of buildings and what uses—residential, commercial, or industrial—are allowed and where.

Some of Austin's most intense, emotional, and even vicious battles were fought over zoning because a change in zoning can drive the price of a property way up or way down. A zoning change can make a property owner richer or poorer with surprising speed, and it can change the appearance, character, and daily rhythms of a neighborhood or a busy street.

Homeowners can get intensely emotional when they're faced with a zoning change in or near their neighborhood. This is especially true when a zoning change affects a person's home. For homeowners, their home often represents the single biggest part of their net worth. Their home is also their best hope for the accumulation of wealth.

The council and I moved to make comprehensive changes in our zoning laws to increase the housing supply and to put downward pressure on Austin's rising housing costs. Among other measures, we pushed for policies like lowering the minimum size of lots throughout the city to address affordability.

A lot is the unit of land on which a single house can be built. Big lots in a neighborhood result in fewer, larger, and more expensive homes. The change in the zoning laws we were recommending would allow property owners to subdivide or cut up their big lots into smaller pieces, allowing for more homes to be built and more people to live on what had been a single, big lot.

The zoning changes we sought would also allow property owners to build taller residences, providing for greater housing density, as well as allowing property owners to build auxiliary dwelling units such as granny flats or mother-in-law units in their side or backyards.

In a city desperately in need of more housing, the new zoning laws would provide for more housing and more people in the neighborhood. When the new laws passed, those previously locked out of the Austin housing market cheered.

On the other side—rooting against the new zoning laws—were those residents concerned that such a change would speed gentrification and alter the character of their neighborhoods: greater congestion and more cars, less open space, and less privacy.

As far as I was concerned, we needed more houses, period. These zoning changes would allow Austin to build more houses. If we built more houses so that there was more supply than demand, there would be downward pressure on prices. More people would be able to afford to live here.

In the summer of 2018, I was invited to a neighborhood association meeting in one of the more affluent neighborhoods of Austin. The topic under discussion was the impact of the comprehensive changes to the city's zoning ordinance that I and some on the council were championing.

I walked into the school cafeteria that evening and was welcomed by the meeting organizers.

"Mayor Adler," one said. "Thank you for participating in the forum this evening."

I then walked past a gentleman leaning against a wall who coughed and uttered under his breath, "The worst mayor Austin has ever had."

As I entered the large hall with school pep posters on the walls and walked up the aisle to the stage up front, I noticed that my presence stopped conversations. I focused on the blank stares in order to avoid facing the anger that seethed from so many of those in attendance.

I felt pretty much alone, though I did have a couple of my staff members with me. I noticed exactly three in the audience who supported my position. They waved sheepishly, letting me know they were there, but they weren't about to support me publicly. As I looked around the room, I realized I could count on one hand those who were supporting me, though I might not reach my thumb.

I want to be home with my wife, I thought to myself.

Emotions in the room were heightened not only because this was such an emotional issue but also because I was in the middle of my campaign for reelection as mayor. In the room was my primary opponent, Laura Morrison, who was billed as Austin's neighborhood advocate. She was a former city council member, and she sided with the majority in the room who feared the zoning changes for which I was advocating. Laura had been invited to the forum, but unlike me, she was warmly received.

The meeting began, and one resident after another took the microphone to address me directly to let me know how opposed they and the community were to this proposed policy—and to me. Each one claimed that he was speaking for the entire community. These people were sending me a message: if you continue to support this measure, you can kiss your reelection goodbye.

During my time as mayor, I didn't enjoy having to mediate or decide between two parties over the use of property. The high stakes for the parties made the arguments emotional and often nasty. It was winner-take-all—there were no compromises—because the parties saw it as a zero-sum game. Either a party got to build what they wanted, where they wanted, or they didn't.

What separated housing fights from other issues was the intensity with which the dispute quickly divided the community into two separate and polarized camps.

There was no achieving a compromise between the two sides on this issue. The two camps not only disagreed with each other, but they came to blatantly dislike and distrust each other. Each side had the same goal: improving the quality of life in Austin. The problem was that each had a very different idea of what that meant—and they both were right.

But they were both also very wrong.

The two sides fought at neighborhood association meetings, like this one, and in the courts, and most vociferously in the city council chamber during public testimony.

In my eight years as mayor, I spent several lifetimes listening to each side argue its case, each insisting it had the moral high ground. Every speaker professed to express the community view, arguing his position was consistent with the most revered of values. Inevitably, the evenings unfolded as if I were watching a Greek tragedy.

To show you what I mean, I have distilled the public fights I witnessed at council meetings over zoning laws into a dramatic over-the-top dialogue. I play the role of referee. The city council plays the role of decider. Those for an increased housing supply play the role of disrupters of the status quo, and finally, there are the protectionists, who virulently oppose *any* material change in the zoning laws.

For this distillation, I will use a worn-out Class C apartment building with ten modest, affordable apartments. Developers purchased the property and applied to the city council to rezone it to allow greater density and more housing units on the site.

If we approve the zoning change, the developers will be able to tear down the existing apartment building and replace it with a new, taller, and larger building with fifty modern, Class A apartments. The new apartments will rent for more than the existing apartments. Existing tenants will not be able to pay those rents and will be forced to move, but the new apartment building will provide homes for a lot more families, and Austin desperately needs more housing.

I called the council meeting to order by asking one of the leaders on the side against the zoning change to make its case.

"Thank you, council," he said. "Our objection to the application is quite simple. The current residents are mostly students at the University of Texas and low-income families. This plan involves knocking down or substantially renovating their building. They will have to leave. And because of rising housing costs in the city, they not only will have to move, but they will have to move far away. They may have to move to another town, away from friends and family. The children will need to change schools, and their learning will suffer. Much of their support group will be left behind. The children will have to make new friends. It'll be harder for the UT students to get to class. They won't be able to participate in school activities. Some won't graduate."

The proponent for the zoning change then spoke.

"The existing tenants will have to move whether you grant the zoning change or not," he said. "All of them. It's not a question of if but when. You can't save the existing tenants. Even if the existing building remains, the rents will still go up. In Austin's rising real estate market, the value of the property and the rent it will command will continue to rise. The real question before the council is whether the city is better served with a ten-unit building or one that will provide five times the number of apartments. Austinites are having trouble finding places to live now. There's not enough housing supply. That's one of the reasons that property values, housing costs, and rents are all going up."

"Meaning," said the side arguing against the new law, "the owner is getting richer by the minute."

"And the real estate taxes the property owner pays are also going up," said the zoning change proponent.

"The tenants' rent pays for it," said the anti–zoning change advocate.

"For the moment," said the developer. "But soon, rents will have risen to the point where the tenants won't be able to afford to live here, just like so many other Austin properties with rising property taxes. What is the owner to do?"

"Why doesn't he sell the existing building to the tenants?" said the anti–zoning change proponent.

"Can the residents afford it?" said the developer. "Even if the property tax and rent increases don't force the tenants out, they will eventually still be forced to leave, even without the requested zoning change. The owner could make more money by not renewing the current leases, refurbishing the existing apartments with more up-to-date appliances, nicer countertops, and other finishes, and then re-leasing the apartments at a higher rent. That would take the property from Class C to Class B. The owner doesn't need anyone's permission to do that under its current zoning.

"Heck, the owner can simply tear the apartment complex down and replace it with a more modern Class A building, with the same number of ten units, and charge even higher rent. That also doesn't require a zoning change since the number of units is not being increased; the owner could start that tomorrow."

He continued, "Or the owner could sell the existing building to an out-of-state individual or corporate buyer. There's more and more of that now, all over the country. In that case, the landlord is barely invested in the property as a rental at all; they're just sitting on the property until its value increases even further. Doesn't it feel like there are more absentee landlords these days? And more of the problems that come with them? Where do you think they come from?"

"The corporatization of housing," said the anti–zoning change advocate.

"Exactly. It's not great. And that's not all. The current landlord could decline to renew all the tenants' leases and turn the building into a short-term rental without a zoning change or increased investment. They could fill that place with tourists willing to pay a resident's monthly rent just for a weekend. And they could get that income every weekend. There are so many ways the existing tenants could be forced out. I'm surprised it hasn't happened already."

"Council," the anti–zoning change side said, "what are you going to do about this? Can't you give apartment residents facing gentrification in Austin a housing stipend or something so they can afford the higher rents their landlords are charging?"

"We do, in many cases," said a council member. "But to do this on the scale you're talking about means having to tax the whole city just to pay landlords. It might slow the tenant dislocation problem down a little, but it wouldn't stop it, and it would be prohibitively expensive. Just ask the group waiting to speak on the next case on the council agenda about how the city is underfunding neighborhood recreation. You want to tell them we took the money for parks and gave it to landlords?"

"It sounds like you've made up your mind," said the anti–zoning change advocate.

"Not at all," said the council member. "The pro–zoning change side has a point about the residents needing to move eventually, but it doesn't mean it's going to happen today. Or this year. The owner isn't underwater on property taxes yet. Maybe one of the different scenarios may happen, but who is to say how long it will take to happen with this particular property?"

"So turn this down! Turn this down. TURN THIS DOWN!" yelled the spokesman for the anti side, as others in the audience against the zoning change cheered.

Many on the pro side then began to try to shout them down.

As a member of the pro–zoning change side leaned over the

microphone, one of the council members began to shout, "Order! Quiet down in here! Quiet! We will have quiet! . . . Sir, were you trying to say something?"

"It's true that we don't know when the residents will get forced out," said the speaker who was arguing for the zoning change. "But you must admit that the landowner has so many options; it's just a question of when, not if. Unless the property owner suddenly decides he's a philanthropist, the existing tenants' time in the property is limited. It could begin to happen at any time."

"Do you even hear yourself?" said a member of the anti–zoning change side. "You just described how the owner can make a lot of money from this property without any new zoning approval, and you're in here arguing that they should get new zoning and make even more money. What about the evicted tenants? Would it interest you to know that most of the apartment building residents are people of color? Does it concern you in the least that they would almost certainly be replaced by mostly affluent white residents, money and race being as they are in this country? Hasn't the city already lost enough of its minority population—and its very character—to gentrification? Do you even know about this? Or do you just not care about Austin's communities of color, you racist?"

At this point, members of both sides began shouting epithets at each other, and there was a brief shoving match in the aisle.

"Stop this! Order in the chamber! Order!" I shouted.

The noise subsided, and the shoving stopped.

"I'm here," said the zoning change proponent, "because I care about Austin's diversity. Changing the zoning is the only way to get more units on the market—the kind that low-income families and working people and students at UT need.

"The only way for us to have enough of the kind of housing that everyone can afford is for us to build more housing. Period. We either do that in Austin, or that housing gets built farther and farther away and outside of Austin, which is what's happening now. And if we let that go on, we'll become a city that's made up of affluent white people, surrounded by a ring of suburbs and exurbs made up of all the people—working people and people of color and everyone else—who couldn't afford to live here. Is that what you want? Is that your idea of diversity? Of equity? *You're* the racist."

"How dare you?" said his opponent.

"How dare *you*?" said the zoning change proponent. "Look, I want to develop the new building in a way that will enable low-income Austinites to live here forever. So, here's my offer: if the council approves this measure and allows the construction of a new, fifty-unit apartment building, the new apartments will keep ten of those units set aside in perpetuity as low-rent apartments, forever affordable for low-income families. The city won't actually lose any affordable units on this deal. And the affordable units will be guaranteed to stay that way forever—unlike the ten existing units that happen to be affordable today but could become unaffordable tomorrow."

"Well hell," said the anti-change advocate to the council. "Why don't you make every landlord in the city do that with the apartment buildings they own?"

"We can't," said the city attorney from the dais. "Texas state law forbids it, along with preventing a bunch of other things we could do to alleviate the housing affordability crisis."

"What kind of sense does that make?" was the reply.

"None," said the city attorney. "The state legislature would argue it's an important check on cities making policy that conflicts with Texas's character as a state and rendering it less attractive to business, but there doesn't seem to be a coherent plan there—mostly they just wait until a Texas city does something they don't like, deem it woke, and then pass a law to prevent cities from doing it. It's called preemption."

"Can we do anything about that?"

"You're welcome to lobby them until you're blue in the face, and good luck to you," said the council member. "Or try to get them voted out of office at the next election. At the moment, though, all we can do under the law is negotiate with a property owner for those dedicated affordable units in exchange for approving a developer's application for a zoning change. We can't demand having affordable units in apartment buildings generally, but we can make the zoning change conditional on a plan that includes guaranteed affordable units. The owner doesn't have to agree—but if he does, he gets his zoning change."

"So that's what this whole thing is about," said the anti–zoning change advocate. "The developer keeps ten units affordable in exchange for being able to build forty more that will bring in more money."

"That's about the size of it," said the council member.

"What about the ten families that would be evicted during construction? These families with their kids are here, now, in council chambers. Let us introduce you to the children. Let them tell you about their schools, their classmates, the fears and anxieties they have about moving to a strange neighborhood in an unfamiliar community."

He went on, "Listen to their parents tell you all the stories accumulated in the decades they've lived here, the trees they've planted, and the memories of their grandparents who used to live with them in this place. Or don't; the press has been talking to them all afternoon, their stories will all be online, on TV, and in print tonight and tomorrow.

"Someday, these families may well have to move. We don't know when. But it won't be today. Maybe the children get another year in their schools, maybe more. These families are not thinking much about five and ten years from now. They're just trying to get through one year at a time. Council, you have the power to keep these families where they are for tomorrow and the next day. Let them worry about when and what comes next."

Those in the audience against the change in the zoning law cheered loudly.

"Let me ask you a question," said an advocate in favor of the zoning change to the anti-change faction. "How many of you live near the apartment building?"

A small handful raised their hands. Most kept their hands down.

"So why are you people here?" the zoning change proponent asked.

"Because," shouted one from the anti-change group who lived across town in West Austin. "We don't want this racist council evicting people of color so developers can make money." And he added, "We're also here to protect the character of neighborhoods all over the city."

Loud shouting erupted from both sides. I banged my gavel, and the chaos quieted.

"That is outrageous," said a proponent of the pro–zoning change side. "You're trying to stop duplexes from being built in your expensive West Austin neighborhood, aren't you?"

"Isn't this what is happening?" said the anti–zoning change advocate.

"The part about people of color being driven out of Austin while developers make money—that's true," said the zoning change proponent. "But that's going to keep happening unless we build more housing, especially housing that is forever dedicated to being affordable. Why don't you want more housing in Austin? What's wrong with three-story walk-ups or duplexes instead of single-family homes? Or taller apartment buildings with more units?"

"It changes the neighborhood character," was the reply. "Neighbors can look down into my backyard."

Loud shouts again erupted from the side against the zoning change.

"Neighborhood character? You mean West Austin neighborhood character. Those big lots? Wide sidewalks, trees, yards?" said the zoning change proponent.

The antis again began murmuring their upset over the idea of changing the zoning.

"Not just those, but yes, that kind of thing," said the anti–zoning change advocate.

"You know how West Austin got those big lots, don't you? You do, don't you?" said the pro–zoning change guy.

"Yes. I do."

"Why don't you tell these people?" he said.

He then went on to answer his own question.

"In 1928, the city passed a zoning ordinance that explicitly required that people of different races live in different parts of the city. People of color on the East Side, white people on the West. One of the ways they enforced segregation was by making the lots in East Austin smaller, so there'd be more density, and yes, houses would be cheaper because they're less desirable. And they kept the lots in West Austin large, so the property would be so expensive that only white people could afford it.

"West Austin is still mostly white, isn't it? Am I right?" said the member of the pro–zoning change side.

"Less so than before, but still, yes."

"That's the 'neighborhood character' you're here to defend? It's just plain racism. At least we're not driving poor people from their homes so rich people can get richer."

Once again, members of both sides began to push and shove and scream at each other.

"Enough! Enough!" I screamed.

The shoving stopped, but the murmurs continued.

"It is anathema to us to approve anything that would force anyone from their homes," said a council member. "Doubly so when those people are already vulnerable. And yet, we need more housing in Austin if we want anyone who isn't rich to still be able to live here. This requested zoning change would give us more housing, a greater housing supply to meet some more of the demand, help slow rising house prices and rents, and guarantee affordable homes to some future Austinites."

"How much are the developers paying you to say that?" yelled one of the antis. "You must be on the take!"

"Shut up, racist," yelled a member of the pro side.

What resulted was total chaos. There was shoving and yelling, and I was amazed that no one threw any punches.

I banged the gavel. I had had enough.

"The hearing is over," I said.

The council and I walked toward the exit.

"See you at the next one," yelled one of the antis.

"Count on it," yelled one of the pros.

A few minutes later, the council chamber was empty.

This was only a somewhat dramatized account of a typical council meeting during which zoning of a particular Austin property was discussed. There were many such cases. During my two terms as mayor, the council had a slight majority of those who supported zoning changes to increase the housing supply. The majority was large enough to act on individual cases but not large enough to make a comprehensive city-wide change.

In September 2015, before I became mayor, Austin had 21,539 subsidized affordable housing units. In 2021, Austin had 46,630 subsidized affordable housing units, and we had 20,508 additional units in the works.

As mayor, I was constantly bombarded by lobbyists on both sides of an issue who wanted to sit down with me and argue their case. My immediate request was, "Please lay out for me the very best arguments that the other side can make."

I did this because I wanted to learn. I often found that the fervent advocates were most familiar with what their opponents were arguing.

They knew which arguments worked best against their position. They would squirm as they made their opponent's case.

I was strictest with the professional lobbyists. They needed to understand clearly that if they didn't do a good job presenting their opponent's best case, they wouldn't be invited back into my office. I was demanding honesty from these lobbyists, and the lobbyists who played it straight were the ones who best prepared me for future debates and the future scrutiny of positions I would be taking. They became the lobbyists I trusted most.

By doing this, each side was forced to recognize that their opponents had some merit to their position. The way I saw it, those who could argue strongly for the other side weren't showing weakness but rather strength. The winning side often was the side that could best articulate the position of their opponents. When engaging in a hotly contested debate, we need to recognize the possibility of humanity and goodwill of the opposition. The best advocates admit they might be wrong in some respects—or at least that the argument of their opposition might contain a kernel of something true.

This is the difference between disagreement and division. Disagreement is about reconciling and being able to hear different notions of what's right, even if the sides are not willing to compromise. Division occurs when both sides identify the other side as being all wrong. This leads each side to take an extreme position and to spend time only in echo chambers where they come to believe their extreme positions are not only right but shared by everybody.

Which brings us back to the neighborhood meeting with the mayoral candidates on the citywide zoning ordinance changes that were being proposed. The room held 400 in attendance, with 397 of them telling me that if I persisted in changing the zoning laws to allow Austinites to build more housing, I was going against the will of the people.

"You're going to get thrown out of office," someone told me.

I'm sure they believed that. They must have been surprised and shocked when I was reelected, beating my closest opponent by forty points. I even won more votes in that particular neighborhood than my opponent. It turns out that most voters do not attend neighborhood association meetings.

The reason I won reelection was that the voters knew why I wanted to increase housing in Austin. We tore down hundreds of old homes and apartments to build more, bigger, and better ones. Most every time we could do it, the new zoning change came with some guaranteed affordability. We did this even though we knew some low-income families would be forced to relocate after their homes were torn down. And a larger number of future low-income families would have a forever place to live.

We had a choice. We could have let some people stay in their homes for a limited but greater period of time, but the council and I instead wanted to guarantee that even more Austinites, from all backgrounds, would have a place to live and a future in Austin.

As you can see, both sides had reasons for advocacy and misgivings. It's why the choice to change the zoning was so hard and why the debates were so emotional and divisive.

There were nights—there are still nights—when I was lying in bed and I could see the faces of the men, women, and children who were being forced to move because of approved zoning changes. These were the vulnerable who didn't have the experience or the money to cope with the decision that went against them. I closed my eyes and remembered what these people were wearing, how the mothers held their babies, and I could hear the desperate pleas in English and Spanish not to do this. They had come to city hall to plead their case and had left saddened, even devastated.

And I was part of that.

I would still make the same decisions today on almost all the zoning cases I heard. I just wish there was more I could have done to help those who were hurting, even as I and the council adopted all the available mitigation measures we could think of.

I hope the permanent affordability we sought to achieve at their expense forever keeps deserving families in our city.

The process of asking a side to present the best arguments of the other side frustrated my staff, who preferred for me to make quicker decisions. The choices we had to make were hard. Rarely was the right choice unambiguously clear. The process we went through in my office often meant we considered the issues and lived with uncertain outcomes longer than other council offices. I wanted to make the best decision. So much was often at stake.

The council and I didn't get all the zoning changes we wanted because the broad comprehensive change we tried to put in place was challenged in court by the antis. The Texas courts ruled against us, holding that we had not met the procedural hurdles set out by state law. Therefore, we changed strategies and tried again, and again we lost in court. By this time, most of Austin had come to want the kind of comprehensive yet targeted city code changes necessary to achieve walkable, dense, sustainable neighborhoods that could support public transit, lower housing prices, and mitigate the dislocation that almost always accompanies gentrification. The council needed a stronger council majority in support of such measures or a different legal strategy to get them done, and that didn't happen until the next council came into office. I'd like to think our efforts, even when unsuccessful, helped focus the issue, move the electorate, and pave the way for future change.

Despite all we did, the housing shortage that had grown in Austin and the resulting increase in housing costs were extreme. In the years

2021 to 2022, rents in Austin rose higher than they did in any other American city. Rents almost doubled.

But then things started to change. In my last full year in office, 2022, Austin was building more new homes than any other city and twice as many as the national average. We were building new homes nine times faster than San Francisco and Los Angeles.

But it still wasn't enough. Reversing the tide and filling the pipeline take time.

During the years 2023 to 2025, housing prices finally began to fall. As I write this book, housing prices are finally stabilizing in Austin.

And yet, there's still more that can and should be done.

Austin still doesn't have enough houses.

9

THE COVID PANDEMIC

I traveled around the country and the world a lot when I was mayor of Austin. I did this for three reasons. The first is that, while every city is unique, there are enough similarities so that we can always learn something from each other. The second is that an important part of a mayor's job is to help build his city's brand and to tout its virtues as a destination for investment and tourism; talking up the city I love was one of the best parts of the job. And the third is that, when cities work together on larger challenges, they can have an effect greater than the sum of their parts.

I paid for virtually all of this national and international travel myself because the mayor's budget wasn't large enough to support it and because I didn't want to wake up to a headline in the *Austin American-Statesman* that the taxpayers had paid for me to travel to some far-off land. Though clearly defendable as a public expense, my right-wing opponents surely would have pounced, and I didn't want to fight the inevitable battle.

My family sometimes accompanied me, which was a delight and provided crucial time together to offset the little time there was for them in this job. For example, my wife accompanied me on a trip to Ireland together with the Austin-based consul general. While there, Diane and I spent almost a full day learning lessons at the Traffic Management and Incident Centre in Dublin, because I know how to show a lady a good time.

My family was with me on my last economic development and international relations trip to the Pacific Rim. It was a visit primarily to China, the highlight of which was a private dinner with the mayor of Beijing and the municipal committee secretary, leader of the Beijing Communist Party. I was fascinated to see what approach the Chinese took to the challenges that confront and define most large Chinese cities, especially on the scale of Beijing. The dinner was indeed memorable, and we talked about the sharing that can happen between cities on matters such as infrastructure, culture, and arts, even while our national governments are working through other contested issues.

I told them about SXSW in Austin and tried to spark interest and a commitment for China to send a large formal delegation to visit Austin.

We never had the chance to follow up on any of it. It was December 21, 2019. A couple of days later, while traveling from Xi'an to Guilin, I passed within 300 miles of Wuhan, where, at that very moment, its Municipal Health Commission was getting the early reports of a mysterious virus.

We know the broad strokes of what happened next because none of us escaped the consequences. On January 5, 2020, China announced that the Wuhan cases did not come from a known virus; two days later, the World Health Organization named the pathogen 2019-nCoV. The first death from this virus was announced by Chinese authorities on January 11.

I didn't realize it at the time, but the United States immediately started screening for symptoms at airports in New York and California. On January 20, a little-known but much-celebrated epidemiologist named Dr. Anthony Fauci, director of the National Institute of Allergy and Infectious Diseases, announced that we were taking the first steps toward a vaccine. On January 21, the first case was confirmed in the United States. Even still, on January 23, the World Health Organization was taking the position that the coronavirus did not yet constitute a public health emergency of international concern. A week later, on January 30, the United States had its first confirmed case of person-to-person transmission, meaning that someone in the country had caught the virus just by being out in public rather than having contracted it while traveling abroad.

We didn't call it by that name then, but the COVID-19 pandemic had arrived in the U.S.

Still, there wasn't a lot of general attention being paid in Texas, beyond a relatively small group of public health officials, to a virus that was spreading from Asia and moving west, even if that was happening with troubling speed.

February 2020 was a busy month filled with other pressing matters. I spent the night of February 3 with my friend, mayor of South Bend, Indiana, and presidential candidate Pete Buttigieg, watching the Iowa caucus returns in his Des Moines hotel room. The other early presidential primaries soon followed in New Hampshire and South Carolina. It wasn't until the first week of March, just as SXSW was beginning to launch, that Pete Buttigieg and Senator Amy Klobuchar endorsed Joe Biden, clearing his way to the Democratic Party nomination.

Austin's elected and executive leadership was not focused on the real-life, impending health disaster but rather on an imagined, different kind of a natural disaster—a fictitious, raging snowstorm.

In a rather fortuitous coincidence during the last week of February, I met with over one hundred of Austin's emergency response officials at the Emmitsburg, Maryland, headquarters of FEMA for the Integrated Emergency Management Course. We had all traveled halfway across the country to participate in a desktop exercise to practice and to prepare the entire Austin emergency response system for an extreme natural disaster.

The hypothetical exercise was built around a fictional winter storm, which would ramp up in intensity, forcing our people to role-play responding to such an emergency so they could work with and get to know the others who would be part of a real response, if we ever needed one.

It was the first such emergency drill the city had done in over ten years, and it happened just in time. In breaks at the workshop, I began to receive early indications that Austin soon might be facing an all-too-real storm back home.

COVID was on the doorstep of Austin. Around the world, people were dying.

Since all of Austin's emergency disaster relief personnel happened to be together, we began to plan for the real and impending public health disaster.

When we returned home a few days later, the virus was getting closer, and I began getting daily medical and scientific advice and data from the experts. My conversations with mayors in other American cities and around the world became more frequent and more pointed. Other mayors were finding themselves caught off guard by the virus's speed and ferocity. When it arrived in their cities, they said, it hit harder and spread faster than they planned, despite all the warnings.

The reality was that this pandemic was way beyond what any of us could imagine.

During the first week of March 2020, Austin had not yet had its first reported case of a resident catching the virus from another resident. But it was getting close, and the first such case had been found outside of Houston. I suspected that there was a good chance that the virus might already be in our community, but we couldn't know that for sure. We didn't know how long it would take before we saw our first case of a local transfer.

In a conversation with Sam Liccardo, the mayor of San Jose, California, where the pandemic had already arrived, he predicted that I would shortly find myself in my conference room surrounded by advisors.

"They will lay out three courses of action for how you might respond to the arriving virus," Sam said. "The first option will cause the least amount of disruption, the least amount of economic and emotional hardship for your community. This will be the most politically palatable action. It's what you will want to do, but you and your advisors will have reservations about whether it would be enough to protect the city.

"They will present a second option that will seem too extreme," he said. "This option will cause immediate and long-term economic hardship. It will be most disruptive to your community and will be an option that would have been unimaginable just a few weeks earlier.

"Your advisors will present a middle-ground third-option response," he said. "This would still be a very difficult ask of a community, but this option, while still significantly disrupting your city, might also slow the spread of the virus. This option will provide a more balanced approach between enduring the physical hardships and suffering the economic and psychological ones as well."

"What would you recommend I do?" I asked.

"I recommend you reject all three," he said.

He advised me to act in a way that would be even more disruptive than the most extreme option they gave me—and more protective.

"Unless you take strong measures immediately," he said, "there will be an initial case of infection and then a couple more, and then there will be hundreds and thousands just like that. The virus will be out of control, and in too many of those cases, people will die."

His advice, which was consistent with advice I was getting from people on the ground in almost every city, was that no matter how fast I thought this virus would spread and how disruptive I could conceive it might be, the reality would be even more extreme.

"More deaths will happen more quickly," he said.

I faced one huge problem: SXSW was only a couple of weeks away. It was scheduled to run between March 7 and March 15. I can't overstate the importance of the festival to Austin's modern growth and international reputation. It brings around $400 million in economic activity to our city. It's comparable to hosting a Super Bowl.

The lineup for the festival was impressive. Among the keynote speakers were Trent Reznor and Atticus Ross, members of the rock group Nine Inch Nails. The two have won an Oscar, a Golden Globe, and a Grammy. Janelle Monáe, an eight-time Grammy-nominated singer, actress, and producer; Academy Award–winning filmmaker Michael Moore; and Roger Waters, a founding member of Pink Floyd, were also among the speakers.

Other speakers included Judd Apatow, Noam Chomsky, filmmaker Spike Jonze, film critic Leonard Maltin, actress and filmmaker Rashida Jones, Grammy Award-winning Ozzy Osbourne, cultural icon Kim Kardashian, actress Julianne Moore, and many others.

The culture and tech festival is the largest, most important public event we hold in our city every year, with a more than thirty-five-year history of strengthening Austin's economy and brand as a center of innovation and art.

For me to close down SXSW was unthinkable.

Local businesses and their employees depended on the festival. Many based their entire year's business model around it. Some made most of their year's income during that festival.

As mayor, I knew that the hardships of festival workers being out of work and facing uncertainty about how they would pay their rent or food would be devastating.

The impact of closure would be far reaching, reaching all the way to the detrimental and long-term impacts of children missing classes if schools were closed.

But those hardships did not rise to the level of someone unable to breathe and begging for a ventilator, even knowing that such an intervention was often a sign that death might soon follow.

I had to consider the possibility that we could end up hosting the first mass virus spreader event in the country.

This presented a horrific choice.

I had to weigh extreme financial and social disruption in my city versus the prospect of a lot of people dying.

At the early stages of the virus, there was very little information and data on how great the disruption might be, how many people would actually die, and how quickly. As I argued with myself as to what to do, I kept coming back to the belief that, while disruptions might be hard, we could come back from them. Death could not be undone.

The contagiousness of this virus was so great, I was told by experts, that it was only a matter of time before it reached our community.

"Is there nothing that can be done to stop it?" I asked.

"Nothing," was the answer.

My job was to buy as much time as possible in hopes that when the virus hit, we would be closer to a vaccine, the protocols for treatment would be better understood and more refined, we would have more resources and protections, and the public health response would be better organized and deployed.

After I met with public health officials and other local officials, I decided that our highest priority had to be safeguarding the physical health of our community as best we could. I resolved to follow the science and the data, regardless of the short-term impact it might have on social interaction and on our economy.

I didn't have an established playbook to follow. It wasn't clear how best to protect public health and safety. If I were to cancel SXSW, many people in our community would lose their jobs and a substantial amount of their annual income. I knew too that the loss of a job frequently meant the loss of health insurance.

If we were to cancel the festival, I knew, we might well be taking away from some vulnerable people the very health care they would need in the months ahead.

What will happen to them and their families? I wondered.

What if the thousands of people already scheduled to travel to Austin still came, even if we cancelled the event? Would an organized gathering with public health protections in place be more protective than a last-minute cancellation?

I lost sleep over these issues.

In an effort to avoid closing down the festival, the city council, my staff, and I conceived scenarios on how we might proceed in the safest manner possible. We thought it might be a good idea to develop and establish best practices for how large events might reasonably be held in a COVID world.

We looked at how we might minimize close-contact interactions in the context of large-scale meetings. Could we move most of the meetings and festival events outside or make much greater use of closed-circuit broadcasting?

If the festival went forward, we posited, maybe we could get people to do the things we thought might be important at the time, like giving a fist bump instead of a hug or washing hands regularly to protect against getting the virus.

Might it even be our responsibility to hold the SXSW innovation festival as a way to help develop such best practices? I wondered.

It was a tempting thought.

But I couldn't shake the feeling that this was also a rationalization for not doing the unthinkable—the one logical choice to keep everyone safe—canceling the festival.

To their credit, Hugh Forrest and the other owners and organizers of the festival never put any pressure on me to continue the event. Though canceling would have the most severe financial effect on them, they clearly loved their city and cared about keeping people safe. They were good and selfless partners throughout. Among the many untold stories of pandemic-related loss and sacrifice is that, as a result of the closure, these longtime Austin residents would eventually lose majority control of the festival they had owned and run for decades.

On the first Wednesday in March, public health officials, the county judge—who is a county-level executive roughly analogous to a mayor—and I held a press conference to report that the virus was coming but that there was no evidence that determined whether canceling the festival would make the community safer in the long run.

We kept gathering and analyzing data. With every passing hour, it was becoming more apparent how fast this virus was spreading and how deadly it was. It was becoming clear to me that sooner than imagined, Austin, as with other cities across the world, would find itself under-resourced and understaffed to deal with a deadly pandemic.

It was becoming more and more difficult to come up with a plan to open the arts festival without suffering the consequences of the deadly, spreading virus.

We couldn't come up with a reasonable best practice for such a large event.

After the Wednesday press conference, I sat down with Austin City Manager Spencer Cronk, who said to me, "You know, the decision whether or not to cancel the music festival is yours alone to make."

"I had no idea," I said.

In ordinary times, I was expected to serve my term as mayor without ever being responsible for making an operational decision like this. Austin has a manager-council form of city government, not a mayor-council form of government. The city manager is at least the chief operating officer, if not the CEO. The mayor's job is more like the chairman of the board of directors.

My understanding of the job when I ran for Austin mayor was that it was mostly about setting governing and policy direction. I needed to know only enough about the daily operations of the city so I could sit down with my colleagues on the city council to review, question, and oversee the city manager as he made his decisions about operations and communicate with and inform the public about what was going on in city government.

Because of the coming pandemic, this was no ordinary time.

Texas state law provides that in the event there is a significant disaster facing a community, the mayor of the city is the one who issues the disaster declaration. And under state law, once such a disaster is declared, the mayor then assumes the responsibility for making the executive and operational decisions concerning that disaster.

Never had I expected to face such a situation.

The decision whether to shut down Austin's signature festival was mine and mine alone.

The next thirty-six hours were the loneliest of my eight years serving as mayor. In some ways, it's a lot easier to make a decision as part of a group or to give your best counsel and advice to someone else who has to make a final decision.

This is not to say that there weren't lots of decisions that I had to make as mayor about important directions and policies with lasting human effect that weighed on me then and weigh on me now, but this decision as to whether to cancel the innovation and music festival would immediately and irreversibly change the lives of over one million people, at the personal and profound level of their health and livelihoods, including the well-being of their children.

Right or wrong, I knew whatever decision I made I would have to live with forever.

The clock was ticking. I had to decide, and soon.

I had the support of colleagues on the city council and other local leaders, especially County Judge Sarah Eckhardt, who promised to have my back if I decided to cancel the festival, which she recommended. Sarah proved to be an incredibly valuable partner, and as county executive, she and I worked together daily and were almost always united. One of the reasons the Austin area responded as well as we did to the pandemic was because local governments spoke with one voice. When Sarah was elected state senator mid-COVID, her successor as county judge, my friend Andy Brown, stepped in, and if such was possible, local governments worked together even more closely.

I read all the books I could find on the 1918 to 1920 great influenza epidemic that infected as many as 500 million people around the world and killed as many as 100 million. The epidemic began before the end of World War I, when a lot of information about the flu was kept secret. By the time news of the deadly nature of the disease became known, millions had died.

Experts were just beginning to develop best practices and rules about how to deal with the COVID virus. I could make a pretty good argument for canceling the festival. I also had an argument to justify proceeding with significant constraints. People from Austin and around the country on social media and by email were passionately pleading with me to both cancel and not cancel the festival.

I didn't know how badly the virus would strike Austin. I needed to buy as much time as possible to slow the virus spread, until our health care system could better respond to the anticipated number of sick people.

With a heavy heart, I decided to err on the side of saving lives.

Only two days after I had announced the festival would go forward, the facts on the ground changed so quickly that on March 6, 2020, I issued a disaster declaration and effectively canceled SXSW.

A day after I made the declaration, at my invitation, I met with the county judge and our state senator at a local restaurant and spoke to the media. We told Austin residents that it was okay for them to go out to eat and to go to clubs to hear bands. Our thinking was that our chief threat was not Austinites infecting other Austinites. My primary reason for canceling the festival was the fear that people coming to Austin from places where the virus had progressed further would more rapidly bring the disease into the city.

I was wrong. The senator, county judge, and I did not recognize the level of danger to the community we were facing. We should have had a different message. I didn't know it, but the virus was already spreading throughout our community.

The day following the cancellation of the music festival, I began work to financially assist those most affected by the cancellation. I met with Eugene Sepulveda, executive director of the Entrepreneurs Foundation, who I introduced earlier as my campaign treasurer, and Mike Nellis, who ran the Austin Community Foundation, to discuss how they could support those individuals and small businesses hurt most by the cancellation. They formed a nonprofit called Stand with Austin, and they raised $687,000, which we awarded to those artists losing gigs who were hit the hardest.

In another effort to support out-of-work artists, the United States Conference of Mayors, Americans for the Arts, and my friend and mayor of Louisville, Greg Fischer, proposed that cities put some of their local artists to work by commissioning them to rally their communities through music. Several cities followed up, some wonderful pieces were created, and the program helped many artists.

I'm biased, but Austin's anthem inspired, united, and brought hope. I urge you to go online and watch the music video "Walk with Me Austin."

Ours is a magical city.

The impending tragedy was unimaginable. The public was hearing disinformation from President Trump, who, on February 27, 2020, declared without scientific backing that "the virus will disappear." Unable to accept the fact that a pandemic could kill a million Americans under his watch, Trump pretended that the pandemic wasn't that great a problem. At the end of March 2020, he predicted that there would be fewer than 100,000 American deaths. At that rate and proportion, Austin would sustain fewer than three hundred deaths. He was making it all up. The ultimate impact to the nation and to our city would be far graver.

In the earlier stages of the pandemic, we gathered the smartest and most expert minds to share knowledge, coordinate, and give me, the public health authority, the health director, and the county judge the best medical and scientific advice on what we should do and what we should be asking of the community.

We assembled an amazing group of experts: CEOs of the three hospital health care systems in Austin, representatives from the Travis County Medical Association, city and county public safety officials, the city and county Homeland Security managers, state agency representatives, other senior staff and county staff, and experts from the University of Texas and the Dell Medical School.

Beginning in early March 2020 and continuing for almost two years, the group met frequently, seven days a week when needed. One hundred members of our metropolitan emergency response system would listen in on a Zoom call centered on the deliberations among the policy leaders.

Beginning with our first meetings, Dr. Lauren Meyers, professor at the University of Texas, presented to me privately and then to the public the most likely scenarios. Her work, which the U.S. government relied on, used historical data, early experience with COVID from around the world, what we were seeing in Austin, the movement of cell phones in our city, and other data focused on how our population was interacting with one another and moving about the city.

The first time she presented her results, there was a long silence—of shock and disbelief. Her models were telling us that unless we were able to cut down the transfer of the virus between people by *over 90 percent*, the most likely scenario was that our city would soon face many thousands of deaths or worse.

If we took mitigation steps, she said, the modeling still indicated the likelihood that up to a few thousand Austinites would die. Even after doing all we could do!

Dr. Meyers was giving me very different numbers than those President Trump was telling the nation. Her assessment of the most probable eventual impact of the virus, guided by science, proved correct—as of early 2024, Austin had suffered almost 2,000 deaths. The national death toll would end up being ten-fold greater than what the president was predicting.

Dr. Meyers shared with me how the virus would likely progress in our community based on the strength of our response.

She showed what different kinds of collective public behavior would mean in terms of the number of new cases, the speed at which those cases would occur, the number of admissions to our hospitals and intensive care units, and ultimately the number of people who would most likely die.

Austinites needed to see this information right away so they could start making choices for themselves and their families and so our community could act together.

I was preparing my public statement when I got a call from Dr. Meyers asking me not to go public with the number of people that her model indicated would most likely die from the virus in different scenarios.

"The University of Texas administration was concerned that going public with that kind of information might create fear in the community," she said.

I wasn't buying it.

"This information has to be given to the community," I told her. "If we're going to ask people to take truly disruptive actions, they must understand the reasons why. Your models, rather than scaring people, will demonstrate that each of us has some control over what is happening and how bad it might get. We are not just the helpless victims of this virus's spread. We have some measure of agency. Through our collective action, we can actually fight and slow the virus."

"I'll get back to you," Dr. Meyers said.

And I knew that regardless of how her next conversation with the university administration was about to go, I would be making the data public.

Later that evening, she called me back and told me that I could go ahead and convey the mortality numbers associated with her model.

I told her how thankful I was that she had gotten approval to share the data.

Dr. Meyers neither admitted nor denied that she had. I'll never know for sure how internal conversations go inside the University of Texas. But I do remember thinking, as I hung up the phone with her, just how valuable tenure is.

Dr. Meyers is one of my heroes.

Her modeling was not designed to tell us what mitigation steps we should take. It only told us about the most likely outcomes for the ultimate spread of the virus based on how rapidly it was being transferred. The models told us that close and sustained social interactions between people led to the transfer of the virus. Even if I limited those interactions by 50 percent, I learned, the virus would still spread out of control.

To control the spread, we would have to limit those interactions that spread the virus by 95 percent. My challenge was that the model didn't tell us how to limit the social interactions that impacted the rate of spread. It also didn't say whether that great of a reduction was even possible.

It was clear to me that we needed to minimize interactions between people almost any way we could. The most effective way to mitigate the transfer of the virus was to reduce physical interactions between people.

As mayor, I was among those responsible for the community's health, and on March 24, 2020, I issued an order that asked my community to shelter in place in their homes.

I had to make decisions even when it wasn't clear what the best answers were. For example, early on, experts recommended that people wear face masks or face coverings to mitigate the spread of the disease. The challenge with that was that there weren't enough quality N95 face masks to go around, and our medical professionals needed them.

With so many infected people showing up at our hospitals, we needed to save the limited supply of N95 masks for hospital personnel and those on the front lines. I asked our community to use lower-quality masks and to fashion masks out of scarves and handkerchiefs, even though no one was really sure how effective these might be.

Adding to the confusion, the advice on the efficacy of masking that came from the federal government and the CDC seemed to be contradictory. They tempered their message about mask efficacy because they were also concerned about causing a public run on the limited supply of the most effective N95 masks. As a result, their message was muddled and confusing.

Requiring people to wear masks also became a polarizing political issue. It made sense that wearing a mask would mitigate the transfer of virus particles, but we did not know to what extent. Hundreds of naysayers sent me internet links to thousands of videos showing people sneezing behind masks, backlit in a manner that captured a significant cloud coming through. The purpose of these memes was to show that mask-wearing didn't work.

Almost unanimously, the physicians around me advised that masking would help mitigate the transfer of the virus. The only unknown was the degree of that protection. That made intuitive sense to me, as I knew I would feel better if a person sneezing in my face had a mask on. Other than the inconvenience, masking wouldn't hurt most people, and the stakes were very high.

In June 2020, I issued what came to be called a mask mandate.

There were myriad decisions to be made on measures that could be taken to mitigate the spread of the virus but that would also hurt the economy. Ordering that restaurants could only deliver or serve takeout meant that people would not be sitting in close quarters, even though I knew many restaurants couldn't survive without people dining inside them. This was an even bigger issue for bars since patrons came for alcohol that had to be consumed on site, so takeout and delivery options were limited.

Some interactions were necessary for people to survive economically. Not everyone was privileged to do their job from home or was able to get food delivered. Grocery stores needed to continue providing food for the community. That meant that people working to stock shelves had to be in close proximity to coworkers and customers who were shopping.

On the night the order banning on-site service in restaurants and bars became effective, I took a walk with Mark Yznaga, a friend and advisor who had been by my side since before I was first elected mayor, in the restaurant-and-bar district in downtown Austin. I was concerned about whether anyone would listen to me and follow the order.

The order was clear, but the burden that I was imposing was so great on restaurants, bars, and people's social lives that I didn't know if *anyone* would comply.

I knew that Austin didn't have nearly enough police officers or code enforcement agents to enforce the order if owners of bars and restaurants and their customers decided to resist. If that happened, my ability to lead the community through the pandemic, I knew, would be cut short right at the start.

I was incredibly nervous and apprehensive at the beginning of that walk. I didn't know if the community would listen to me or whether they'd heed those mostly Republican voices around the state loudly claiming I was overreacting.

This was a test of my political power and standing in my community.

As I turned the corner to enter the district, I knew I was about to face an early referendum on me personally.

I was scared.

The street was mostly empty. As we walked, I saw a few cars go by since there was no ban on intracity travel, and there were reasons a few people might be driving. I passed the first restaurant and saw no one inside. It was closed.

It's hard to describe the relief I felt.

The farther I walked, the greater the relief. The restaurants and bars were empty. An order like mine only works if people agree to follow it, and from the looks of it, the city had agreed to shut down.

Later that evening, I took that walk again. I'm not sure why. Maybe there was a need to make sure I indeed had seen what I saw. Maybe people had changed their minds and were now gathering. Maybe I just needed to be alone.

I was back in the middle of the block on a still very deserted street. I sat down on the curb and privately celebrated that our community had understood what needed to be done. It was so quiet on that street. It had the eeriness of a snowed-in street with no traffic under the silence of the streetlamps that I remembered from growing up back east.

As I sat there, the silence soon became a ringing that at first sounded distant but drew closer and grew louder. The feeling of relief didn't last but a few moments. It was displaced by the deafening realization that the economic and social harm that was just now beginning in my city and in communities across the country and the world, even though necessary to save lives, would be unimaginable.

The people missing from the restaurants and bars, ostensibly in their homes, were far from safe. This was going to be hard. Many people were going to die. The economy was about to be devastated. Our children would suffer immensely.

Our lives were being changed forever.

Almost every evening, beginning in March 2020, I made a live broadcast on Facebook from my home to share with my community the latest information and data concerning the virus. I began each evening's episode by asking, "Do you have a minute?" That became its name, even though most evenings the live Facebook broadcast would go on for more than twenty minutes.

I shared with the community the daily numbers of how many new cases we had, how many new admissions there were to the hospitals, the occupancy of our intensive care units, and the results of the modeling that the University of Texas was providing.

Most of this information was also available on the internet for anyone to get themselves, but I was able to add a little background and color. I also shared photographs that neighbors had sent to me of them and their families coping with the restrictions on ordinary life, like sheltering at home. The shots were of family activities, forming small social pods, and avoiding interactions with most others. This part of these broadcasts may have been the most popular, as we could see that even though we were by ourselves, we were not alone.

I worried that Governor Greg Abbott would play down the epidemic à la Trump, but early in the pandemic, Abbott was telling residents across the state the same message I was giving them. Governor Abbott and I each publicly declared that in responding to the pandemic, we would be guided by the science and the experts.

I took great comfort in the fact that we were both pledging to follow the science. Because many of the people advising me were also advising him, I knew our messages would be so much more powerful because I mistakenly thought we would be aligned.

At the start of the COVID scare, Governor Abbott encouraged local communities to set their own rules for how to respond to the pandemic. I was working very closely with the mayors of many of the other large cities in Texas, including Houston, San Antonio, Fort Worth, Corpus Christi, and El Paso. We spoke individually and regularly as a group. We shared the content and timing of our draft orders so that the actions of cities would affirm one another.

Governor Abbott, at times, was hands-off to a fault. It was as if he didn't want to accept the responsibility of making decisions. In one telephone call, initiated by him and attended by many, a Republican county judge from a rural area in West Texas asked him to issue a statewide mask mandate so that he could enforce it in his community. The county judge thought it was the right thing to do but thought that he'd run into political resistance if he acted on his own, so he was asking for cover from the governor.

Governor Abbott left him hanging.

"These are local decisions that need to be made by communities for themselves," Abbott said.

Governor Abbott's commitment to local control didn't last, however, and conflict followed.

When I issued our shelter-at-home order, it exempted essential workers and allowed critical operations to continue. At that early point, it was not clear what was or wasn't an essential job or a critical operation.

In Austin, we were confronted with the question of whether large-scale construction was critical and thus able to continue. I had a difficult call to make. The cost of stopping construction activity on large projects would be immense, I knew. But I also knew that construction workers were disproportionately Hispanic and that the virus was hitting the Hispanic community the hardest. Many of these workers were living in multi-generational homes, living in close quarters in small spaces. If one worker became ill, many others would follow.

I asked Dr. Meyers to model for us the spread of the virus in our community if construction activity was allowed to proceed versus if we declared a construction hiatus. Her results were dramatic. Thousands more people would die not only in the construction industry but in the general population if we allowed construction to continue unabated, she said.

Construction activity was not necessary for the city to survive from day to day, like the operation of utilities or the ability to get food and drugs. But the projects were so big, involving so many people and so much capital, delays of any kind would have a huge economic impact.

Once again, I had to choose between a better economy and the death rate.

I entered an order that included construction activity, at least until we had a better handle on a clearer path forward to mitigating the possible harm and more ventilators in our hospitals.

Immediately, the order was controversial.

My office and I started getting emails and calls.

One caller was Anthony Precourt, the owner of the Major League Soccer team who had just moved his team to Austin in the year before the pandemic. He was in the process of building a new twenty-thousand-seat stadium. I very much wanted him and the new team to be successful. Before he chose Austin as the team's new home, we were the largest American city without a professional major league sports team.

I had worked hard to help build the political coalition necessary to have the team in our community. In fact, the final council vote to approve the agreements to bring the team and allow the building of the stadium passed by only two votes. I had kept the council in session until after 4 a.m., in a council chamber still full of people. Those opposed tried both on and off the dais to run out the clock. I held the session open until we could call the vote because I knew we had the numbers. Sometimes politics is about strategy, and sometimes it's just plain endurance.

I was now on the phone with that owner. He wanted an exemption to the halt on construction activity for the stadium. He was asking me what could be done. He had a very large investment caught in the moment, and I understood the validity of his concern.

I ran through the scenarios in my mind. Was there a way I could justify the stadium construction moving forward because it was so important for the city and, honestly, to me personally?

But there was no way. We needed to figure out how to best keep construction workers safe before construction projects could continue.

The modeling from Dr. Meyers was clear in its conclusions. We were early in the virus, and we didn't have all the answers, but we knew people were dying. We also knew that we were going to have to live with the virus and allow more interactions between people, even as we tried to mitigate the virus's impacts. We just weren't there yet.

I told the owner I understood the challenge he was facing, but I didn't give him the answer or encouragement he wanted. The conversation between us went south. A year later, after the vaccine was available, the team would open its first season in the new stadium. The team honored me with a framed jersey and a game ball. But in that inaugural season, I was never invited up to the owner's box.

I'm sure the governor's office was getting the same phone calls I was getting from builders and property owners involved in construction. In response to my order, Governor Abbott issued an order that contravened mine. Abbott declared construction activity to be an essential operation and decreed that it be allowed to continue.

I don't know if the governor ever saw the study from Dr. Meyers or whether he saw it and didn't believe it or whether he thought increased deaths among those most vulnerable—the workers who most needed to work and were least able to protect themselves—was a necessary cost to keep the economy open and functioning.

In any event, I chose not to go to the courts to fight him on this. I would have to pick my battles.

Mayors and county judges have almost unlimited power to respond to local disasters. The governor was given similar powers, but arguably, his came with certain limitations that didn't come with mine. Rather than challenge the governor in court, I chose to amend my order to be consistent with his, and at the same time, I worked with the construction industry in Austin to impose masking and other restrictions on construction sites that would at least make them as safe as possible for the workers. We watched the effects carefully. Construction projects, like the Q2 stadium for Major League Soccer, went forward.

I didn't relish being in conflict with the governor. I didn't think it served Austin well, as conflict sends confusing and unsettling messages to the people. Governor Abbott had discretionary control over the allocation of certain resources among cities, and I didn't want him to punish Austin. I also had a growing realization that Governor Abbott was using his disputes with me and other mayors of predominantly Democratic cities to organize politically and fundraise, and I didn't want to help him do that.

There were other times when I had no choice but to meet the governor in court. The advantage of getting engaged in such a dispute, regardless of the legal outcome, was to send the message to the Austin community that what we were doing was important enough to force us into a confrontation, that we needed to do everything we could to protect our community—including being in court with the governor.

Our messaging to the community during the pandemic was critical.

The media frequently asked me whether I could actually enforce our local orders because of limited enforcement resources.

I answered by first recognizing that we didn't have enough police officers or code enforcement agents to enforce the orders.

"If the orders are to be followed," I said, "it will be because the community chooses to abide by them. If people see others cooperating, they're more likely to cooperate themselves."

Sometimes all I sought and needed was a temporary victory. Prior to New Year's Eve on December 31, 2020, I issued an order that required restaurants and bars to close at 8 p.m. Public health officials and I were afraid that an unrestricted New Year's Eve would become a citywide super-spreader event.

I also knew when I issued that order that the governor might issue a contravening order, that he would have the state attorney general seek an injunction. But I also thought that we might be able to keep my order in place long enough to get past New Year's Eve.

And that's what happened.

The bars closed for the holiday at 8 p.m. The courts didn't hear the case until later. I would like to think that we saved lives by taking that action and by the newspaper coverage and other media attention that the controversy brought. I wanted my community to understand that it was still very important that we maintained vigilance.

COVID would go on to devastate Austin. We lost almost 2,000 of our area residents, and as in other cities, the virus hit our most vulnerable with its greatest fury. Added to the tragedy is the fact that even now, thousands more haven't recovered from the physical harm and the financial hit. Some still suffer from long COVID, and some children may never recover from the time lost in school.

In part as a result of my orders, the COVID mortality rate in the Austin area was less than one-half of the mortality rate in Texas as a whole. In fact, if the State of Texas had had the same mortality rate as the Austin area, more than 25,000 fewer Texans would have died. The numbers are even more stark for the United States, generally. Thanks in part to President Trump's refusal to warn the public about the deadly nature of COVID, our country had an even higher mortality rate than Texas. If the United States had had the same mortality rate as the Austin area, more than 636,000 American residents would *not* have died from COVID.

We may never know for certain why so few died in Austin compared to most other large urban areas around the country. It's likely that our atypically strong COVID response coordination under the leadership of Dr. Mark Escott (City and County Health Authority and Medical Director) and Stephanie Hayden (Austin Public Health Director), the cooperative interaction of our major private health care providers, the wide community adoption and support of aggressive mitigation measures, and a particular focus on equity in health care delivery contributed greatly.

More than anything, it was the selfless individual decisions of so many Austinites working together as a community that saved so many as the pandemic raged around them.

10

HOMELESSNESS—"A CHALLENGE"

When I took office, homelessness wasn't even on my radar screen, and as I was setting priorities for my second term, I remember telling my staff that I had no intention of being known as the Homelessness Mayor, as the issue was not among our priorities. We were making great strides on infrastructure, jobs, the economy, climate change mitigation, equity, and justice, and I wanted these issues to be my continued focus. And yet when I left office at the end of my second term, even with additional progress in each of those areas, the homelessness issue exploded in Austin, and that issue may be linked more with my time as mayor than any other.

Will we solve the problem?

Only time will tell.

A year and a half after I left office, Diane and I, at the last moment, were disinvited from a dinner for a couple of hundred attendees, mostly successful tech entrepreneurs who were gathering for networking and a discussion of economic development.

"Adler is not welcome in my home," said the host, "because he allowed homelessness to nearly destroy our city, because he was okay with tents all over, and because his actions in office are evidence of a disregard for public safety."

He wasn't the only one who felt that way. While most people I encounter are very kind and appreciative of me and my time in office, there are those who even now follow my family and me down the street and blame me for allowing tents and creating danger on the streets of Austin.

I learned a lot from how we dealt with homelessness. I'm proud of what we did, and there's much I would have done differently if I had known then what I know now.

I ask myself, *Was the disruption the council and I brought to Austin to set a more strategic and comprehensive plan regarding homelessness the right and effective thing to do?*

I hope it was. There are very encouraging initial results. But there is no denying that this was and is a very divisive and disruptive issue, one that will forever be linked to my time in office.

I admit that I and my fellow city leaders actively and affirmatively caused significant angst in our community. I also believe in my heart and continue to contend that it was the right thing to do, as I'll explain.

Homelessness, to be sure, is the great Achilles' heel of successful American cities. Los Angeles, San Francisco, Seattle, and Portland—great cities with fantastic growth, all desirable places full of exciting potential—have been significantly shaken by the spiraling crisis of homelessness.

The recent mayoral elections in each had homelessness as a major if not *the* major issue in those races, a testament to civic angst on a grand scale. Many of the people moving to Austin from those cities point to homelessness as the reason why they left and came here. Homelessness in Portland was a critical issue in the 2022 Oregon governor's race. The winner, Tina Kotek, made homelessness her highest priority as she began her term.

When a community is faced with a challenge that it doesn't sufficiently address, the people lose faith in their government. It becomes too easy to doubt a government's ability to do anything at all when it can't fix the specific problem that is driving the angst. Failing to deal with homelessness in a community where the problem is growing has far-reaching implications.

Frustration and disappointment turn into a sense of helplessness, followed by anger.

A community that had been resolved to help people in need can become a community that sees a person in a tent as a threat and an enemy. Instead of trying to solve the problem and stop the suffering, public opinion can turn to wanting the problem to just go away, and at no cost or as little cost as possible.

When parts of a community turn like that, it can be hard—even impossible, as I found out—to win back the naysayers. The issue becomes politicized and polarizing. The very real nuances and complexities are lost and devolve into two sides that will no longer talk to or listen to each other, as each uses the issue as a tool to organize and raise money.

Homelessness is an issue that has the greatest potential to send a successful city on a downward spiraling path. Homelessness and public safety meld into the same issue; finding homes for people who don't have them inevitably ends up with debates on issues like police funding, violent crime bail policies, immigration, and fears of being unsafe. Homelessness is the tool that politicians and special interest groups exploit to cause fear and drive wedges.

This is the story of San Francisco, Los Angeles, Portland, and Seattle.

I was determined not to let it be the story of Austin.

For years, most Austinites didn't notice the homeless population very often. It just wasn't a big part of their lives. The people without homes were mostly living hidden in places the community never saw. Occasionally, someone would encounter an unhoused Austinite and it led to tension. The violations that resulted most often were of space, decorum, respect, and aesthetics. Sometimes an individual would fear for their personal safety, whether or not there was actual danger.

When I began as mayor in 2015, most people in Austin who didn't live near the few visible encampments only encountered homelessness when they drove through east downtown by the Austin Resource Center for the Homeless shelter facility, also called the ARCH shelter. Those who were homeless and their predators gathered in an open-air drug market outside the shelter, which only admitted a small number for the night.

This shelter was created about fifteen years earlier at what then were the outskirts of the downtown business district. Not understanding how Austin would grow, the leadership at that time didn't anticipate that the business district would come to surround the ARCH. Greater interaction and conflict were inevitable. Nor did they realize that creating the ARCH—what was presented as a solution—would also hide the real challenge. It removed the impetus to find permanent homes for those without them and to build a homelessness response system fit for the purpose.

Building the ARCH by itself was an example of a small, ineffective solution that looked big at the time, as the politicians of the day were eager to make quick, visible splashes rather than doing the harder, long-term, and comprehensive work of solving this very difficult problem.

The ARCH was a ticking time bomb. Eventually and inevitably, it would explode.

For almost twenty years, in a city of almost one million people, a city of great and increasing wealth and seemingly unlimited resources, the politicians who ran Austin were unable to find homes and hope for the few thousand people who were left living on our streets and hiding in our green spaces and wooded areas on any given day. With homelessness relatively small and not very visible, there wasn't the citywide public outcry for politicians to ramp up efforts to try to meet the scale of the problem.

The need to set up an effective homelessness response system was easy to ignore because providing needed homes and associated services meant spending a significant amount of money. Large constituencies were clamoring to spend that money elsewhere: for parks, libraries, more roads, and more police.

Building and locating homes for the homeless population, moreover, meant the nearly impossible task of identifying appropriate places somewhere in the city in the face of objections that constituents would raise, no matter which location we suggested.

A howl would arise.

"It's too near my neighborhood, school, or business," people chorused.

The alternative was to suggest a site so isolated that no one without their own ready transportation would want to live there, a site too far away from the services, odd jobs, and resources those without homes need to survive.

Why was homelessness hidden? Austin's prevailing strategy for dealing with the homelessness challenge was similar to that of most large cities: criminalize it. No camping, sitting, or lying on the ground was allowed, and if you got caught doing any of these, you could receive a citation or a fine or be arrested.

A business owner could call the police and report someone out front who was scaring away potential customers. The police would arrive and threaten arrest or a ticket if the homeless person didn't move along.

Most often, that person would go elsewhere.

"Just the threat of a ticket," our Police Chief Manley proudly said, "resulted in nearly complete voluntary compliance with the law."

But those moving along had no safe place to go. No matter where that unhoused person went, he was still violating the law. The only way to avoid arrest or a ticket was to hide.

From 2014 to 2016, the Austin Police wrote 18,000 tickets for the homeless who were camping, sitting, and/or sleeping in public areas. Because very few of those who were handed tickets showed up in court on the appointed day, a bench warrant would almost automatically be issued for their arrest. Months later, if the support system was able to find the unhoused person a home or apartment or, even better, a job, an arrest record and outstanding warrant would frequently appear, and that person would be disqualified and denied.

The system was defeating itself. It was cruel. And it sure wasn't doing anything to solve or limit the increase in homelessness.

Most people on the street and without homes were and are victims of a perfect storm.

The road to homelessness can begin simply when a family gets a medical bill it cannot pay. Hounded by bill collectors, the family suffers from anxiety over finances. They make the difficult decision not to make the car payment in order to pay the medical bill. And then they lose their car. And because getting around becomes harder and less reliable, either the husband or wife loses a job. And then the spouse also loses their job.

And then they get the eviction notice.

One spouse leaves with the children. The other, usually the husband, is on the streets, after having burned through all the family and friends who might otherwise take him in or intervene.

The difference between keeping a home and losing it in most cases is a matter of a few hundred dollars.

Addiction and mental illness often follow, though most people are not on the streets for this reason. The longer someone is living on our streets, the data shows, the more the incidence of substance abuse and mental health challenges grows. These issues become increasingly severe for those suffering chronic homelessness.

If a person is newly on his own on the streets and can quickly get a place to live and find service support for just a few months, in most cases, he will be able to right himself and his life. The opposite is also true. The longer a person is left on the streets, the harder it is to get off them.

In Austin, if a homeless person asked for help during the years 2016 to 2018, it could take a year and a half to find him a home. By then, for many, it would be too late for the speedy exit from homelessness.

While I was mayor, the number of those stranded on our streets was beginning to grow, but most Austinites didn't know.

It's not that homelessness wasn't an issue. It just wasn't a priority interest among most people. They knew about the ARCH downtown because it was visible, especially to those leaving downtown and heading to the airport. It was also visible to those who frequented the nearby downtown entertainment district, East Sixth Street. For many in Austin, the perceived homelessness challenge was the ARCH.

During my first campaign for mayor, the Chamber of Commerce and other downtown business interests wanted me to promise that I would move the ARCH. The problem with that was that the social justice activists understood that if the ARCH was moved, the homelessness challenge would be even more removed from sight and mind, making it even less likely that the problem would get solved.

I met with the outgoing Austin mayor after I had been elected. He brought up the subject. Mayor Lee Leffingwell had bolstered my run for mayor. He publicly endorsed me just two weeks prior to the election over two of his council colleagues, and his endorsement may have helped seal the victory.

When I met with Lee, he asked me to make him a promise.

"Steve," he said, "if there was one missed initiative I wish I had been able to move on, it would be ending veteran homelessness in our city. Promise me that you'll complete what I started."

Mayor Leffingwell had been a champion for veterans, having created a city Veterans Office and providing significant support to the Honor Flights program. In Leffingwell's last year in office, First Lady Michelle Obama and Second Lady Dr. Jill Biden launched the Mayors Challenge to End Veteran Homelessness. Mayor Leffingwell had been one of the first mayors to sign up his community. But there had been no time for him to take action on that commitment.

"Mayor, you have my word," I replied, without knowing much about homelessness, much less veteran homelessness. On the campaign trail, this issue had not been something I had heard much about.

Because of my promise, in addition to dealing with transportation, infrastructure, housing policy, and other recognized priorities, I moved to address veteran homelessness.

It took two years to end it. It was that quick. In August 2016, Julian Castro, the secretary of Housing and Urban Development, came to Austin to announce that Austin had achieved net effective zero veteran homelessness. Almost seven hundred veterans had been on our streets. Now they had housing and services. We also built the infrastructure necessary to house and provide services to the veterans who fell into homelessness thereafter.

We now had a formula that could be applied to address homelessness in general. We had formed an unprecedented coalition between the business community and interested social justice and service organizations to create new innovative tools like the de-risk fund outside of government that opened more housing spots. Surely, I felt, we could now quickly address homelessness citywide in a major way.

Except we couldn't.

And we didn't.

Homelessness is a national problem, and when the federal government decided to end veteran homelessness as a priority, it moved resources for housing vouchers and support services to veterans, and it got the job done in cities across the country. Austin received millions of federal dollars to support our effort to get veterans off the streets.

What the federal government did not do was make ending homelessness a priority for other target groups.

I discovered that many of those who supported ending veterans' homelessness did so because they were motivated specifically to help veterans. It turned out that the political will in the community to spend the money to end homelessness in general didn't exist.

Without the necessary resources, expanding the success we had with veterans wasn't possible.

Austin, like so many cities, was dealing with homelessness on the cheap. Criminalizing the homeless population had kept the issue out of sight for most people.

The challenge, unseen, was beginning to bubble up.

Not long after we had achieved success with veteran homelessness, one of the most significant mistakes I made as mayor came after a visit to a large homeless encampment in the woods near the railroad tracks. Many homeless people had been living there in tents and under tarps for a long, long time. Trash had rarely been picked up. There were piles of it everywhere. It looked like a stereotype of the poorest parts of the developing world. It was clearly a health hazard and a safety risk.

I was appalled. And as a member of local government, I felt ashamed.

I went to the city manager and asked that he clean up the trash from the encampment.

"If the media finds out about these conditions," I said, "the city government will be embarrassed, and we will be blamed."

It was a big mistake, and I'm sorry I did this.

Leaders tend to hide problems because they don't want to preside over failures.

I was guilty as charged of this thinking.

Yes, the trash needed to be removed for the benefit of both the housed community and those living in tents, but I should have invited every reporter and photographer who'd take my call to join me there the next day after my visit. I should have better understood that the anger, shame, and embarrassment I was feeling would also be how my constituents would feel.

After all, the people living in the encampment had no other place to put their trash, because garbage trucks don't regularly show up where they live. I should have known that unless my fellow Austinites saw this, *really saw it*, they wouldn't be moved to act to help these people lead better lives.

In the time since and even today, social media trolls post videos on their feeds of the homeless living in squalor around the city. Accompanying the videos are posts blasting the city for not doing more to clean up such encampments and to get rid of these people. But these trolls don't offer suggestions as to how to solve the problem. They virulently oppose spending the resources to get people out of such encampments and into shelters and homes. They want the trash and the people to just somehow disappear. They're quick to point fingers and complain but slow to be part of a constructive solution.

Ordering the camp cleaned up was the right decision, but I missed an opportunity to clearly highlight a problem and, in so doing, build support for finding and executing a constructive solution.

What we were doing was not working. Our community was not moving to meet the scale of the challenge of homelessness. The overarching public policy we had to offer was to continue to criminalize homelessness. As the out-of-sight places that hid those without homes began to burst forth at the seams, sending people to more visible places, nearby neighborhood anger began to build. I learned just how much when I was invited to attend a meeting of the Onion Creek Homeowners Association.

By then, emotional and even antagonistic neighborhood town hall meetings were familiar terrain. I listened carefully, responded honestly, and usually knew where to find answers to questions raised. We could identify a path forward to resolve the issues.

I was confident in my positions and, with my legal training and experience, could communicate and defend them even in rooms where few if any agreed with me. It was easy and part of my nature to be open and transparent. That meant I was comfortable talking to crowds wherever I was. Knowing all the answers was not something I expected of myself. I assumed everything I said and did was always being recorded, posted, or reported, and that meant my safest place was always being consistent, which is what happens when you're being honest.

Many times before, I had gone before a room of several hundred neighborhood members to hear objections to land-use changes I was supporting—changes that some neighbors felt would hurt their neighborhood character or would devalue their chief asset, their home.

Many times, I spoke to business owners to defend pushing for initiatives like mandatory universal health care for employees, knowing such a policy would cut into their bottom-line profitability, at least in the short term, in exchange for a healthier and safer community.

I knew how to find and speak from common values, to identify and correct misinformation, to be willing to accept and to value learning things I did not know, and to appropriately question myself even on the spot and in real time.

I knew I would not always find friends and convince others of the correctness of my positions, but I had been elected to do a job, and I was determined to do it. I also knew that my agenda was in accord with what most of our city wanted. With honesty and transparency, I felt I could build goodwill even with people who disagreed with me. That was usually true, until the partisan divide over the issue of homelessness became such an impenetrable wall as to end most people's ability to hear views not their own.

That evening meeting of the Onion Creek Homeowners Association was *so* different, I was blown away. I felt frustration and fear in the room, unlike anything I had ever felt before. The neighborhood wanted to talk to me about a homeless encampment under a nearby highway overpass. They wanted the encampment and those living there gone, and they didn't care how I did it.

They were sure that all the petty vandalism and crime in their neighborhood originated from that encampment. It seems that every father and homeowner had a wife or daughter or knew someone who had a wife or daughter who had had what they felt was a frightening encounter with someone they believed to be homeless and living under that overpass.

After the meeting was over, an angry man and several others ran over to me.

"If you don't fix this," the man told me with cold eyes and a red face, "I have a gun, and I'll fix this myself."

I didn't know whether he was threatening the people under the overpass with harm or whether he was just incredibly angry and scared, but just in case, I alerted my security detail after we walked away from him.

I never saw him again.

But here I was at this meeting, the mayor who was presumably in charge of the city, and I had no answers to the ninety minutes of questions, comments, charges, and accusations hurled at me about what the city was going to do about the homeless problem.

What we were doing was too small, too temporary, and too ineffective to address the problem. I could make no satisfying or meaningful promises, and I could not give the gathering any real sense of future hope.

I didn't disagree with much of what I heard. The fear those people felt was real; their frustration, justified. It was just that I had nothing to offer the people attending that would address their angst. What I knew was that the issue was not seen as important enough for the city to make the problem of homelessness a priority.

Driving home from the Onion Creek Neighborhood Association meeting, I realized that I had just seen a glimpse of what Austin's future well might be. I couldn't go to sleep that night because I had seen a live ember in my city, and I had not put it out.

Even more troubling, I had no path forward for putting it out.

We were headed to a crisis point.

Our community should not rely on using the threats of tickets or arrests to make those without homes move somewhere else, after people complain about their presence. Wherever they moved, they would still be breaking the law, only now, they'd be upsetting a new neighborhood or a new shopping area.

The farther out we pushed them, the farther away they were from the resources found close to downtown, the harder it was for them to survive, the more desperate their behavior, and the greater the chance for petty crime and unwelcome advances.

Their numbers were growing, and our city was doing very little to get people off the streets, out from hiding in our green spaces, and into homes with needed support.

Left unaddressed, I knew, the scale of our challenge would grow from one that was still solvable to one so large it would be difficult or impossible to fix.

I knew that our city's way to deal with the symptoms—threatening arrest and tickets to get people without homes to move and become invisible—gave the false perception that homelessness was an isolated phenomenon—not a problem that needed to be solved as one of our highest priorities.

It was becoming apparent to me that tickets and arrests were not only not solutions but were untenable morally. We shouldn't be arresting people or giving them a ticket if their only crime is that they are broke, have nowhere to go, and are living in a tent.

The way I saw it, as long as someone wasn't posing a public safety risk or presenting a public health hazard, we as a society should be *helping* them—not making them criminals.

Criminalization of the homeless is not, nor should it be, a long-term civic strategy. It may address a symptom of homelessness, but it does absolutely nothing to fix it.

The city of Austin didn't have the number of homes and the level of services necessary to address homelessness. In fact, our policies had made the challenge worse when we tried to address it by investing in more and more police resources.

The police wanted to be fighting real crime and didn't want to be doing this work. It shouldn't be the role of the police to be the mechanism or tool that cities use to address poverty and meet the mental health challenges of the homeless population.

An even more bitter irony lays at the heart of this issue: homelessness is one of the only large municipal social challenges for which we definitively know the answer.

We know how to make homelessness rare, brief, and nonrecurring. After all, we made the homelessness of veterans disappear. Well-resourced Austin organizations that provide both a home and support services are more than 90 percent successful in getting and keeping people off our streets and out of tents.

Why can't we do it for everyone else on the streets?

Because it costs a whole lot of money to build the homes and shelters and set up the service-provider infrastructure that will allow a community to attain net effective zero homelessness.

Why won't a community spend that money?

Because the homeless and their advocates have *zero* political clout.

Whenever an American city seeks to invest resources in the homeless, a faction with far more political clout always steps in to redirect the spending of that money to their cause.

That was certainly true in Austin.

Until it wasn't.

The city of Austin was prospering. The demographers and economists predicted sustained growth, increasing vitality, and new jobs. As mayor, my job was to maintain the trajectory while helping steer it in the most equitable direction, giving all a chance to share in that prosperity. I wanted to keep that train on the tracks and moving forward.

Part of the job of mayor is to anticipate future threats to that success. I was watching homelessness accelerate in Austin. We weren't unique. Other cities were dealing with this challenge, too, but it was clear to me that this was the one challenge that could derail Austin's momentum.

Big cities don't usually fail, in the sense that they lose population. That has happened, rarely but occasionally, to mid-sized cities when a steel mill or a car manufacturing plant closes.

A city can fail because of war. The Cypriot vacation resort of Varosha, once one of the most popular destinations in the Mediterranean, was abandoned during the island's civil war in the 1970s. It has largely remained abandoned, gaining dark tourism fame.

Failure can come from a natural or man-made disaster. Pripyat in Ukraine was once a city of fifty thousand. Then came the explosion of the Chernobyl nuclear power plant. And then there are the numerous small mining towns that were abandoned when the oil or silver or diamonds ran out. And there was Centralia, Pennsylvania, which became unlivable because a coal-seam fire has been burning since 1962 and is expected to keep burning until the twenty-second century.

Big cities don't fail like that, but they can lose momentum. Their conditions can degrade. They can lose their vital spark, their essence, sometimes for generations at a time.

Most of the issues that we debate in municipal policy don't have the potential to lead to such failure. Cities don't lose their way because they don't build enough parks. They don't cease to exist because their convention center is too small. And despite what some of my fellow Austinites might say, they don't fail because too many people want to go there. It's not as if, as Yogi Berra said, "It's so popular, nobody goes there anymore."

Our city was strong enough to survive everything thrown at us—except a failure to deal with homelessness.

We had time. Homelessness in Austin hadn't yet reached the level of other cities. We weren't yet San Francisco or Los Angeles. The encampment I came across and the neighborhood association meeting were isolated events, though growing in frequency.

But the clock was ticking.

I needed to learn what we might do and what we needed to avoid. I traveled to the cities with the most substantial homelessness issues—Los Angeles, Seattle, San Francisco, and Portland—and I spoke with experts on the ground and to the mayors and their staffers about the challenge.

I was there just to listen—and a good thing, too, because I had nothing to offer them. The scale of their challenge and the political immovability around the issue were far greater than anything we faced in Austin. I wanted to learn what these cities wished they had done ten years earlier to avoid being where they were now.

Each city had its own unique experience with homelessness, but their stories had common themes. This is what I learned:

- Homelessness holds the greatest danger in cities with rapidly increasing housing costs. (And Austin was the poster child for rising housing costs.)

- Homelessness can be successfully addressed, but the solutions take real resolve to achieve and require the joint participation of public, private, nonprofit, and philanthropic parties.
- A successful response system requires a multi-prong approach. Emergency shelters are important because they address immediate suffering and give people a safe place to live, but if the city only focuses on immediate emergency sheltering, it fails. To keep people off the streets, they need to be able to leave temporary conditions and have a more permanent home. Otherwise, they'll be back on the streets. And if a city only focuses on permanent supportive housing and services, it fails to meet the immediate suffering. Success requires both shelters and permanent supportive housing, plus all the other elements of a complete and integrated homelessness response system.
- This comprehensive system is expensive relative to the number of people who use it, but it isn't nearly as expensive as failing to deal with the issue until it becomes too big to solve.
- Criminalizing homelessness helps a city deal with the symptoms and temporarily hides the challenge by forcing the homeless into the woods and along the creeks. Not only is this fundamentally unjust, but it dangerously allows the challenge to grow unseen and unsolved until it grows too large to stay hidden (not a solution), or it renders the city unable to get help without support from state and/or federal governments.

I asked the elected officials and senior staff of each city why ten years earlier they hadn't built out the necessary homelessness response system (housing, support services, sheltering, diversion, jobs, and reintegration programs), when it would have cost so much less than they were currently spending to not accomplish as much.

One message came back loud and clear: if they had wanted to prioritize and solve the problem ten years earlier, they could have.

"It was never a question of not knowing what to do," I was told repeatedly. "It was a question of political will."

The problem had been manageable; it just wasn't enough of a priority.

By the time it became the most important thing in each of these cities, it was too late.

People prioritize problems based on their experience with them. For years and for most people, the homeless in Austin were invisible. The laws against camping, lying on the ground, and even sitting in public pushed unhoused people out of sight and out of mind.

Many think we should have kept it that way. There was a lot of support for us to continue to threaten tickets to keep the homeless out of visible public spaces. When the city council was considering decriminalizing homelessness, our police chief stoutly defended the existing policy. In his defense, it was not his job to solve homelessness. The way he saw it, if the police got a complaint call, responded, and could get a homeless person to voluntarily move along, the problem the officers had been called in to address was solved. End of story.

I felt we needed to do better than that. And quickly.

Change wasn't going to be easy, though at first I thought it might be. We had a working model for this solution, after all, when we effectively ended veteran homelessness.

But there weren't enough people who were interested in helping the rest of the homeless population.

We needed the commitment over time of hundreds of millions of dollars to build out an effective homelessness response system. But with the challenge hidden, in large measure by our city's criminalization policies, there was no priority expressed or community will to address it.

Not that we didn't try. For several city budget sessions in a row, I and some of my colleagues on council, especially Kathie Tovo and Ann Kitchen, tried hard to get significantly more resources to end homelessness.

We didn't get very far.

We were unable to move much past the stasis and inertia of the status quo. How do you get a city to prioritize a challenge that may be inevitable, but that is presently unseen? We needed a fundamental change in priorities and in understanding. I and my colleagues on the Austin City Council came to believe that the only way to achieve that kind of fundamental change was to directly and visibly confront it.

On June 20, 2019, I and the Austin council voted to decriminalize homelessness. We didn't know it when we did it, but this was a move that hit Austin like a crashing cymbal.

The homeless community could now live where they wished without penalty, so long as they did not create a public safety risk or present a public health hazard. Effective the last weekend in June 2019, the police could no longer write a homeless person a ticket or arrest them for merely not having a home.

Homelessness was no longer a crime in Austin, Texas.

After we passed the ordinance, I spent time speaking with members of the homeless population in and around their tents. I would often go with organizations like Antony Jackson's We Can Now, a wonderful organization whose volunteers bring food, supplies, hope, and friendly faces to those living on our streets.

I spoke with Mary, a longtime street resident whose eyes filled with tears as she held my hand and described what it had been like to be a woman unprotected in the woods.

"I had a life," she said, "where men would grab at me almost nightly. Unless you get with someone who will protect you." She added wistfully,

"But that has problems, too. But now I'm safer out in the open, and it's not just me. People leave me alone more," she said.

Squeezing my arm, she said, "Promise me I won't have to go back to the woods."

I couldn't make her that promise.

"I'll do what I can," I said.

11

HOMELESSNESS–"A RESPONSE"

Our new ordinance didn't increase the number of those without homes, but it certainly made their presence more visible. On the positive side, that visibility moved the issue to the top of the priority list for public (and private) action, and that meant we were able to devote real dollars to this challenge.

On the negative side, if we had set off an explosion in the city, we couldn't have done as much damage.

Many people ended their weekend drive home the Sunday evening after the ordinance was effective following routes they'd taken many times before, like horses heading for the barn. There wasn't a lot of looking around, and nothing stood out. Few knew when they drove under the highway overpass on the way to their neighborhood that they were passing people who were living there in the crevices of the highway structure, hidden from view. It's in the corners and cracks where we let reside those we don't want to see.

The next day, July 1, 2019, the city council's action decriminalizing homelessness went into effect.

On that Monday morning, Austinites left their homes and headed for work and the new week. Many drove under that familiar overpass. What they saw that morning rocked their world.

The prior evening, in anticipation of the decriminalization, Philip Berber, a good Samaritan and founder of the wonderful A Glimmer of Hope Foundation, delivered thousands of tents free of charge to people living on our streets, in our fields and woods, down by the railroad tracks and small streams, and in those crevices.

Many of the tents were *bright orange.*

And so, on that Monday morning, drivers set out and saw a sea of bright orange tents. Overnight, there seemed to be thousands of them everywhere.

Our phones started ringing.

"Where the hell did all these homeless people suddenly come from?" the callers wanted to know.

The answer: they hadn't mysteriously come from anywhere, except out from hiding. They had always been there—in many cases, literally right there, sleeping out of sight where their orange tents now stood. The orange tents were what was new.

For the first time, on that Monday morning, much of Austin saw homelessness, really saw it. And many people went off the deep end, including our governor, other state leaders, many of Austin's business leaders, and, frankly, many regular folks who now had a sense that their tranquil world had been attacked or was just falling apart.

Texas Governor Greg Abbott posted on Twitter, "If Austin—or any other Texas city—permits camping on city streets it will be yet another local ordinance the State of Texas will override. At some point cities must start putting public safety & common sense first. There are far better solutions for the homeless & citizens."

The Travis County Republican Party expressed support for state intervention in a news release on July 3, incorrectly stating: "Homeless given more rights than property owners under new camping policy."

The Republicans later admitted the statement was incorrect but defended publishing it since they had gotten it from the Facebook page of the Austin Police Association, the police union.

I responded in an open text message that Austin remains "laser focused on public safety and health."

"We will still act on public safety threats," I said. "But arresting homeless people is generally not an answer to city problems. What do we do with folks experiencing homelessness who are presenting neither such risks or hazards? The person sitting up against the building, dealing with swirling demons the rest of us can't see, needs our help. The answer is not to arrest them. We need to be able to tell people not only where they can't be, but also where they can be."

Governor Greg Abbott wasn't buying it. He adamantly threatened to overturn the new law. He cited public safety and common sense as the reasons.

In response, Council Member Greg Casar, who sponsored the ordinance change, criticized Abbott and the State of Texas for not doing enough to fund mental health care.

"We did more last week to address homelessness—from funding services to buying a new shelter to fixing laws—than Gov. Abbott did in his entire six months of the last legislative session," Casar wrote. "Austinites are coming up with solutions to these issues, but Gov. Abbott insists on being part of the problem."

We knew our action would have visible consequences. My goal and that of the city council, however, was to end the immoral and ineffective practice of punishing someone without a home rather than finding ways to help them. Nonetheless, we also thought that seeing the accelerating challenge of homelessness could not help but encourage the community's will to act on it.

Instead, we got more disruption than we anticipated.

We made some serious errors that resulted in our inability to get the community to focus on what people without homes needed because the general population was overwhelmed by the sudden unmasking of the challenge.

The city manager never came forward with the guardrails our ordinance instructed him to bring back to city council, identifying where people should and should not sleep. When he didn't act, the council and I could never figure out how to step in for him because we couldn't agree among ourselves on how to manage shared public spaces.

Orange tents were everywhere.

I repeatedly told the city manager that we needed to be doing more to manage our shared public spaces, even if it meant changing where city resources were going. He convened department heads to meet with me weekly to report what they were doing, but those meetings were mostly meant to placate me. They certainly did not lead to the action that was needed.

I wanted to be in control, but I wasn't. My frustration grew.

On the positive side, our city's hidden challenge had burst into the open. People everywhere were demanding the homelessness crisis be fixed.

The decriminalization ordinance was singularly successful in focusing the attention of the city on the challenge.

The Downtown Business Association and the Chamber of Commerce had a solution: build shelters and move these people where they wouldn't be seen. They wanted people without homes quickly taken from the downtown, where businesses and hotels were complaining that their customers were discomfited by frequent encounters with people living on the street. They wanted more emergency shelters, but they wanted those shelters to be placed somewhere other than downtown.

On the opposing side, the social and criminal justice reform activists wanted more permanent supportive housing. Rounding up people and putting them in shelters where people would not stay and where supportive services have a much lower success rate, these activists knew, was not the answer.

For years leading up to the disruption of the decriminalization vote, those two sides—downtown business and the activists—argued and fought each other at town hall meetings and in the hearts and minds of the community generally. Downtown businesses did not support permanent housing because it cost too much and took too long to execute, and also because, bluntly, their primary goal was to remove homeless people from downtown. Solving the problem was secondary.

The activists didn't support a focus on emergency sheltering because it didn't provide a permanent resolution to the issue. People off the streets might move into a shelter, but if it became clear that there was no housing to graduate into, most shelter residents chose to go back to the streets.

This battle was long and drawn out because there wasn't enough money available to do either strategy, much less both at the same time. Rather than joining forces to demand more total resources, the politics of poverty had claimants fighting over the too meager dollars available.

This same dynamic frequently has played out in cities across the country in a myriad of issues, such as housing, public health, education, and poverty programs. When dollars are scarce, multiple well-meaning and wonderfully constructive groups end up fighting against each other for resources. The result is a kind of long-running cold war.

Neither side had a viable solution.

The downtown business group wanted a solution that was the quickest and least expensive. They wanted group housing—a big tent structure with a lot of bunk beds. Social services would be provided.

There was a serious problem with what they wanted to do: the success rate for those in such group housing to stay off the streets for three years was only 18 percent.

The advocates wanted a more permanent solution, where each homeless person would have a unit of his own with a key to the room to ensure privacy. Social services would be provided. The success rate for keeping these people off the streets for three years was over 90 percent.

But there was a serious problem with what these advocates wanted to do: it was a lot more expensive, and it took a lot more time to build.

The disruption caused by the decriminalization of homelessness forced both the downtown businesses and the activists to meet and see if they could build even a modicum of trust.

A meeting was set up by an organization called ECHO, an acronym for Ending Community Homelessness Organization. The idea was for the two sides to get together and talk. Maybe there was something they could agree on. Maybe if they talked, they could build some measure of trust.

I was invited to participate, and so was Lynn Meredith, a local philanthropist who was the wife of one of the very early Dell computer executives. She was involved in many Austin civic causes, including this one. We met with Matt Mollica, the executive director of ECHO, and he suggested the two sides sit down with a homeless response expert to conduct something like a marriage counseling session.

The disruption pulled these players together with nonprofits and foundations, other businesses, and the public sector. Because finding a solution became the imperative—so much more important than rehashing past differences—as if by miracle, they all got on the same page. United for the very first time, the opportunity existed for the community to move forward to address the issue of homelessness in a meaningful way.

The outcome was surprisingly positive. Each side came to realize that if they got what they had been seeking for years at the expense of the other, they would fail. It wasn't a matter of the city choosing between sheltering or permanent supportive housing—it had to have both and everything in between or nothing at all.

We started talking. We asked, *What if we worked together? How do we set goals? How would we structure a plan? How would we get that done?*

Our group came up with a plan that was built around housing an additional three thousand homeless people over a three-year period. This plan, we agreed, would make an impact on getting a sizable number of people off the streets and would force us to set up the kind of homeless response system that could effectively end homelessness.

That became the goal.

Solving homelessness is a particularly frustrating challenge because doing so requires a great deal of resources that affect the lives of a relatively small number of people. A city needs a complete response system: prevention; diversion; emergency sheltering; bridge housing; permanent supportive housing; and job, substance use, and other counseling and support.

Part of the plan was a recognition by both sides that we couldn't do just one element of the plan. We couldn't just make or build emergency shelters, though getting the homeless off the streets was important to do. We couldn't only do permanent housing.

We needed both—and we needed *all the steps in between.*

We needed to pull people out of shelters before they got frustrated with being sheltered and went back onto the streets.

We needed a whole response system, and each one of the stages had to be scaled to the other stages. We had to build a support system. We had to hire social workers and case workers. We had to provide job training, and we had to provide the tools, the education, and the mental health support.

You're beginning to see how difficult it is to solve the homelessness challenge. Each of the component elements of the response system not only needs to be in place, but they need to be at a scale that fits with the other elements. There are no partial solutions or half measures—a city either commits to ending homelessness, or it doesn't.

After decades of an inability to come up with a consensus approach and plan, we finally had one.

Because of the community angst arising from the proliferation of tents, we had the community demanding action.

We just needed to find the money.

It is extremely expensive to build out a homelessness response system on the proper scale. And in Austin, we had to fund additional capacity for every aspect of the plan.

The plan we developed cost out at $515 million over three years.

A loosely formed organization grew out of the informal group in order to broaden its reach and enable it to put the plan into action. The idea was to bring in more interested people and eventually to design and implement a comprehensive plan to address homelessness.

That ad hoc organization was called Finding Home ATX, and its purpose was to help facilitate the implementation of the three-year plan. That meant circulating, socializing, and getting support for the plan. And it meant helping to find the money to get it done. At any other time, the cost alone might have doomed the effort.

Then the otherwise horrific pandemic arose. Because of the pandemic, we were able to find a once-in-a-generation path to the kind of resources the plan would need in the form of the ARPA COVID

Response dollars the federal government was making available to local governments across the country.

Remarkably, the community unity on the issue of homelessness was forming just as the ARPA COVID Response dollars were arriving, and that money gave the city, county, and Austin housing authority the political will necessary to devote most of the federal funding to this one issue of homelessness.

This was a rare, unified approach for local government, where large sums of money ordinarily get chopped up into a thousand tiny pieces. This customary practice is the safest move for an elected body because it can give at least some money to all the interested constituent groups, each doing important work. But when dollars are cut up this way, no organization gets enough dollars to truly do something that's transformative.

To spend money on one central priority means to deny the requests of many valid claimants, which is hard on policy grounds and even harder politically.

Because of the community's reaction and angst arising from the disruption of the decriminalization of the homeless, we finally had the community will to address the issue in a substantial way.

The stars were aligning. We had a plan. And we had most of the money in hand.

The city council contributed more than $200 million to the effort. County government chose to lead on several elements with over $100 million. The local HUD-funded housing authority directed over $50 million of its grant funding to incremental funding for the homelessness response system. Private philanthropy stepped up with over $50 million.

When I left office, we were only about $75 million short of our goal, which was darn incredible. We had created three new emergency, non-congregate shelters operating in Central, North, and South Austin. We were closing some encampments by moving people into shelters instead of forcing them into hiding. Our city was increasing social service and support capacity. We had funded and begun to design, approve, and build the permanent supportive housing projects that, after two to four years of construction, would increase that housing capacity tenfold. Impressed with our successes, the federal government and HUD increased Austin's annual federal grant level, providing additional revenue into the future.

But meanwhile, back at the ranch, as Texans say, while the homelessness response plan was being put together, while the political alliances were being built to raise and sequester the funding, all the public was seeing were tents—thousands of tents—in parks, under high-trafficked overpasses, and along our sidewalks in downtown Austin.

For two years, neighbors and friends turned against one another. One group wanted the homeless population to go away and disappear. People led by their feelings of compassion were driven to greater action and increased tolerance. Many, if not most, felt real compassion but also believed that there had to be a better way than letting the men, women, and children without homes sleep in tents.

The question of what to do about the homeless was ripping apart our community.

The presence of tents in all parts of our city was causing many to lose faith in government and in their elected officials, me included—and maybe even especially me.

Anger and frustration rose at the visible camping around the city. Those who were angry saw the tents as evidence that the city was ineffective and unable to deal with the challenge. Another contingent, with considerable help from social media disinformation, believed the outrageous suggestion that I and city leadership were not only okay with it but wanted the tents to become a permanent fixture.

There was no general agreement about how to solve the homeless challenge, and over time, our community became increasingly divided. A lot of people became angry and stayed that way, even as others became even more resolved and focused on finding answers to the challenge.

I'm not convinced that the loudest complaining voices wanted to solve the problem. There was a contingent that professed to want to solve it—they said they wanted homeless Austinites to have a good and safe place to live—but many were adamantly opposed to spending public money to provide a solution. These people wasted valuable time and were really trying to divide the community for a longer-term, partisan political advantage.

Many people supported criminalizing tents so that they would disappear. They didn't connect the disappearance of tents with its impact on the people who lived in them. "Tents," they said, "should be banned because that's an inhumane way for people to live"—as if forcing people out of tents and into hiding was somehow more humane. This contingency wasn't about solutions because they didn't have any. They were just "wishing away" a challenge.

I found these people the least sympathetic. At least those angry people who were open about the fact that they didn't care if the problem was solved so long as they didn't have to see it were honest, clear, and consistent.

I was proud that many Austinites took the decriminalization of the homeless as a clarion call to real action, to do what it would take to get those folks into homes with services so they could be safe and stabilized and could return to a more secure and established life. But setting and realizing that constructive course of action did not come quickly enough.

While we were working to bring people together to execute a consensus plan, some Austin residents, led by the chair of the Travis

County Republican Party and by a woman who lived near the location of a proposed permanent supportive housing facility, initiated a ballot proposition to reverse the city council and to once again ban camping, sitting, and lying on the ground.

The measure was presented as a vote against the inhumaneness of having people live in tents, but it didn't contain any funding authorization to actually help those without homes find one. The measure would just return us to the days when it was illegal not to have a place to live, and it would force people back into hiding to avoid ticketing and arrest.

The resulting campaign was emotional and polarizing, and it reflected the depth and widespread trauma the whole city suffered after homelessness came out from hiding.

Most of the public felt that the visibility of the homeless living in their orange tents had gone on for too long. The COVID pandemic made the problem worse when it froze our ability to help many unhoused people relocate from their encampments, as health experts warned that we shouldn't move this vulnerable community for fear of spreading the virus. For health reasons, the epidemic also made creating congregate group shelters impractical. Leaving people in tents is one reason Austin's citywide COVID mortality rate was less than half the national rate. The virus never got out of hand in our homeless community. We miraculously didn't lose any from the homeless population to the virus.

Ultimately, the vote became a referendum on whether people hated seeing orange tents.

Both the opponents and the allies of decriminalizing homelessness voted for the proposition. The measure had the strong support of those who just wanted the tents to go away and didn't care how it happened. It also had some support from allies of reform who were hoping the vote would force the city to move more quickly to fund the homes and a response system necessary to get people off the streets, into shelters, and then into more permanent housing with services.

On May 1, 2021, Austin voters went to the polls and reversed the city council action that had decriminalized homelessness. The camping ban election was the only one of the more than twenty bond elections, referenda, and voter initiatives that I lost in my eight years as mayor.

The truth is, if I had been one of the regular voters, I might have voted for this proposition too. I would have wanted the tents to go away and go away quickly. There needed to be a more constructive and helpful way to address homelessness. Most people didn't know about the Finding Home ATX plan, the coalition that was forming around it, or the money in the pipeline that was becoming available to support solutions to homelessness. Yet voters were being offered no other proposition than this one.

I learned a lot of lessons from the lead-up to the vote on the proposition. First, as I said, the council and I should have imposed some guardrails on where people could and could not put tents. The disruption didn't have to be so traumatic. We should have done a better job of managing shared public spaces. It was not necessary to let those without homes camp nearly everywhere. We shouldn't have let tents be erected in parks the public wanted to enjoy or even in the few gazebos we had in those park areas. We didn't need tents under overpasses near traffic where hundreds of thousands of cars passed daily and where traffic created a safety risk.

The council had voted to have the city manager present a plan to manage shared public spaces at the time we voted to decriminalize homelessness. I called for it publicly. But because the council was divided on how that management should be done, the city manager never really responded to the council or to me.

The council and I failed when we couldn't agree on how to impose such guardrails and controls on our own in the absence of the manager's help. We all agreed that some guardrails would be better than none, but because we couldn't agree on what they should be, we got none.

We also should have put another proposition on the ballot at the same election—an initiative to establish guardrails, a timeline to set up a response system that could constructively take people off the streets, and the authorization for dollars to fund the creation and expansion of that response system. I believe that this is the proposition that would have won the day. But we didn't do this, and it was a failure on my part.

The final lesson is that we should have done a better job of keeping the public informed of the work being done by Finding Home ATX, the joint work being done by the business community and the social justice advocates, and the future prospects of the federal funding we would get.

I'm not sure how our city will do against this challenge in the long term. In November 2022, after I was term-limited, Austin reelected Kirk Watson, who had been mayor of Austin from 1997 until 2001. He left that post in 2002 to run for attorney general, only to lose to Greg Abbott. He was then elected to the Texas legislature for sixteen years. He was now returning to an office he had held before.

When he was a state senator, Watson would get very frustrated with me and the city of Austin because we were doing things like helping the homeless or working on citywide health care. He was a Democrat in a very red state capitol building, and we were making his job harder because he was having to defend us all the time, and he thought we were needlessly antagonizing the Republican state leadership.

When he became mayor for the second time, Watson tried to differentiate his administration from mine, and so initially, he didn't prioritize the issue of homelessness. He had watched me jump into the middle of this cauldron, and it would not have been an unreasonable decision to avoid that path.

More generally, Mayor Watson ran on fixing problems he accused me and my council of creating, and he blamed us for almost all the challenges he believed Austin was facing. I never heard him mention the name of the Finding Home ATX community effort. He never got in front of the initiative or its comprehensive plan, and he started pushing what sounded a lot like the rejected plan the business community had been pushing: a primary focus on congregate shelters, and he got one done. He ignored our efforts to rally energy and resources for a comprehensive plan to get those without homes off our streets.

Mayor Watson began his second mayoral service focused on what he could do quickly and what would have the most visual impact—a three-hundred-person emergency congregate shelter. Such facilities successfully get some people off the streets, which is good, but only temporarily because most residents don't want congregant sheltering where they can't sleep with their partners or their pets, where their personal property too often disappears at night, and where there is little promise of an exit into permanent housing.

My council and I funded a historic increase in permanent housing units that would start coming online a year into Watson's term in office. From 2023 to 2025, Mayor Watson went to many of their groundbreaking and ribbon-cutting ceremonies, but he did not fill the pipeline with additional projects that would come online in the following years.

Solving the challenge of homelessness is more important than who gets the credit. And after he won reelection a second time for a second term, Watson began to recognize and more actively act on the priority the community has given to this challenge.

Watson seemed to understand that something very important was lost with his decision to abandon much of the past effort when he first came back into office. Finding Home ATX represented a consensual, comprehensive plan and joint action between all levels of government, the business community, and the social service infrastructure. These groups had established momentum that led to the private sector investing tens of millions of dollars in helping to address the challenge. The prospects for continued and increased support were good. But much of that momentum was lost when the newly returned mayor chose not to recognize the value in that effort and to keep it going. The consensus went away, the plan lost the all-important city of Austin endorsement, and the supporting private investment significantly diminished. I hope the stakeholders involved in that prior effort are able to resurrect it.

Disinformation, discussed generally in Chapter 16, was and remains a significant threat to meeting the challenge of homelessness. One of the most pernicious myths about homelessness is that the solution to the problem—a professional, comprehensive response system—makes the situation worse by giving unhoused people from elsewhere an incentive to flood into our city.

This is an urban myth. A working homelessness response system doesn't invite homeless people from all over the country to come to Austin or anywhere else. There is no such thing as a Fodor's guide to cities for the homeless.

We have enough of a challenge getting someone on our streets to move to another location where housing is available, much less changing cities. It's hard to advocate and rally support and consensus to end homelessness when the issue is so politicized and partisan that you begin to wonder whether the politicians want the issue to remain so it can be used for political fundraising and organizing.

The overwhelming majority of people living on Austin streets lived in our city before they lost their homes. Few came from elsewhere.

More than four years after homelessness was decriminalized in Austin and more than two years after the ban on camping was reinstated, homelessness remains an extremely emotional issue in Austin.

In some ways, this is a good thing because it may keep the issue as a community priority long enough to establish and institutionalize a homelessness response system that can house people who are on our streets with no place to live.

In hindsight and with all I wish we had done differently, the disruption that I and the council created by decriminalizing homelessness was essential to enable Austin to avoid the scale of the challenge faced by Los Angeles, San Francisco, Seattle, and Portland. Without the visibility—without those orange tents—we would never have mustered the political will to put ourselves in the position to try to solve homelessness.

If local government and its leadership continue to support and execute the plan to solve homelessness, Austin will be one of the few cities in the country to claim success in ending homelessness. In early 2025, led by Austin Mayor Pro Tem Vanessa Fuentes, the recently elected Austin City Council directed an additional $350 million be spent over ten years on the comprehensive homelessness response system, in order to keep the momentum going and maintain homelessness as one of the city's top priorities.

"I am really proud," Fuentes said, "that one of the first items that we'll take up at our first council meeting is prioritizing investments in homelessness. That includes having additional funding for shelter, for housing, and for prevention."

I hope we get there. Austin could be on the cusp of effectively ending homelessness. If we're successful, we will know that we couldn't have done so without the tumult and discord of disruption.

The jury is out. It could be that the disruption we caused so polarized the community that too many citizens have given up on the idea of government being able to meet the challenge of homelessness.

In any event, I know that I spent every penny of my political capital on this effort because I believed that confronting and addressing the challenge of homelessness was the most important thing I could do as mayor. That challenge presented our most existential risk, and I rolled the dice as to whether my legacy will be that I was helpful in leading the city to achieve big things—mobility, equity, infrastructure, and homelessness—or whether there would be such uncertainty on homelessness that all my other achievements might be forgotten.

Today I sometimes get stopped walking downtown Austin streets by those without homes who remember me from my time in office. Some come over to thank me. The other day, my wife Diane and I were walking a few blocks from our home, and we encountered Jack, as we often do, sitting on his favorite street bench. This time, he stood up and came toward us. One at a time, he handed me some coins and counted out to twenty-seven cents.

"For your grandson's piggy bank," Jack said with great pride. He was giving back.

Addressing the homelessness issue unabashedly wasn't just a risk I chose to take; it was a risk I had to take.

Even though we did not solve the challenge, we helped raise awareness and make addressing this issue the city's highest priority. We helped many people get off the streets. We dramatically increased the city's permanent supportive housing inventory and expanded supportive services. I believe our community will someday be one of those that solves this challenge, both because I love this place and in part because of what we did. I'm very proud we took the most difficult challenge head-on.

Was it worth it?

Only time will tell.

12

TECH AND GOVERNMENT: THE UBER AND LYFT WAR

It wasn't unusual for me to be confronted at a reception by someone like the gentleman emboldened with one too many drinks who introduced himself by saying, "So, you're the mayor, huh? You know, government doesn't fix problems; it *is* the problem."

Immediately, I looked to see if I had staff nearby who could take over the conversation.

Mayors go to a lot of parties because showing up to events is part of our job and because people seem to like to invite us. It's tempting to go into a deeper analysis than that, and my inimitable scheduler, Barbara Shack, someone capable of bending both space and time if the occasion requires it, could no doubt give an eloquent disquisition on why I was sent to one party versus some other event.

But the reason behind it is simple. A mayor has the unique

combination of having a high profile and a profound responsibility in a relatively small area. For most people, the mayor is the highest-level elected official they can reasonably expect to talk to.

Meeting and talking with people and being seen as part of the community are essential parts of the job.

Sometimes that means going to a party, which is either a perk of the job or a drawback, depending on the party. Some parties are memorable; mostly, they kind of run together. But conversations usually start off better than this one did.

In fairness to this gentleman, the sentiment he expressed is one held by many others. His specific gripe was about traffic congestion. No matter that we were just getting started on a decades-long backlog of projects to give Austin the mobility system that it needed. The $10 billion total investment needed was still just a gleam in the transportation coalition's eye.

My policy in conversations like this one, in which people are essentially venting about their concerns, is just to listen. Listening is another part of the job, and telling people who are frustrated with traffic that they'll feel differently in ten years is not exactly a way to make people feel valued or understood. So, not for the first or the last time, I was treated to a screed about how the problem with government is that it isn't nimble or innovative enough.

"What we need," the extremely animated gentleman told me, "is for government to look at things like the private sector does."

That the city was simply too hidebound by rules and regulations and by conventional thinking and that it lacked talented people to find or execute the best solutions fits into a neat and common narrative about government: that it's inherently stodgy, slow, and limited, while the private sector—especially tech—is the real home of innovation, speed, and ideas. This is why our private sector has such a large share of what, in other countries, would be considered public services like health care, education, and, of course, transportation.

I didn't blame the guy for believing that narrative. It's a common one and not without some truth—government process can be extremely slow. But the idea that government cannot do new things—cool things—that compete with or complement the tech industry is, quite simply, wrong.

In a perfect world, at the intersection of technology and government, the public and private sectors help each other do better what they each do. Too often, though, the private and public sectors do not trust each other and are not open to the possibility of working together.

Austin's combative battle with the rideshare companies Uber and Lyft was just such an example.

In 2015, there were worries in Austin about public safety after reports of sexual assault by rideshare drivers became public. It wasn't clear whether Uber and Lyft drivers represented a greater risk than traditional taxi drivers, but a growing number of Austin residents began to pressure the city council to address rideshare passenger safety.

One solution, proposed by some members of the city council, was to require Uber and Lyft drivers to undergo fingerprint background checks rather than their cursory driver's license checks, as a better way to weed out untrustworthy and potentially dangerous drivers.

Uber and Lyft objected. They felt that a fingerprint requirement was an unnecessary complication for getting people to sign up online as drivers.

"There will be fewer drivers," the companies said. "And our business model will fail if we don't have hundreds of drivers out on the road at any given time providing the quick response time customers want."

Uber and Lyft criticized the idea as an example of government overregulation of private business, and some Austinites agreed.

Uber and Lyft were among many new companies that were launching and disrupting existing markets, such as Airbnb and other short-term residence rentals. These new, disruptive companies were coming into cities with an adversarial approach to government, having already decided that cities would try to regulate them out of existence.

I didn't buy that paradigm. As the mayor of one of the most innovative and tech-savvy cities in the country, I thought the Austin City Council and I could help demonstrate how mutual innovation and cooperation might avoid confrontation.

The old way cities regulated businesses might be outdated, I thought. *Maybe there needs to be a new way to approach these new economies.*

I wanted government to be as innovative as the new economy, and I wanted to try to find ways both to empower new technologies as well as to ensure public safety. Most of my council colleagues were willing to give me the chance to find the right solution.

I could see how requiring rideshare companies to get prospective drivers fingerprinted for background checks could be something that fundamentally was inconsistent with the business model of these new services, so my team and I tried to figure out how the city could help get drivers fingerprinted without making online sign-ups cumbersome.

I posited that if the city could get drivers fingerprinted for the companies, run like a traditional government workforce development program that trains workers in the community, then we would get the desired security check and Uber and Lyft wouldn't have to change their onboarding process.

We proposed that the city would have a third-party company take fingerprints and do background checks, meeting prospective drivers where they lived, worked, or went to school. Our system would allow the applicants to arrange the fingerprinting at their convenience and within a fifteen-minute window of the appointed time at the chosen location.

I approached Uber and Lyft to make sure that moving in this direction was a good way to meet everyone's concerns.

But right from the start, Uber and Lyft arrived in Austin with their established culture and game plan ready to do battle.

Uber and Lyft responded with an emphatic, "No."

They said they didn't believe better background checks were needed. And in any event, our proposal would make it too hard to recruit the number of drivers needed for their products to perform as customers required, they said.

We went back to the drawing board to innovate further.

What if, I asked Uber and Lyft, the government didn't require drivers to get fingerprinted but instead merely encouraged drivers to voluntarily get fingerprinted?

"No," was their answer. "You'll never get enough drivers to voluntarily get fingerprinted. We've tried that before in other places and failed."

We went back to the drawing board once again. We talked to a lot of drivers about what might give them an incentive to voluntarily get fingerprinted for a background check. They wanted it to be easy and convenient—as we had proposed—and they wanted to be rewarded if they volunteered.

When we proposed holding a lottery drawing for a free new Tesla for those drivers who had chosen to participate, there was near unanimous driver willingness to get fingerprinted.

We had a real shot at getting most drivers to get voluntarily fingerprinted.

Would Uber and Lyft work with us? We asked them if they would give consumers the choice of a fingerprinted, background-checked driver by putting that choice on their phone app "slider," just like a customer requests a certain size or condition of rideshare car.

"No," was the answer. "It's too hard and complicated for us to customize our slider to address a one-off Austin solution," they said.

They wouldn't budge, but we weren't ready to give up. We enlisted some of our brightest tech programmers, and they confirmed they could code the slider application we wanted. It wasn't hard and could be easily installed.

We went back to Uber and Lyft and told them we'd create the entire system for them, soup to nuts. All they had to do was let us solve the problem for them.

Not only did they again say no, but they told us to stop trying because "you cannot solve the challenge."

Uber and Lyft were at last being honest enough to tell me that they would not work with the city on this issue at all, period.

Then what could the government do on its own without asking anything of the rideshare companies? I wondered.

I pulled together some of our top tech innovators, including Josh Baer, Josh Jones-Dilworth, and Eugene Sepulveda, and I asked them how we might provide what was perceived by some as being a safer background check without impacting the new platforms that were achieving greater and greater popularity.

I loved the concept of the new platform they came back with. Thumbs Up would be a new, innovative, and cutting-edge equivalent of the legacy Good Housekeeping seal of approval. This independent, third-party app would validate someone's background.

It wasn't hard to do. You went online and arranged for a quick, easy, and no-cost fingerprint background check (conducted by an independent third-party and qualified entity), and, once cleared, you got access to a virtual Thumbs Up badge that, when added to your online profile, certified that you had successfully completed a biometric background check.

Drivers on Uber and Lyft could put it on their profiles. In fact, users of Uber and Lyft could also put the badge on their profiles so that drivers would have the option of only accepting ride requests from safe-certified riders, a boon to people who wanted to earn extra money as rideshare drivers but who were uncomfortable picking up strangers on the street without knowing anything about them.

The Thumbs Up badge could also be used by Airbnb hosts who

were marketing rooms in their home so short-term rental tenants would know that the person whose home they would be sharing had passed a background check. Moreover, the Airbnb host who was inviting a stranger into his home could choose only renters that had no criminal background.

A vendor with a requisite good history on eBay can qualify to be a recommended or qualified seller on that site. That entity, however, can't take that certification to Amazon.

Wouldn't it be great if a vendor were independently certified as a "Reliable Seller" by Thumbs Up and could place that validation badge into their profile on whatever website or platform they were trying to sell something on? I wondered.

The Austin entrepreneurs and innovators started to get really excited about this idea of having a cross-platform, third-party web app certificate that could be widely recognized.

There seemed to be no limit to the kinds of background, skills, track record, performance, or evaluation that could be independently qualified and awarded a Thumbs Up badge for that characteristic. The app went right to the heart of one of the biggest tensions within the digital economy—how often are we asked to trust our money and our safety to people about whom we know essentially nothing?

We asked Uber and Lyft if they would allow their drivers and maybe even their customers to make a Thumbs Up certificate or badge part of their online profile. We told them that Uber and Lyft would not be endorsing or guaranteeing the certification, only allowing notice that it had been obtained.

We weren't asking them to do anything about the challenge—all we wanted was for them not to obstruct us from solving it ourselves, at no cost to them.

They turned us down flat, but still we would not be deterred.

One of the things that I enjoy most about the entrepreneur and innovation community in Austin and globally is how relentless they are when they believe in an idea. The tech and business team we'd assembled to work on Thumbs Up refused to surrender. There had to be a way to get this working, including for the rideshare industry, without burdensome regulation.

The team started to develop plans for there to be an actual physical Thumbs Up decal for fingerprinted drivers to put on the back windshields of their rideshare cars. Prospective rideshare customers could scan that decal, get a picture of the person who had been checked, and then visually confirm that they had the correct driver.

As an added incentive for drivers to voluntarily get fingerprinted, the city said it could allow rideshare drivers with a Thumbs Up decal to drive one-half block closer to a big event to pick up customers or to park closer to large events so they'd have a better chance of getting customer requests for service.

We were very excited about the development of a plan, which we thought could provide our residents with the ability to have a fingerprinted and background-checked driver while, at the same time, innovating and developing a strategy to do this without engaging in heavy-handed regulation.

Could this be the beginning of finding a twenty-first-century way for business and local governments to work together? I wondered.

Not according to Uber and Lyft.

"If you do anything like this," they said, "we will leave your city."

In the course of my time as mayor, I had some wild conversations. I argued with then-U.S. Attorney General Jeff Sessions in his office early in President Trump's first term about their draconian and inhumane immigration policies. I was regularly confronted and accused of being both an anti-business communist and a corporate shill, often while taking a single position.

I had joined London Mayor Sadiq Khan in a meeting to urge U.N.

Secretary General António Guterres to give cities a larger role in the international COP climate change conference. There was my private dinner with the mayor of Beijing and the secretary of the Beijing Communist Party to discuss the importance of direct city-to-city communications separate from those of nation-states. There were many conversations I had as mayor that I'll never forget.

But I don't know that I was ever as taken aback as I was when Uber and Lyft threatened to pull out of Austin rather than let us accommodate our residents at no cost to or involvement by them.

"What do you mean you're going to leave our city if we do this?" I said to them. "We're not asking you to do anything!"

No matter. Uber and Lyft wouldn't budge.

The Austin City Council and I could not and would not be intimidated. There was something seriously wrong with a city being blackmailed and thus prevented from doing something on its own that didn't ask anything of an industry.

In response, I drafted a resolution to be sent to the city council to adopt ordinances necessary to put the Thumbs Up plan into action—we would incentivize drivers to voluntarily get fingerprinted, work with a third-party independent app to qualify fingerprinted drivers, and allow our city traffic officials to manage traffic in a way that prioritized fingerprinted drivers.

In the face of Uber and Lyft's unwillingness to work something out, some of my council colleagues took a hard line. They put forward an ordinance that required Uber and Lyft drivers to get fingerprint background checks.

During the several weeks before the final vote, we made last-ditch efforts to find an innovative solution that might head off this more traditional regulation. We needed to reach an agreement with Uber and with Lyft, and we needed to get it with enough time left for my council colleagues and the community to study and consider it.

No such luck. The day of the meeting came, and Uber and Lyft still would not seriously consider a resolution that might forestall what the council was going to do.

I was the chair of the city council meeting, and I kept delaying consideration of the matter so I could sneak up to my office to talk to the representatives of the rideshare companies to see if we could get an agreement.

For a while, it seemed as if they were reconsidering their response, but it wasn't until the end of a thirteen-hour council meeting that Uber and Lyft finally agreed to allow us to implement the innovative solutions we had proposed. (Even so, Uber added annoying last-minute demands, such as reducing operating fees, to which they had previously agreed.)

There was insufficient time for my colleagues and the community to read and evaluate their proposals. Lyft had signed on to an outline of the proposal earlier in the evening while there still may have been time to gain the necessary support on the council. But its agreement was subject to Uber also signing on, and Uber took too long and asked for too much. To this day when I need a ride, I will not call for an Uber vehicle if there's another choice.

Most of the city council members would have been willing to support a cooperative relationship with Uber and Lyft, if only the companies had agreed to it in time. When they finally agreed to collaborate in some measure, it was too late.

When the vote was called, the council was by then set on a course to pass a mandatory fingerprint background check for all rideshare companies—the kind of regulation that my team and I had tried our best to avoid. The chance for a compromise—and with it a new model of how government and tech might work together—had gone up in smoke.

On reflection, it wasn't that the city and our tech and entrepreneur team had lost but that we were never in the game at all. Lyft might have shown some flexibility toward the end, but it was my impression that Uber never intended to work with us.

Like many of the new tech companies, Uber and Lyft made a big show of attacking cities for not being willing to accept the disruptions that they would bring to traditional markets. But in Austin, quite the opposite was happening. There was neither a mayor nor a city in the country, perhaps in the world, that would have been a better partner for new emerging and disruptive players than me and the city of Austin. We bent over backward to try to meet new innovation with new innovation. We took to heart the concerns that twentieth-century city and government regulation might very well not be the way that government needed to interact with new industries and economies today.

But we were stopped.

The grim irony is that although Uber and Lyft had only been operating for a few years, they were already acting like the worst stereotypes of stodgy, old companies—inflexible, dogmatic, and strangely inert. It was the city and our coalition of tech and entrepreneur allies who showed the flexibility and inventiveness that the disruptors claim as their cultural hallmarks.

In the months leading up to the council meeting, faced with the possibility of a municipal mandate for fingerprinting drivers, Uber and Lyft went on the offensive. They directed a local and national social media campaign to mischaracterize Austin as the Luddite in this situation. Swamped by their messaging, young tech entrepreneurs around the country couldn't understand why Austin, a bastion of tech innovation, was trying to over-regulate this new disruptive economy—mobility innovation—a mischaracterization that follows me to this day.

There was, of course, a strategic reason why Uber and Lyft were promoting this falsehood. Unwilling to work with me, the city council, and city staff, Uber and Lyft believed they could go around all of us by initiating a petition to be voted on by Austinites. They took their case directly to the voters of Austin to persuade them to order the council to leave the companies alone. They hired outside operatives and gathered three times the necessary 20,000 signatures to put on the ballot a proposition that would prevent the city council from instituting any of the regulations the council had enacted, as well as those forward-looking measures my team and I had proposed.

Uber and Lyft were sure that they would win at the polls. This wasn't their first rodeo.

They spent a ton of money to fund their messaging—between $8 million and $10 million—to persuade Austin voters to limit what the city council could do. They ran commercials on TV. They paid the mayor before me, Lee Leffingwell, $50,000 to come out of retirement to support their cause. They tailored their rideshare app for Austin specifically—everyone requesting a rideshare received a message urging them to support their proposition and mocking the city council.

To put this in perspective, the election cost more than seven times as much as the next most expensive municipal election in Austin's history. The opposition to the rideshares' referendum spent only about $175,000.

Uber and Lyft also played their most valuable card. In the lead-up to the election, Uber and Lyft threatened that if their proposition didn't pass, they would pull out of our community. It's no wonder they thought this would be an effective gambit. Rideshare usage in Austin was among the highest in the world and, I was told, was the highest in the world for Lyft. Would our community put this service at risk? Uber emailed its Austin users the day of the election that it would leave Austin in three days if they lost the election.

It was less a referendum than an ultimatum—give us carte blanche, they said, or we're out of here.

They had done this before in other cities. Uber was operating in Houston with a fingerprint background check requirement (Lyft had already left), but as the election in Austin was heating up, Uber announced it would also leave Houston if that city didn't change its rules (which were much more burdensome than what we had suggested we'd do in Austin).

In a similar dispute over safety provisions, Uber and Lyft had stopped operating on alternate days during San Antonio's citywide Fiesta celebration. Residents were so frustrated and angry by having such a valuable service one day and then not having it the next that they put the necessary pressure on the local city council to force it to back down and reverse direction. That's what Uber and Lyft thought would happen in Austin.

They were wrong.

I was frustrated with the election because neither choice on the ballot represented the best outcome. Uber and Lyft tied our hands by putting their measure on the ballot, which, if passed, would have imposed a solution that compromised the council's ability to address public safety. On the other hand, if the proposition failed, the ordinance that had been adopted after Uber and Lyft failed to come to the table would be in force, and it would impose a regulatory framework that was not appropriate to the new sharing economy, especially as compared to the better and more innovative solutions that could have been implemented.

On the night of the May 7, 2016, election, almost 56 percent of the voters in Austin told Uber and Lyft, "No." The election turned out not to be a referendum on the value or benefit of rideshare but rather on whether companies disrupting markets could bully and disrupt cities with no regard to the communities into which they were entering.

Even though Uber and Lyft were vowing to leave Austin, I went to sleep that night very proud of our city.

After the election, I sat down and met with Joe Liemandt. Joe is one of Austin's most successful innovators and entrepreneurs, a man with a big reputation who is given both respect and some disdain in the tech industry. He was the founder of Trilogy, which helped to establish Austin as a new tech center. Also, he knew Lyft's management well.

I described to him what had happened in my behind-the-scenes negotiations. I also told him what we had tried to accomplish and how we were hoping to do it.

"Let me make some phone calls," Joe said.

Though Uber and Lyft were threatening to leave Austin, he thought he might be able to broker a deal that would work for everyone. Key to this, he said, was that the city had offered cooperation rather than intrusive regulation.

True to form, Uber and Lyft also told him "No."

There would be no negotiation, no compromise, they said.

"We are leaving," they said.

And they left.

Joe, no fan of government regulation, liked that the city had been trying to innovate on incentives, and the companies' refusal to engage with us and with him clearly got his goat. He unleashed his army of coders and developers. In a matter of just a couple weeks, he developed and launched a new rideshare platform called RideAustin.

RideAustin proved to be an effective replacement for Uber and Lyft, even if rideshare wait times increased by an additional minute or so. It worked just like Uber and Lyft, but it was set up as a nonprofit. Drivers were happy to sign up with RideAustin, because it paid closer to a living wage than either Uber or Lyft. It invented new functionalities like rounding up fares to the nearest dollar to make charitable contributions (as later adopted by Lyft).

And not only was RideAustin available in our community, but other new rideshare companies came to Austin. With the withdrawal of Uber and Lyft, we had become the only competitive rideshare market of any major city in the world. Only in Austin, among major cities, was the rideshare market not controlled by the big two.

Uber and Lyft left Austin believing that our residents would beg them to return on whatever terms the companies wanted, but because of the success of RideAustin and the other rideshare platforms, that didn't happen.

But Uber and Lyft, determined to return to Austin, did what companies in red states with blue cities do. They turned to Governor Abbott and the Texas state legislature. They lobbied to get the Texas legislature to pass a law that prevented or "preempted" cities from doing anything in the rideshare space.

Under the law, we couldn't require or even incentivize drivers to get fingerprinted. We couldn't provide locational advantages to drivers who were fingerprinted. We had no choice but to accept these out-of-state companies operating subject only to the State of Texas oversight, and the oversight provided by the state was so small as to be no material oversight at all.

Uber and Lyft came back into Austin. They operated at below cost until they ran out of town all of the rideshare competitors that had arrived and were developing new functionalities and improving their products. The last company that Uber and Lyft forced to shut down was RideAustin.

Contrary to what some of my more inventive critics might tell you, I am not a doctrinal anti-capitalist. I understand the desire to build something that is distinctly your own, and Austin itself is a testament to the magic that develops when creative people of all kinds have the drive and means to turn ideas into reality. What we saw with Uber and Lyft in Austin, however, was also a distinctly capitalist tale, and one that has nothing to do with celebrating and rewarding bright ideas and determination and energy.

Government can, indeed, be slow. That is a consequence of its definitional responsibility to represent a lot of people at once; being deliberate and consultative is part of the mandate. Put differently, government's natural tendency is to move carefully and try not to break stuff.

Which, of course, is the exact opposite of the old tech industry maxim of "Move fast and break things." That line is usually credited to Mark Zuckerberg, but the American tech industry prioritized boldness, excellence, and risk tolerance long before Zuckerberg ever learned to code. In its early iterations, the tech industry (by and large) had a kind of libertarian, even anarchic and Darwinian ethos to it. Status came from making something cool; sometimes money followed. If you didn't invent then innovate fast, you died. As the industry evolved, money began to follow invention more frequently—and in huge amounts.

As those amounts got bigger, though, some parts of the young tech industry began to act like the aged corporations they proposed to disrupt. What was once a chaotic, dispersed industry (think: "Let a thousand flowers bloom and then let them fight") became centralized into the tech behemoths that now feel as much a part of the American cultural and political landscape as the Rocky Mountains are to the physical one.

Those tech giants behave the way that big corporations always have—which means that, for them, innovation is not always the path to profit. Sometimes the opposite is true. Sometimes they seem to actively stifle innovation and progress if it's not something they own.

Austin's goal throughout the totality of the Uber and Lyft saga was to institute a measure that would provide an option to make rideshare passengers feel safer. The companies' intransigence led us to consider all sorts of new ideas, most a blend of tech, behavioral economics, and sound management principles—the basis of most successful tech firms today. Ultimately, they led us to envision an entirely new platform, Thumbs Up, and to create an entirely new enterprise, RideAustin.

We took great pride that RideAustin, a nonprofit developed with government and the private sector working together, compared favorably to the disruptors Uber and Lyft. It provided rides at a competitive price. It had a few technical glitches as it rolled out. It had fewer drivers so the wait for service was a touch longer. It had safety measures its competitors did not have. It paid a higher wage than its competitors, keeping money in Austin. And it was profitable. Not hugely so, but then—and this is the critical point—it did not need to be.

RideAustin's job was not to make titanic profits. I should point out that it took Uber fourteen years to achieve a profitable quarter; Lyft didn't post a profit until eight years after this Austin experience.

RideAustin's job was to provide the riders of Austin with safe, reliable ridesharing at a good price in a way that treated drivers and passengers fairly.

It did all of that.

Despite that, Uber and Lyft got rid of it not by creating a better product but by using millions upon millions of investors' dollars to lobby the public and lawmakers to own the Austin market, and, once they were back, they used loss-leading practices that distorted the market and choked out the competition—whereupon their prices went right back up.

The result is that the innovative, disruptive rideshare champions of the tech sector now provide Austin with products that are, in some ways, inferior to the government-developed one they displaced, at no savings to their riders and to the detriment of their drivers.

When we see private companies operating in areas that in other countries are considered part of the public good—transport, health, and education—it's worth questioning the common assumption that they're there because they were more nimble or more inventive or more efficient than government can be. Maybe they are. Or maybe they just used their resources to manipulate the political system in a way that government agencies can't.

Often someone from the business community will run for elected office with a platform that's a form of "Vote for me, and I'll make government run more like a business."

I've gotten to the place where I rarely listen to the next words that the would-be politician might utter as they promise to make government more efficient.

When my partner and I ran our own law firm business for the thirty-five years I was in the private sector before I ran for mayor, we did try to run it as efficiently as possible. While we also wanted to be principled and competent, among other values, certainly one of our goals was to run our business efficiently and save money where we could.

Truth is, when I ran for mayor, I was one of those candidates who touted my private sector experience as a way to make Austin City Hall more efficient. But then, when I got into office, I learned some things I hadn't known.

Two important values the public expects from their government, especially their local government, are transparency and engagement.

Transparency is critical for residents to know that their government is being an honest broker between competing and often conflicting interests and that it's acting ethically and fairly. A government that operates in the dark and behind closed doors does not instill confidence and cannot be held accountable.

Engagement is the opportunity the community expects and needs, especially the advocates and focused interests, to feel that they are heard and that they have the chance to make an impact on their government's decisions and actions.

In the context of government, the values of transparency and engagement are held more highly than the value of efficiency. In fact, being truly transparent and allowing for engagement are most often inherently inefficient.

Private and public sectors each bring different but important priorities, dynamics, access, and skillsets to the table that, together, enable them to achieve what neither can achieve alone.

The Uber and Lyft saga could be read now as an old and dated story of what had once been cutting-edge technology disrupting an economy that has since continued to change at an escalating frequency. Now, as an operating partner at Commonweal Ventures evaluating deal flow and advising founders, I see the lessons of this chapter to be even more salient today than they were then. Technology companies and governments that partner are uniquely positioned to unlock value and innovate real solutions. Government intervention, including investment, has driven 24 percent of all venture-backed unicorn outcomes (companies valued at $1 billion or more) over the last twenty or so years, catalyzing $1.6 trillion in corporate valuation.

The private and public sectors in our society both have more in common and less in common than most people think.

And when that animated gentleman at the party told me that Austin's traffic woes might be solved better by the private sector if only the government would leave them alone, you'll understand why I just listened, smiled, and walked away.

13

POLICE AND PUBLIC SAFETY

The people of Austin, as people in many cities, have a love-hate relationship with their police. Most residents most of the time fully support and respect law enforcement, especially when they're scared or in trouble and need someone they can call.

And yet, they all have seen too many videos and read too many news stories of police officers who have abused their power in situations that seem to escalate into someone getting hurt or killed—too frequently someone Black.

Law enforcement was at its best when, as laid out in Chapter 1, it gathered from all across the country to protect and calm a community under attack from an anonymous bomber. Very clearly, these public servants not only did their job at the highest level, but they also put their lives at risk to keep our city safe.

That anonymous bomber launched a surprise attack on our city, immediately causing fear that, in the absence of knowing what was going on, quickly morphed into generalized concerns for safety, the rapid spread of rumors built on historic injustices, and an immediate loss of confidence in and a questioning of our public institutions.

Austin Police, together with an extensive federal and other public safety network, blanketed our city and our airwaves, visibly delivering all that could constructively come to bear. They were as transparent and communicative as circumstances allowed. As mayor, they empowered me to be the eyes and ears of the community and positioned me to help reassure and rally a community under stress. They ended the siege, restored order, and returned a feeling of safety. Police officers promise to run toward danger to protect our lives, and as shown in graphic videos, they delivered on that promise when the bell rang.

But concerns about policing persist. There are some that argue that today's political controversies regarding the police in major U.S. cities arose during the creation of police forces in our country. In our colonial era, we had no standing police forces as we know them today. We had night watchmen on lookouts for fires and other singular events and part-time local constables that served warrants and collected taxes, and as needed for specific incidents, members of the community formed posses. Each of these focused on protecting the property and public order that undergirded the social hierarchy at the time.

Later in the South, the development of organized policing was centered on slave patrols to enforce slave codes, capture escaped slaves, suppress rebellions, and generally regulate the movement of Black people. In the North, cities formed police in response to industrialization and immigration and focused on threats to the economic base—like riots, strikes, and newly occurring urban crime.

Even when these evolved into full-time officers, central command, uniforms and beats, and preventive patrol rather than reactive justice, the focus was on protecting commercial interests, managing labor and immigrant populations, and enforcing prevailing moral norms (alcohol, vice, vagrancy). The emphasis was not on widespread individual safety and protection but with the police more focused on providing enforcement for political elites.

Even as policing reformed in the progressive era with advancements such as civil service exams, police academies, and standardized procedures, historical legacies run deep. There exists today a dichotomy in the perceived role of police as either efficient, effective paramilitary enforcers or as community guardians and protectors. Each leads to different public expectations, self-images, and choices of police tactics.

An example of how this manifests on our cities' streets is the May 25, 2020, Minneapolis arrest of a Black man by the name of George Floyd. Officers said they arrested him because he used a counterfeit twenty-dollar bill to make a purchase in a convenience store. While three other officers looked on, Derek Chauvin, a forty-four-year-old white officer, handcuffed Floyd behind his back and laid him on his stomach. Chauvin then put his knee on Floyd's neck for more than nine minutes until Floyd suffocated and died.

"I can't breathe," Floyd kept telling Chauvin.

Chauvin didn't seem to care. It even appeared to many that Chauvin wanted Floyd to die or was indifferent to the possibility. Chauvin would be convicted of murder and sentenced to twenty-two and a half years in prison.

In the immediate aftermath of the George Floyd murder, demonstrations broke out in major cities across the country, including Austin. Most of those protesting in the cities were non-violently exercising their First Amendment right to express the anger and frustration they were feeling and to make what they felt was an important statement. Some of those involved in the demonstrations, however, were engaging in or precipitating violence.

Different cities and their police forces responded differently to the public safety issues the protests presented.

In the face of large, mass demonstrations, law enforcement agencies can show up seeking to demonstrate strength and control with such a presence that agitators are deterred from doing violence. The downside to this approach is that it creates the perception that the police are battling all of the demonstrators, and it can escalate confrontation even among those who had been disinclined to participate in destructive behavior.

An alternative is to recognize that almost all the demonstrators are engaging in non-violence and do not present a danger to public safety. The police could treat the crowd as what they are—residents exercising their rights. Only a very small group needs to be controlled.

Either way, during a demonstration, the police and that small group are competing to win over the hearts of the large mass of non-violently inclined protestors.

Police present two entirely different moods, depending on whether they show up in uniform riding bicycles wearing Bermuda shorts or whether they show up in police vehicles wearing riot gear. These two approaches require the police to act in very different ways and with very different mindsets. I believed in the former approach. Unless there is clear evidence that a demonstration is about to turn violent, the police presence should be focused on facilitating peaceful protestors' constitutionally protected expressions. I believe police arriving in a manner that says they're most focused on being ready for battle plays into the hands of those who want to turn the peaceful protestors to violence.

On the evening of Saturday, May 30, 2020, curfews were called in Minneapolis, Seattle, Portland, Denver, Atlanta, Los Angeles, Cleveland, Columbus, Pittsburgh, and Philadelphia.

But not in Austin.

During the first weekend of demonstrations in Austin, the police force attacked the demonstrators with beanbag munitions, projectiles intended to incapacitate but not kill the protestors. The issues of provocation are complicated and disputed.

Austin's experience with the police using this weapon was horrible. Some of the demonstrators hit with this weapon weren't threats—they were observers. Some who were hit suffered permanent disabling injuries. The city ultimately paid out over $20 million in settlements to victims and their families.

After the first weekend of demonstrations, I as mayor and members of the city council demanded that the use of beanbag munitions be discontinued, and they were. The public was no less safe.

The job of a police officer is incredibly hard, and I'm not sure if I could do it. After the first weekend and over the course of the George Floyd demonstrations, I stood to the side as our police officers and the demonstrators faced each other literally nose to nose.

A number of the demonstrators approached the Austin Police, yelling their disapproval of the police conduct that had led to the murder of George Floyd and the questionable death of Michael Ramos in Austin just a month earlier. Ramos was sitting in a car at an apartment building. The police showed up, and as he started to drive away, the police shot and killed him.

Inches away from the officers, the anger of the protestors was nearly overwhelming. Yet, in almost all situations, our officers did not react and were not provoked.

That was their job. They had trained for it, and most did it well. Again, it was something I don't think I could do.

My most direct involvement as mayor in the response to the demonstrators was to make the decision about whether Austin would impose a curfew. In my conference room, I met with our police chief and special agents from the regional FBI office in San Antonio. They recommended to our city manager and me that we proceed with a curfew.

They were reacting to the violence they had seen in other cities, and they had read on social media that violent actors were planning some kind of action in Austin. I thought the social media postings they brought to the meeting were few and vague.

This was a tough call. The advice from the public safety professionals was clear. They wanted me to impose a curfew. But I knew that members of our community would protest the curfew itself on the streets. Rather than avoiding a dangerous situation, I was concerned that we might be creating one.

We had seen a convenience store broken into and its shelves cleared. A restaurant had its front vandalized. A car had been set on fire.

But these were isolated incidents rather than a hint at increasingly dangerous behavior.

I looked across the table at Spencer Cronk, the city manager. He was looking back at me. Together, we shook our heads no.

We would not impose a curfew.

It's lonely making final decisions. Make the wrong one, and there's no one to hide behind. Usually, I would take the recommendation of the professionals, but here I didn't. If it was the right choice, no one would notice. If not, I would receive and deserve significant blame.

My role as mayor in this event differed from my role during the anonymous bomber. In the latter, the police did not need or want my tactical input. But to order a curfew meant civilian leadership participating in finding that an emergency situation existed that required this measure be taken.

That night, like so many other nights as mayor, I held my breath. As the evening progressed, I watched for reports of mobs of people in the streets. There were none. There was a call about a breaking and entering at a Target store, but it seemed isolated, and the police were quickly on the scene.

By the next morning, it was apparent I had made the correct decision. Some cities that had imposed curfews sustained terrible confrontations, and some suffered from horrible police brutality against protestors. Denver later paid over $4.7 million to protestors who claimed the police enforcing a curfew had violated their First Amendment rights.

But the city, our police, and I did not always get things as we might like. As I discuss more completely in Chapter 14, the issue of race casts a shadow over policing in Austin and in all major U.S. cities.

In the years just before I came into office, Austin had one of the highest rates of police shootings of minority residents in the country. It was only a year into my first term that I got my first call as mayor telling me that the horrible pattern had struck again. On February 8, 2016, one of our officers shot to death David Joseph, a seventeen-year-old Black teenager. The officer who shot him was also Black.

Joseph was a senior at Connally High School in Austin, where he played football and soccer, and was scheduled to attend college in the fall. For weeks, Joseph had been acting strangely. People who knew him said he was a genial kid. A cousin said he was "open, honest, and kind." But starting in January 2016, they said, he began making bizarre proclamations. On February 7, the teen spoke gibberish with his friend's mother over the phone. He told her Lucifer was after him and that he was one of the three kings and two of them had to die.

On the morning of the shooting, two neighbors said Joseph walked up to them and said, "I'm going to see Jesus tonight, and I'll see you there."

Later that day, the Austin Police responded to a series of calls about a naked young Black teen running through the streets making noise and scaring residents.

Officer Geoffrey Freeman responded, and when he saw Joseph, he ordered him to halt. When Joseph, naked and clearly unarmed, ran at the officer, Freeman opened fire and killed him.

What is the correct tactic to employ as a police officer, armed and ready, standing next to and able to enter his police car, when he is approached and confronted by a naked, out-of-control teenager? This is certainly a tactical question long the domain of police professionals.

Yet the city council and I also thought the question could go beyond mere situational tactics and that it gave rise to broader issues of whether greater resources and understanding of mental health might provide officers more tools to use on the streets or whether a more significant emphasis and training on tactics for disengaging and de-escalating might lead to better outcomes.

On this day, Officer Freeman killed David Joseph, and the city needed to give an immediate and long-term response. The mayor's job is to help facilitate and direct both.

Public officials have a routine immediate response for what happens in such critical circumstances. To the family, we convey some version of our "thoughts and prayers." The sentiment is sincerely meant but of very little comfort. The city's leadership—I, the council, the city manager, and the police executive team—communicated with Black leaders, primarily the older and established clergy from East Austin. We promised a rapid and transparent investigation.

"The family will get answers," we all said.

This was a well-known drill, a repeated and practiced response that serves two purposes. The first is to show the community in general and the Black community in particular that we care. The second is to head off any spontaneous, large-scale response to the tragedy that might include violence or disruption.

I participated in the ritual, but in doing so, I felt guilty and complicit. How many more press statements like this could I make? If my colleagues and I in city leadership really cared, we would have had to offer something more than sympathy every time this happened. And I knew too well that it would happen again.

While it was the city leadership's job to maintain public order and safety, we had to ask ourselves, *Is there an appropriate community response to something like this other than some kind of large-scale civil disruption?*

We needed to do something that went further than just reacting, promising, and placating. I couldn't escape the feeling that participating in this ritual was horribly wrong. It felt totally insufficient.

While David Joseph's death was the first police-involved killing I had confronted in my relatively new term as mayor, in the recent years before I was elected, such deaths of Blacks had been occurring at more than a fourfold disproportionate rate.

As discussed in Chapter 14, police killings, like David Joseph's, are not just a series of unrelated but similar incidents with identically tragic endings. They are a systemic and institutionalized part of our culture. Just before I became mayor, there was a police call communication that became public, where Austin officers, sitting in their car, watched a long-established Black social club burn down. You could hear the glee in their voices, especially as one crowed, "Burn, baby, burn!"

That was, of course, one moment, but it's one in a pattern of examples in which certain members of the police force have shown contempt—or worse—for those they are meant to protect.

In 2023, the vice president of Seattle's police union was recorded saying that the life of a twenty-six-year-old graduate student from India killed after being struck by a police cruiser "had limited value." In 2020, fully armored riot police in Buffalo, New York, violently shoved a solitary, elderly protestor, resulting in a serious head injury that kept the man hospitalized for over a month.

As pointed out at the beginning of this chapter, the list is long and growing.

Not every case of police antagonism toward civilians involves a white officer and a victim of color, but in the three preceding examples, race was a factor. The burning nightclub speaks for itself. The young woman in Seattle, Jaahnavi Kandula, was of South Asian descent, and the white protestor in Buffalo was taking part in the public response to the murder of George Floyd. His demonstration against racism led to his injury.

Before I go further, let me make clear that I don't think most police officers are racists. In fact, most of the police officers I've gotten to know in Austin are very good people, willing to do a really hard job. Many I grew to greatly trust, respect, and admire.

So long as our society does not sufficiently deal with the underlying causes of crime, there will be a need for police to protect and serve, and they deserve our support. Maybe someday we'll no longer need police officers, but crime still exists, so that day is not now. That's why Austin's city councils have always supported our police and why during my time in office our police officers were always among the highest paid in Texas.

And yet, when there are all too frequent shootings of civilians of color, something is wrong. Something is wrong when our police academy's training videos present all police officers as white and all criminals as people of color. Something is wrong when the second highest ranking Austin Police officer for years disparagingly characterized minorities in private communications with other officers without ever being called to task.

The city council and I launched an effort to examine and "reimagine" these policy issues and how we approached public safety and policing in 2020.

Something is wrong when our community uses our police as the way we deal with the challenges of poverty.

Something is wrong when so many of the incidents that go badly on our streets involve officers having to be social workers dealing with mental health challenges without the extensive training that would best enable them to handle such situations. Something is wrong when police officers, instead of mental health professionals, are the first responders called to those situations.

Something is wrong when the police department trains officers to be warriors ready to do battle with their community instead of to be guardians. Something is wrong when our police are firing at demonstrators and observers who are not threatening violence.

Maybe there should be some limits on the use of force?

Maybe police officers should be focused on solving crime and keeping the community safe and spend less time giving parking tickets and taking accident and crime reports (after dangerous situations have passed), maybe they could do what they were trained and sworn to do, while others without such specialized training could assume those more bureaucratic tasks? Maybe we'd need fewer police officers, but have more effective police forces?

These are all questions for the mayor and the city's civilian leadership. And they began to come before us with a new sense of urgency in June 2020, shortly after George Floyd's murder and in response to the way our police reacted to the associated Austin demonstrations.

The Austin City Council passed a measure restricting the use of deadly force by the Austin Police Department. The council ordinance banned the use of less lethal munitions (beanbag projectiles) in response to protests. It also directed the city manager to review the police budget and propose possible reductions.

Two months later, as part of the 2020 city budget approval process, we considered redirecting up to $150 million of the police department's annual budget to civilian entities—like violence prevention, food, abortion access, victims' services, and forensic sciences. After consideration, however, we decided to move only about $20 million or about 5 percent of the annual police budget, mostly from funding for unfilled police positions that would not have been filled, to expanded mental health services and shelter for domestic violence victims trying to escape dangerous situations (then our city's biggest source of violent crime).

The number of police officers on the streets—patrolling, responding to emergency calls, investigating crimes, maintaining public order—remained relatively unchanged. So did the public safety–related operational budget. Nonetheless, and as discussed in the later Chapter 16 on disinformation, I and the city council were wrongfully accused of "defunding" the police.

At the time this 2020 budget conversation was occurring, the level of trust between the police officers and me and the city council had already been significantly damaged.

Two years earlier, in 2018, I and the city council unanimously voted to reject a proposed police contract. It would have cost the city an additional $80 million over five years to give a 9.5 percent salary increase to officers who were already the highest-paid in the state.

This earlier contract dispute had a profound impact on the relationship between the police officers and me and the council. It was the moment that many officers lost trust in us.

As council deliberations of the proposed contract began, many in the Austin community wanted its civilian leaders to use the contract as a vehicle to examine and possibly rethink public safety, as the community had concerns over policy questions such as those I previously set out. The community wanted there to be greater civilian oversight over police conduct and sought to change police culture from a "warrior" culture to a "guardian" culture.

On the night of the vote on the proposed contract, a couple hundred members of the public addressed the council. Most argued angrily against the contract because they felt it provided insufficient police oversight and because this group, frankly, did not like the police. They made this latter point very clearly.

I've been told that most of the police officers who watched the public comment came away with the perception that they weren't supported in the community. The council members, accustomed to hearing community advocates, knew better and knew that most Austinites support and appreciate their police.

Yet it had to have been hard for the officers to listen to the accusatory public comments that night. Some officers, I was also told, were angry at me for failing to cut off speakers who were particularly negative about the police. It wasn't something I could have done since my responsibility and job, as I chaired that meeting, was to provide each speaker with their First Amendment right to speak their mind.

When the council ultimately chose not to approve the proposed negotiated contract, many of the officers thought that the council and I were endorsing the anti-police views of most of the speakers that night.

While some of the substantive and constructive arguments voiced at that meeting raised issues of legitimate concern, the council did not vote against the contract because it didn't support the police.

Money and policy were the reasons. Most council members voted against the contract because it would have cost the city more than the city could afford to spend, especially if the city also expanded the police force as the officers' labor union was requesting. The proposed contract also didn't address the oversight and use of force policy issues the community was raising.

The damage to the relationship between the officers and the council and the associated loss of trust was a very unfortunate outcome of that contract debate. It also fueled the beginning of a years-long disinformation campaign on the part of the police union, discussed more fully in Chapter 16, that caused harm in the community. My inability to correct the record and to maintain what had been a good relationship with our police department is one of my regrets as mayor.

Over my two terms as mayor and despite the ups and downs, I and the council were able to achieve early reforms to establish the path to reimagining how policing could best keep our community safe. We gained greater permanent expansion of civilian oversight authority, structural separation of some non-police public safety functions, a city-wide acknowledgment that policing alone cannot deliver public safety, and a political normalization of alternatives and enhancements, such as a mental health first response. We made ground in changing the policing culture to one of guardianship. We changed policies to lessen police use of force and create greater reliance on the tactic of de-escalation.

We didn't achieve a durable, scaled alternative response system to replace police and police functions at volume. We weren't able to sustain reductions in armed police workloads. We remained victims of state preemption of local control over how we managed police, public safety, and trying to keep our own community safe.

As I pointed out in Chapter 7, when I became mayor, our city was spending around 68 percent of its discretionary general funds budget on public safety (police, fire, and emergency services). When I left office, that percentage had decreased to closer to 63 percent. With a general fund budget of about $1 billion, that change in funding percentage meant that every year there was an additional $50 million to spend on more mental health support and intervention, job training, health care, and safety net protections. One of the reasons that Austin was one of the safest big cities in the U.S. was because we were spending relatively more on these social services that go to preventing crime rather than spending more on responding to crime once it occurs.

That it is difficult in today's world to have an objective, dispassionate policy discussion on what makes for the most effective law enforcement agency is unfortunate. The issues are real, still unresolved, and open to honest debate. People on all sides of the related questions, despite the prevailing rhetoric, are rarely soft on crime or uncaring about public safety, actual racists, or proponents of fascism. Residents in cities across the country could get to a consensus on reimagining policing and keeping our officers and communities safe if we could just talk with one another without the name-calling, the disinformation, and the use of the "public safety" issue by many on all sides as a tool to organize and raise money.

14

RACE, RACISM, ACCESS, AND OPPORTUNITY

George Floyd died at the hands of the police in May 2020. Here is a short list of some other Black victims who died at the hands of the police in that same year: Google them. It's horrifying. Breonna Taylor; Rayshard Brooks; Daniel Prude; Michael Thomas; William Wade Burgess III (shooting officer later indicted for murder); Kurt Reinhold after he was stopped for jaywalking; Mickel Lewis, whose family was awarded $30.5 million; Jonathan Price; Dana Young; Frederick Cox, who was shot in the back at a funeral; and Casey Goodson, shot entering his home holding a sandwich that the officer thought was a gun.

Many times, the officers said the victims had a gun. Almost every time, they didn't.

The complete list of Black victims killed by police in this country during the time I was mayor is too long to print. Black Americans are killed by police at more than twice the rate of white Americans. The racial disparity is even more pronounced for unarmed victims. In fact, Black men and boys face approximately a 1 in 1,000 chance of being killed by police over the course of their lives. Police use of force is among the leading causes of death of young men of color.

If you're a minority, those aren't stories you witness from afar. They are a repeated reminder that you're not as safe as others. White children grow up believing that the police are their friends; Black children, especially boys, are taught from an early age by their parents to be cautious around the police and not to provoke them for fear of what might happen to them.

Sixty years after the '60s civil rights movement, the racism that plagued the South for hundreds of years has not disappeared. When that old evil manifests or is reflected today in an abuse of power by someone who should be trustworthy and has a gun, the impact on the community is horrific and devastating.

As mayor, one of my priorities was to see that the officers of the Austin Police force treated all residents fairly. I have to say that the great majority of our officers do that—but not all and not all the time. Because the resulting betrayal of duty can be so blatant and has the potential for such great harm, even an occasional incident can be seen as part of an observable pattern, evidence of a culture gone wrong, and undercutting the standing of what has to be a totally reliable civic institution.

As raised in the last Chapter 13, in the years just prior to my becoming mayor, Austin had one of the highest rates of police shootings of minority residents in the country. And as discussed with the experience of David Joseph, early in my first term in 2016, I found it hard to escape the conclusion that the difference between police violence against white Americans and against Americans of color, in Austin as in other major U.S. cities, is not a difference of degree but a difference of kind.

Whenever police officers improperly mete out violence against Black Americans, the excuse is often that it is violence by "just a few bad apples." This excuse is way too facile. The real truth of the statement is found in the original phrase from the fourteenth century: a rotten apple quickly spoils its neighbors. Yes, it may be just a single officer that was shown to use improper force against a Black American, but prudence would require a look to see if there may be reasons that the department might have others, too.

Ironically, this isn't the defense the "bad apple" proponents have in mind.

Nor could I in 2016 accept that violence against Black Americans is a series of separate accidents. My response, as an elected leader, as well-rehearsed and rote as a religious ritual, was that this happens way too often to be accidental.

I was confronting a brutal truth, known in the Black community for generations: racist, and specifically anti-Black, violence was not an accident or the natural consequence of law enforcement and criminal justice. And it was more than the unjust and targeted work of a few racist outliers. The design, values, and customs in our institutions carry forward, even inadvertently, the racist work of those in our past who helped create these institutions.

Injustices will keep happening until we do something to end this continuing connection.

As mayor, my job was to try to figure out how to do it.

One thing was very clear from the data. The same historic patterns of denying fair treatment to Black Americans that manifested as police violence against them are also present in all other aspects of modern life: Blacks have less access to capital, health care delivery, education, housing, and civil and criminal justice.

We weren't just dealing with the racist acts of a few outlier individuals, although we did have some of that. My—and our—bigger challenge was dealing with the institutional racism and systemic inequities that are part of and baked into nearly all our institutions.

A truly constructive and transformative action required a response that was so much broader and more inclusive.

As I formulated a meaningful and constructive response to David Joseph's killing, I encountered one of the most intransigent obstacles to progress that I would meet during my tenure at city hall and since: those who stoutly deny that racism is ever at play anymore.

"Those who commit acts perceived as denying justice aren't racists," they proclaim.

What they refuse to see is that injustice too often is the by-product of institutionalized racism.

What is the difference?

Let me present this difference with an imagined game of Monopoly. The twist for the four people playing our imagined game is that the rules provide that one of the players cannot come into the game and roll the dice until the twentieth round. The game starts, and the other three players roll their dice, moving their pieces around the board, passing Go, buying properties, adding houses and hotels, and collecting their money.

As I said, the fourth player doesn't get to roll his dice until the twentieth round.

Of course, the newly participating player, finally entering the game and as hard as he tries, can never catch up to the others.

When the fourth player starts to move around the board, there are few if any properties to land on that he can buy because they're already owned by the other players. And, to make his position in the game even more difficult, most of the properties he lands on have houses and hotels on them, and so he must pay some pretty high rents—more than he can afford.

As we get to the last rounds of the game, the relative positions of the four players become clear. The three players allowed to start the game at the beginning have built their fortunes based on some combination of skill and chance.

For the player who spent the first twenty rounds watching, once he began playing, the other three treated him as an equal but certainly not equitably.

He owns less. He pays more.

He has been allowed to play but at a considerable disadvantage. The rules, as applied, don't seem fair. It's very clear the rules weren't written to benefit someone who wasn't able to roll until late in the game. In fact, quite the opposite—the rules were written to favor the players who have been accumulating money and who have a valuable portfolio of properties and hotels.

This is the way the game of life is played in real life in America. It has become clear that for many Black Americans, they aren't playing by the same rules as white people in America. Too many Black Americans draw Chance and Community Chest cards, like everyone else, but they're hit with a higher rate of hospital fees, doctor bills, and other costs and fees. And there is one card in the fictional Monopoly game that Black Americans never see—a bank error in their favor.

More often than the other players, they get sent to jail—Do Not Pass Go, Do Not Collect $200—and the fines Black Americans pay to get out go into a community pot that is always, always won by someone else. When many Black Americans finally land on a high-value property that isn't already owned and they have the money to buy, it turns out there's a little note on the back of the property card that says, "Sell to whites only," unenforceable but still there.

One of the three players might even be appalled by the apparent unfairness of the situation and might be willing to sell him a property, but at an inflated price—not because they wish him ill but because this is real-life Monopoly, and you don't win by giving anything away.

This analogy does not suggest or imply that the other three players have anything but the best hope for the fourth or that they treat him badly or differently after he starts rolling the dice. The disadvantage is not something born of the present behavior of anyone playing but rather is the lasting vestige of the fact that this player had been excluded for twenty rounds.

In the real world, it's hard to differentiate between racists and the systemic racism in an institution made up of good-hearted people who merely find themselves working where injustice is so baked in that the institution itself is unjust and unfair because it perpetuates past discrimination. This is what's called "institutional racism."

In some Monopoly games, the first three players, recognizing the advantage they are enjoying, might choose to give the fourth player $400 instead of $200 when he passes Go for a few rounds just to try to mitigate the unfairness otherwise present. It would seem to be the fair thing to do. If they did, it would be called "affirmative action."

An observer, arriving sometime after round twenty to watch and unaware of the history of the game, would probably assume that the player who was barred from starting the game at the same time as the others was losing because he was not very good at Monopoly, wasn't very smart, or had been outplayed by the other three. But then, how could that observer possibly understand the state of the game at any subsequent round unless they were told the full history?

As applied to the experience of Black people in this country, this knowledge of centuries of slavery and of segregation—what happened earlier in the game—is called "critical race theory" or CRT.

Teaching history should not be very controversial, but after elections that empowered Donald Trump, Elon Musk, Stephen Miller, Steve Bannon, and right-wing governors like Texas's Greg Abbott and Florida's Ron DeSantis, teaching critical race theory is now being banned from the classroom in a growing number of jurisdictions and states. As a result, many of our schools are prohibited by law from teaching our children to understand the world in which they live.

While it's true there are moments in the history of humankind of which we're not proud, that doesn't mean they shouldn't be taught. In fact, this history needs to be taught so that past failings are not repeated.

The staunch opponents of CRT, afraid that white America is losing ground to Blacks and Latin Americans, insist *without any evidence* that learning about this history makes white children feel guilty and bad about themselves.

I cannot see how teaching history needs to make children feel guilty about something they didn't do. But it would help those students understand why someone might be disadvantaged and only appear not to be good at the game of Monopoly—or life.

If some children are made to feel bad about themselves from the teaching of history and its present impacts, if that teaching suggests history brands broad groups of individuals in today's society as racists or oppressors, or if the history being taught is factually incorrect, then the challenge is with how that history is being taught, not *whether* it should be taught.

We should be focusing on helping teachers teach better rather than on banning the teaching of history itself.

The demonization of critical race theory was so successfully used by Trump, Governor Abbott in Texas, and Governor DeSantis in Florida as a political tool to separate and divide us that the tactic has and continues to spread.

First, we see the banning of teaching about the formative role of race in our country and how our history shapes our present. Then we see government offices, public universities, and even private companies put into the position where they must cancel programs that promote diversity, equity, and inclusion, what are commonly referred to as DEI initiatives.

What's wrong with valuing diversity, equity, and inclusion? As

Minority Leader Hakeem Jeffries said, "These are American values." Our country's motto is "E Pluribus Unum" or "out of many, one," and that's diversity. The Fourteenth Amendment provides equal protection under the law, and that's equity. In this country, we pledge allegiance to the flag, and in that pledge, we promise "liberty and justice for *all*," and that's inclusion.

Yet DEI programs that promote these core American values are being demonized by the Trump administration, in the same way the administration has demonized critical race theory.

"DEI is about so much more than just hiring people from minority communities," said Judith Crowell, chief diversity and inclusion officer of Springfield, Massachusetts. "It includes issues like how to make services and opportunities available to people with disabilities, how to include seniors, and how to make sure that city job or contract postings are widely distributed to reach people from different backgrounds."

What can be wrong about ensuring that no one is systemically denied access and opportunity?

I recently attended a gathering of an annual retreat with primarily younger tech startup founders and C-level executives whose politics run the spectrum. One of the more conservative and very successful participants in one of my small group sessions said that he was adamantly against the practice of DEI and that he worked with our governor and others to outlaw the practice.

I asked him why.

"I oppose any policy that would require the hiring of anyone other than the most qualified for an available position," he said. "I handle the hiring for my company, and I refuse to engage in DEI.

"Besides," he added. "It's not needed. I have one of the most diverse sets of employees among all the tech firms with which we compete."

I was intrigued.

"Congratulations," I said. "How do you hire your employees in a way that results in such a diverse workforce?"

"First, we recruit widely," he said. "Not just from the traditional places, so we find very good people that might otherwise be under the radar. Then I personally talk with everyone we hire to get a really good feel for who they are, their strengths and weaknesses, and I don't just rely on the standard indicators of someone's talent and character. We end up with diverse and very successful people."

He was so proud of what he and his company were achieving, and deservedly so.

"You should be proud," I said. "In fact, the process you just described is exactly what DEI initiatives are supposed to be. DEI is not about hiring unqualified employees. It's about making sure that all qualified people get a shot at your jobs. You find the best workers by widely casting your net and not just hiring from the standard pools. You give applicants a chance to impress you by finding better ways for them to share who they are. You don't just rely on standard measurement tools.

"These practices end up with a diverse workforce because real talent can be found in many places among many kinds of people. Not everyone has the chance to be in the top schools or to score highly on standardized measures."

Another tech CEO in our group added, "My company does what you just described, too, but it's gotten too big for me to do all the interviewing and hiring by myself like I used to. I've hired a great team to help me with that. They find candidates in uncommon places with practices that allow the best and most qualified to shine. I call my team the 'DEI Office.' It's inside my HR department."

The second CEO and I nodded to each other, and together we turned to the conservative tech executive.

"You are the model for DEI," I said.

The room was quiet while several members of our small group

grappled with the thought that maybe DEI wasn't damaging, threatening, or scary, and that it might well just be the best practice.

Knowing our history, understanding that some people don't have the same access and opportunity enjoyed by others through no fault of their own, and recognizing that offering some people an affirmative lift might mitigate some of the injustice they face and that our core American values and the building of this country are centered on diversity, equity, and inclusion are all demonized as being woke.

These are core American principles and objectively rational.

President Trump on January 31, 2025, ended all federal programs that promoted DEI. Without any evidence, Trump went so far as to blame DEI for the crash of an airplane and a helicopter at Reagan National Airport. When asked how that was possible, Trump responded, "It's common sense."

White supremacists all over our country cheered.

In a debate among Republicans seeking the presidential nomination in September 2023, Senator Tim Scott (R), who is Black, stated that "America is not a racist country."

I don't know what the senator meant by this. Did he mean that most Americans aren't racists and that most of the rules in today's society do not explicitly discriminate based on race?

Because both are true.

Or did he mean that race is no longer one of the most significant determiners of any American's standing in life?

Because that's *not* true. All aspects of our lives are impacted by race.

Why is life expectancy so much lower for Black people than white people, even after adjusting for education and economic level?

Like the Monopoly player who enters the game late, the reality is that many Black Americans begin life at a disadvantage that touches almost everything—even something as obscure as lower SAT scores for Black children. Income level has been shown to impact scores. Black children from families with higher incomes receive higher scores than Black children from lower-income-level families. But at each level of family income, even controlling for income, Black children score lower than any other race or ethnic group.

I watch the wide, excited eyes of my students at the LBJ School at the University of Texas as they see doors and networks open with the promise and potential of unlimited opportunity for those willing to take advantage. Yet my extremely bright and hardworking students at Huston-Tillotson University, the oldest institution of higher learning in Austin and a Historically Black College and University (HBCU), have to work harder to find the same scale of invitations to internships and interviews that could lead to similar future opportunities. I do not see merit as the differentiator as much as I see access as the decider.

You don't get generations-long disparities in wealth, health, and prospects through prejudice alone. What we see in this country are the effects of prejudice backed by power.

Prejudice with power is oppression.

I still encounter the inability of many whites to distinguish between the explicit intentions of an individual and the effects, rules, and culture of an institution. So many necessary conversations about race never move forward or even get a chance to start because there is such an overwhelmingly and frequently emotional and passionate reaction to the use of the words "racist" and "racism," as if they mean the same thing.

The scale and intensity of protests against the teaching of critical race theory reveal that there's more at work than an academic argument over pedagogy. Indeed, much of the anti-CRT movement was catalyzed and organized by a conservative political operative named Christopher Rufo, who was very public and open about identifying CRT as a politically useful wedge issue and a way of engaging a certain type of white American who was looking for a socially acceptable way to push back against the George Floyd protests and the increasing conversations about race and racism that were occurring after his murder.

As mayor, I was given a staggering amount of data about Austin and the people who live here. The numbers I was looking at demonstrated a clear reality: racism is so much bigger than the wrongs faced by a single generation of people.

It's bigger than one Black person denied a job or another Black person refused by banks for all but the most predatory loans or another Black person arrested on a triviality or another Black person shot by a uniformed representative of the state because of his skin color.

The consequences of American racism compound over generations, a sort of devil's interest on the country's original sin. We see it everywhere; I saw it in Austin.

For example, the life expectancy of a resident from the old Black communities of Austin was ten years shorter than for those who resided in the West Side of Austin, where neighborhoods are more affluent and mostly white.

The most significant variable is that Blacks don't live as long as the better-off whites.

The human cost is awful to contemplate. Consider the years of lost love, support, and guidance by Black elders—the things that people work their entire lives to be able to offer to their families as they get older. An analysis reveals the terrible cost of that shorter lifespan, not to mention the shorter health span, the period of life when a person is in good enough health to be active.

The American health care system is rife with problems, but it is particularly good at keeping people alive and healthier longer. These added years are usually a gift. One who lives longer has more time and opportunity to make a greater material contribution to his family.

When parents and grandparents decline and die at an earlier age, their children and grandchildren suffer the loss of what their presence and incomes could have provided—greater food security, help with medical access and care, experiences like trips and vacations, even help with cars and computers. By dying early, Blacks have less time to generate family wealth that could be used to help children make a down payment on a home or help a grandchild pay for college. Imagine the effect on grandchildren after three generations of elders die early. Consider too the effect on today's generation of children of color from twenty generations of early death. How could any Black family or community ever recover from this?

The data couldn't have been clearer: the effects of racism are a compounding phenomenon touching every important aspect of the community. A police shooting may have been the catalyst for my inquiry, but to really understand and deal with institutional racism and systemic inequities found in policing and criminal justice, we had to look at the causes and effects of historical racism across other areas, such as access to capital, health care delivery, education, and housing.

It was increasingly clear to me just a year into my first term as mayor that Austin wasn't different from America when it came to discrimination. The question for me became how best to address discrimination that had been baked into our banks, clinics, schools, and law enforcement and that existed no matter how progressive, fair, and just the current players in those institutions were.

What, within the law, if anything, should or could we do about how the police respond when a Black person is the subject of a 911 call?

I chose to adopt an approach inspired by President Barack Obama's 21st Century Policing Initiative, in which his attorney general, Eric Holder, was given the assignment to study and provide a list of achievable and specific initiatives or programs that, in a very short period, could be adopted and implemented.

Holder's initiative made fifty-nine recommendations to change policing around the country. Many were designed to change the cultural ethos of policing.

More than 40 percent of American police forces changed their training practices to comply with Holder's recommendations. In February 2016, I wanted to repeat a process that was designed to quickly result in specific, actionable steps we could take in Austin.

The long-term effects of the federal policing initiative were as yet unknown. But I was struck by its timeliness, the clarity of its mandate, and the thoughtfulness that went into it. I wanted to do something similar in Austin, not only for policing but in other significant areas of life where communities of color—especially the Black community—were suffering the ill effects of generations of institutional discrimination.

To lead this effort, I enlisted two friends with wide community credibility, including within our minority communities, to look broadly at institutional racism and systemic inequities in our city. Colette Pierce Burnette, the president of Huston-Tillotson University, a Historically Black University, had recently arrived in Austin like a shooting star. She seemed to be everywhere raising the HTU flag, inspiring trust and respect in every corner of the city.

Paul Cruz, the superintendent of the Austin Independent School District, headed our largest public school system. He had Austin's second-hardest job—the hardest being the head coach of the University of Texas football team—and he did it very well.

I asked Colette and Paul to look at racism in five different areas: access to capital, health care delivery, education, housing, and civil and criminal justice. I told them it wasn't enough just to restate the challenge we face but to return to the community in just ninety days with specific and enumerated examples of remedial or mitigating work that could and should be done.

Initiating the Mayor's Task Force on Institutional Racism and Systemic

Inequities, I reached out to many members of the Austin community. The response was overwhelmingly supportive and nearly unanimous.

The glaring exception came from leaders of the Austin Police union. They told me that they supported the review generally but wanted me to take the word "racism" out of the task force's name.

"The word is too incendiary," they said.

They said the title implied that the Austin Police officers were racist and that if they participated, they would be admitting that the charge was true.

"That's not true," I told them.

For the first time, I was directly faced with the conflation of the words "racism" and "racist." This is the challenge faced in our country's political debate on race.

"I'm not going to change the name of the task force," I said. "To really deal with institutional racism requires us, at least, to call it by its correct name."

The police union chose not to participate in our conversations, and I regretted that.

The city fired the officer who shot David Joseph, though never charged, and he sued to get his job back. We settled his wrongful termination claim for $35,000 on the condition he drop his claim for reinstatement. The settlement avoided even more expensive litigation.

In February 2017, the city agreed to pay Joseph's family $3.25 million. None of us labored under the delusion that any sum of money could undo or redress or even adequately atone for what happened. The money would not bring David Joseph back to life. He never would get the chance to attend college.

The task force presented its report to council and the public in April 2017. It issued 207 specific recommendations, most of which have been implemented or initiated. As I expected, there were more recommendations to improve equity in banking, finance, and industry than in criminal justice, although the report had thirty-eight recommendations in that field, too.

In my eight years as mayor, the council and I tried to address the institutional racism all around us. We created the Spirit of East Austin initiative as the city's first community-owned look at how to accelerate economic prosperity in our disadvantaged parts of town. The participants coined the name Eastern Crescent for Austin's historically economically disadvantaged area.

We created an Equity Office in city government to be a watchdog over all we did. The work was difficult, and there have been controversies because it's not possible to right the harms of several hundred years of slavery and racism in two terms.

Here's why there were controversies about this: one side resisted change and saw it as being too abrupt. The other side saw what we did as insufficient.

I am proud of what I and the council achieved, including the following:

- We ended legal penalties for truancy. The result was to stop a system that disproportionately and too early brought Black youth into our criminal justice system.
- We stopped arresting and prosecuting for low-level criminal violations like the possession of a small amount of marijuana. This ended another practice that disproportionately created criminal records that caused greater harm than their legal offenses ever did.
- We required employers to give those with non-disqualifying criminal backgrounds much-needed second chances in employment applications, not to give them jobs but to ensure worthy people are considered.
- We created a Civil Rights Office and implemented greater and more meaningful community oversight over the police department.

- We raised the minimum wage for city employees and contractors by over 50 percent and set it at a living wage.
- We focused on responding to homelessness, where Blacks, who make up 7 percent of the city population, make up 40 percent of those living on our streets.
- We piloted a guaranteed income program to help people in poverty. We felt this practice would be the most cost-effective way for taxpayers to help keep people in their homes and off our streets.
- Thousands of Austinites, including C-level executives, attended Glenn Singleton's two-day Courageous Conversation race training or a similar workshop (and I later became good friends with and an occasional advisor to Glenn; Diane joined his foundation board).
- As a result, more Austinites understood our history and the reality of institutional racism. They had learned the vocabulary to discuss and address the issues of race and of police brutality that they could use several years later in the aftermath of the George Floyd murder in Minneapolis and the very disturbing Michael Ramos killing in Austin.

In all this work, I and the council tried to help make Austin a fairer and more just community for those who didn't have the same access and opportunity that I was given. My focus was on race because, with the wider view that I enjoyed as mayor, it became apparent to me that race is the single greatest determinant of someone's life in this country. This is true whether you're white, Black, or any shade in between.

The Black Lives Matter movement reached its pinnacle during my time as mayor in the aftermath of the George Floyd murder. When you say Black Lives Matter, that doesn't mean that other lives don't matter as well. It's merely a recognition that the Black experience in this country comes out of slavery, which is uniquely damaging. No other single group of people in this country has so directly and for so long been denied access and opportunity. Though some in the Black community have been able to rise above the challenge, that doesn't mean that many others aren't held back by the barriers of lost access and opportunity denied.

Against all that I have laid out in this chapter, six months after I left office, the United States Supreme Court held in *Students for Fair Admissions v. Harvard* that affirmative action based on race was unconstitutional. The court ruled that racial preference at the University of North Carolina and at Harvard must end. According to this court, our Constitution does not require equity but rather only equality. Everyone has to be able to play by the same rules, as if that were enough.

But as the imagined game of Monopoly demonstrates, being able to participate late in the game using the same rules doesn't provide the same access and opportunity to those who didn't start with the same advantage and privilege.

For that reason, I was very critical of the Supreme Court decision. I question whether everyone who plays by the same rules does, in fact, receive the constitutionally guaranteed equal protection under the law. It seems to me that those who are playing with such a built-in advantage benefit from rules that preserve the existing inequality, ensuring that some people will never catch up.

In his recent reelection, President Trump rode a rising backlash among working-class white and Hispanic men against affirmative action policies favoring Blacks. This has made me question my views on the twin concepts of fairness and equity. My focus as mayor on the unique harm suffered by Blacks in our country and the need to correct that historical injustice meant that I didn't target just as directly or as diligently the need to correct the lack of access and opportunity found in poor white and Hispanic communities.

Not all Black Americans face the same measure of denied access and opportunity.

Not all Americans that face denied access and opportunity are Black.

While it is true that Black Americans are disproportionately represented among those sleeping on our streets, everyone without a home needs help—regardless of who they are or how they got there.

To recognize that many white and Hispanic children are not getting equal opportunity because many of them are also starting out far behind is not to discount the Black experience in this country. Shouldn't all children who are being denied equity, regardless of the reason, receive special attention to help them make up the ground they need to have an equal shot at opportunity?

Many in this country don't have a fair shot with an equal application of the rules. Those without economic opportunity can't compete with those who have greater resources and connections. Shouldn't we fight for all those denied real access and opportunity?

I've now come to believe that the burdens of implementing progressive policies aimed at correcting historical injustices sustained by Black Americans are unfairly, unjustly, and disproportionately borne by whites, Hispanics, Native Americans, and those of any other identity who also lack access and opportunity because of their financial position and other hardships. The cause of their status is different from those suffering from a history of slavery and racial discrimination, but their individual (not collective) need for a level playing field to achieve access and opportunity is similar. I support the positions taken by the Reverend Dr. William Barber II as I understand them. He is a leader in the movement to lift all poor and working-class people.

Many affluent white progressive communities that support affirmative action programs based on race do not lose much from the existence of these programs because they already have such an advantage in life that they will have access and opportunity regardless. But if your status in life means you are being denied access and opportunity and you are not among those receiving the benefits of affirmative action based on race, then those programs are doing you real competitive harm. You would correctly resent and oppose such programs, which, as applied to you individually, are neither fair nor just.

The Supreme Court in the affirmative action case did not say that our society cannot or should not provide greater access and opportunity to those who are in poverty or who are being denied such privilege. It said that our Constitution does not allow a government program or policy that favors only some of those disadvantaged based on their race or membership in another protected class, like ethnicity or sex. The Supreme Court allows and our laws should provide for our federal and local governments to affirmatively provide what's necessary for each person to be able to fairly compete when all the rules are being equally applied.

No matter how unique the Black experience in this country, no matter the unmatched degree with which that experience has denied the Black community access and opportunity, no matter that race is the single most significant determiner of someone's status in this country, there are others in this country who are also being denied access and opportunity. A just and fair country, or city, should be trying to provide equitable access and opportunity to *every one of them.*

This is not to deny the special historical and lived experience of Blacks in this country and the unique burdens and thus manifestations imposed. It is only to recognize that everyone is entitled to a fair shot at success, regardless of how they got to a place where they don't have it.

Yes, there is a fair rationale for providing greater mitigation measures for Blacks in our country because their historic injustice is more extreme and more uniform in its impact. Even among those equally without access and opportunity, Blacks still exhibit greater health and other disparities that arise from generations of compounded harm. The Supreme Court holding does not account for this. There are also mitigation measures (of varying effectiveness) that address institutionalized racism that isn't a product of economic injustice, such as the Rooney Rule, which ensures that Black football coaches are at least considered for NFL head coaching jobs.

And yet, providing the full and direct measure of racial justice, if it also turns a blind eye to the barriers confronting all stressed economic classes, comes with several significant and associated costs and challenges.

First, fighting over who is most deserving of fundamental fairness distracts from the righteous fight against unfairness for all.

Second, in-fighting between worthy groups serves to divide those who would be stronger together, each having a better chance of realizing fairness if they fought as one. Frankly and at the end of the day, those who seek access and opportunity for those to whom it is denied need a bigger army of both allies and those on the front lines.

Finally, until a subsequent Supreme Court revisits affirmative action, racial preferences in governmental action are against the law as it is being applied.

While imperfect and not the most direct or efficient way to address the Black experience in this country, a focus on denied opportunity or class rather than a racial focus will best serve the Black community and our country generally.

The accomplishments achieved in Austin in the list I previously set out in this chapter, many initiated with racial injustice in mind, help all people who are dealing with poverty and lack of access and opportunity, not just those in the Black community. Even while race-neutral policies and programs to address poverty and lack of access will help all races and ethnic groups, they will disproportionately help those who, by identity, most suffer from a great historical and systemic disadvantage.

Regardless of their paths in life, *everyone* should be entitled to opportunity and access.

The greatest danger of affirmative action based on race is not that it divides Blacks, whites, and Hispanics in this country. It's that it divides poor Blacks, poor whites, and poor Hispanics from each other and their common battle for universal opportunity, in which they should be engaged together. During my time as mayor, the most fervent racial and ethnic conflict I saw in my city was the one between the Black and brown communities, as each thought the other was taking away their chance for greater access and opportunity, as if these were finite resources.

All those who are being denied access and opportunity should be on the same team, helping and supporting one another. It's the politics of poverty that frequently has disadvantaged communities competing against one another for the small slice of the pie available to them.

We should support those communities as they join to insist that their collective slice of the economic opportunity and access pie must be bigger.

We should be calling on the business community and our political leaders not to retreat from DEI hiring practices that seek to ensure that all of the best candidates are found and have access to universal opportunity. This is what the best DEI practitioners have been doing all along. These companies should be supported in this work, and they should never feel isolated or fearful of those who would seek to make this country and all of its citizens less than their promise and potential.

The Democratic Party should change its policies and positions to those that seek justice and equity for *all in need* rather than leading with any identity factor, including race, that may have contributed to creating that need.

This policy North Star would widen the Democratic base because it champions all without advantage, access, and privilege. As a practical matter, such a policy will benefit Black communities and communities of color the most because they have suffered the greatest actual and the most omnipresent institutional racism and discrimination.

Understanding what we need to do to ensure greater justice for all will require us to know how we got to where we are, and the history of race in this country needs to be part of what we all must understand.

In the most recent presidential election, too many people who would benefit from affirmative action based just on need didn't believe they could find in the Democratic Party the recognition that they, too, were deserving and entitled to such attention and focus. They turned to a Republican Party that deceived and sold them a bill of goods by recognizing their plight and making them feel they were heard, even though Republican policies do not reflect that feigned concern. It's unlikely that the Republicans will ever deliver on any of it. It has become clear that the Republicans in 2024, aware of the dissatisfaction of the white male voters in the Democratic Party, misled them into voting for MAGA Republicans, and I'm certain that many of these voters are very sorry they did.

These disenfranchised white and Hispanic voters turned away from a Democratic Party that they perceived as too focused on race rather than on universal opportunity, even though its programs generally aid all who lack access and opportunity.

Even still, the Democratic Party will not be the party of the entire working class unless its policies and priorities lead with a concern about universal access and opportunity rather than race, ethnicity, sex, or any other identity. When someone disadvantaged for whatever reason is looking for a political party to join, they will join a team that champions full opportunity for them.

The challenge for the Democratic Party is not primarily a communications issue. Our policies have placed undue hardship—an unfair share of the burden of achieving equity—on the poor white and Hispanic communities that need help too. Our policies have been wrong, not merely misunderstood. Recent national Democratic candidates have broadened their messages to be less identity-oriented, but the implementation of their programs and policies, the substantive work, has not caught up to and thus does not support that messaging.

The Democrats need to be the party of universal opportunity and access.

If the Democrats focused on all who deserve a greater shot at access and opportunity and if all in this community were united in bettering the positions of all the others, then maybe, just maybe, more people would see the Democratic Party as being focused on them and their hopes and aspirations.

And if it prioritized them, more of the working poor and the working class would trust the Democratic Party to be their team.

15

SANCTUARY CITY ON ICE

One of the most serious issues I had to deal with in President Trump's first term was his insistence that all undocumented immigrants be thrown out of the United States. What Trump wanted to focus on, what he wanted done, was for ICE—the U.S. Immigration and Customs Enforcement Agency—to gather up, arrest, and deport these folks in our community.

Trump gave a speech while first running for president in which he said: "When Mexico sends its people, they're not sending their best. They're not sending you. They're not sending you. They're sending people that have lots of problems, and they're bringing those problems with us. They're bringing drugs. They're bringing crime. They're rapists. And some, I assume, are good people."

Like much that Trump says, he was making up his "facts" from whole cloth. The truth is, the crime rate among immigrant communities, including among those undocumented, is lower than in the general population. I would tell people all the time in a tongue-in-cheek but still honest way, "If you really want to lower our crime rate in the U.S., we should bring in more immigrants. It would average down our crime rate."

There had been ICE raids and arrests of undocumented immigrants under President Obama. One key difference between what Obama had done and what Trump did and is doing is that when ICE in the Obama administration would target and arrest an undocumented immigrant, he or she would most often be a criminal who had a violent past. In Trump's first term, ICE would not only go after that person and arrest him, but if there were four or five other undocumented immigrants in the area, they would be collaterally arrested even though they had no violent or criminal past.

In Trump's second term, there's not even a pretense of targeting only criminal undocumented immigrants—the policies target any undocumented immigrant.

Trump's untrue and demonizing characterization of undocumented immigrants was like his boast that he would build a wall between the United States and Mexico and Mexico would pay for it. Neither was true. But his effort to throw undocumented residents out of the country has brought a lot of pain to this community.

Our city was drawn into the controversy. As with many cities, Austin had a large population of undocumented residents, and Trump was calling on us to use our resources, including our police and jails, to help ICE deport them.

Our city's undocumented community was scared that we would acquiesce.

I met with our police chief, Brian Manley. He told me the same thing he would later tell the Texas legislature. He said that using local police to arrest non-violent and non-criminal immigrants was bad public policy because it would make our community less safe. Why? Because our police department was already strained by not having sufficient resources to deal with violent crime in general. Moreover, if our police were assisting ICE and acting as federal immigration agents, our officers would lose the trust that the immigrant communities need to have in the police.

It's very important for people to trust the police so they're not afraid to go to them and point out bad guys or to be a willing witness at a trial to put a bad guy away. If a woman is being hurt by someone, she needs to trust the police enough to go to them to get protection from the evil doer.

"But," said Police Chief Manley, "if the greater fear is that she or someone in her family might end up deported if she gets involved, then she is going to hide. She is not going to show up as a witness, point out bad people doing bad things, or turn in people who are hurting her. Bad people causing injury will not be stopped."

He continued, "People should see us in uniform as protectors. They should not see us as threats and worry most about their immigration status."

That made a lot of sense to us, and it was the policy that I and the city council directed.

The biggest dispute we had with ICE concerned a detainer document that ICE presented when it wanted local law enforcement to hold an undocumented immigrant. If ICE wanted time to investigate someone soon to be let out of jail, who they believed was undocumented, ICE would present a detainer to the sheriff.

The document said: "We want to investigate this person who you are about to release to see whether he should be deported. Please continue to hold him until we can complete our investigation."

The problem was that ICE was asking the sheriff to hold this person beyond the time he was supposed to be released. Even if he had posted bond or a court had ordered him released, ICE was asking for him to be held longer.

Unlike some cities around the country, which acquiesced and did as asked, we didn't think ICE had legal authority to do this.

Here's the issue. Our police can't arrest someone, and our jails can't hold them, unless they are suspected or guilty of committing a crime.

Many who are undocumented in our country aren't criminals. Someone who comes into this country legally but, say, overstays their visa or fails to renew it properly is undocumented, but this is a civil violation, not a criminal one. This differs from someone who has committed the crime of entering the country illegally.

Without a special grant of authority, local law enforcement can neither arrest nor detain an undocumented immigrant for a civil immigration violation.

Only federal immigration agents, like ICE, have the general authority to detain and hold someone without documentation for both a civil and a criminal violation. Trump and ICE didn't care about this legal distinction. To them, an undocumented immigrant was to be deported, and any tool available to assist in this effort, including local law enforcement or jails, was something they wanted to use.

We in Austin pushed back. We had no way of knowing whether someone the sheriff was asked to hold over in jail had committed a civil or criminal offense—or even no offense at all. We believed ICE needed to establish probable cause before it could demand that local authorities detain people.

Another reason not to hold undocumented people outside the law was that President Trump and ICE weren't only going after violent criminals, as they said. In fact, most of those arrested and detained were not violent criminals. These were hardworking people who were raising families, paying taxes, and making our economy work.

I repeat: Trump was lying. Most were not violent criminals.

We said to ICE, "We will detain people as required by law, if you make the appropriate legal showing and get a court to order that they be held."

If the person to be detained the extra days was a criminal or a suspected criminal, ICE should have easily been able to get a court order to hold them. But they rarely, if ever, did.

Our local sheriff, Sally Hernandez, quite rightly said, "We just can't hold people not shown to be violent or a threat and not suspected of having committed a crime."

Were Austin and Travis County violating the law by not honoring the detainers and affirmatively helping ICE? No.

We would have been violating the law only if we arrested or held someone in custody for whom there was no probable cause to believe they had committed a crime, absent a further state law or a formal agreement whereby local law enforcement agencies agreed to serve as federal immigration agents.

Nonetheless, to pressure cities to assist ICE with immigration enforcement, President Trump and then Attorney General Jeff Sessions falsely charged that cities not willing to help ICE detain immigrants were intentionally violating the law to allow immigrants to endanger public safety. They added that those cities would be punished with the loss of federal funding.

They called the cities they targeted sanctuary cities and promised to go after them.

There was a real question of what exactly a sanctuary city is. There is no legal definition. President Trump and the right-wing media claimed that a sanctuary city is one that violates the law by protecting undocumented immigrants.

The challenge with this definition, however, is that I didn't know of a single city that was violating federal law to protect or give preferential treatment to undocumented immigrants. For a time, some cities were declaring themselves sanctuary cities, but their definition was only that they were a city willing to publicly express their support and provide services for immigrants. None was touting practices or even a willingness to violate the law.

In response to the threat to go after sanctuary cities, we joined other cities and went to court to see whether the U.S. Justice Department could legally withhold funding from us. The key issue was whether it was a violation of the law for a sheriff to refuse to honor a detention request that was unaccompanied by a court order.

There was another important issue: if it wasn't illegal or against the law for a sheriff to refuse to honor a detention request, could the U.S. attorney general withhold funding in order to promote the president's immigration policy?

We waited as those cases wound their way through the courts.

While all this was happening, Austin's immigrant communities were scared to death, as were the nonprofits providing services to these communities that were facing the possibility that their funding would be cut off if we didn't cooperate with ICE.

There was a lot of funding at risk. Tens of millions of dollars a year. A lot of money.

I convened the executive directors of the larger nonprofits supporting and aiding folks in the immigrant community who would be impacted by the threatened funding loss.

More than fifty directors of nonprofits sat around a large table in a big room, two and three deep in spots, and I said to them, "We all need to really think about what happens if we lose funding, because if we lose funding, then you're not going to be able to provide the services your clients need. And that is going to hurt people."

I went on. "Whatever we decide, we will be making a choice that puts people at risk. Which choice to hurt people are we going to make?

Which is the better of the two evil choices? What shall we do?" I asked everybody in attendance.

The executive directors in that room were familiar with what was going on, and they were very concerned. They understood the threat to their grants if we didn't help ICE.

"What shall we do?"

Immediately, everyone started talking about how helping ICE was going to make our community less safe. They ran through all the reasons.

"We can't help ICE," said the executive director of a nonprofit organization that helps provide medical care to poor Hispanic communities. "The ICE raids aren't only going after people who are violent or other kinds of criminals. They are arresting and removing people who aren't even suspected of a crime."

Said the executive director of a nonprofit protecting constitutional rights of undocumented immigrants, "If the local government participates in federal immigration enforcement, it will increase the fear in the immigrant community that they will be discovered and deported. We will see greater numbers of our community go into hiding. If people go into hiding so they can't be found and deported, they are less likely to go to the clinic when they or their children are sick. They're even less likely to go to church. This will make our entire city less safe and will put all of us at a greater risk."

"I appreciate what you have said and how quickly you have said it," I said to the room. "But I don't want your answer right now. I want everybody to think about this. We'll reconvene in a week, and during that period, I want you to really think about the answer to this question. I want you to go and talk to your boards and to your staff. Do we participate with ICE knowing the harm that will cause, or do we refuse and risk the loss of funding?"

They all left, and a week later, we reconvened. When we were together again, I repeated the same question I had asked before: "What shall we do?"

I was anticipating a hard conversation and that there would be differences of opinion. I expected a very emotional meeting because there didn't seem to be one perfectly good or correct answer.

"Let's see where each of you has arrived. But first," I said, setting the stage for the anticipated disagreements, "let's recognize that we are all on the same team and share the same goals but may have very different opinions on what is the best path to follow. We are all in this together," I said. And then, "What shall we do?"

I asked for a show of hands to see who was willing to cooperate with ICE so that we wouldn't jeopardize our funding.

Not one hand went up.

These people are so courageous, I thought.

At that moment, I was so proud to be an Austinite.

Many of the nonprofit directors said they hoped that our community would find another way to make up any funding loss, if needed. In fact, I was asked if the community would step forward. I told the group that I thought it would. I also promised that, as mayor, I was ready and eager to provide the very necessary aggressive, visible, and political leadership that is required to deliver such a result.

Direct advocacy and work by a mayor can be determinative in such a situation. A mayor has a powerful bully pulpit and is in a unique position to raise the needed campaign and communication funding to rally general public support. I did this over twenty times as mayor, and we had a near perfect record of getting voters' approval of ballot measures for funding social initiatives. Unfortunately, Austin lost that edge in a recent, unsuccessful 2026 voter proposition to support these social service organizations when my successor as mayor chose not to play such a role.

As it turned out, back in Trump's first term, finding funding to fill a gap never became necessary. Federal funding was never withheld because the courts ruled in favor of the cities.

In many states, that became the end of the story, but not in Texas. The Texas legislature was in session in 2017, and Governor Greg Abbott, appalled that some cities in Texas weren't facilitating illegal measures to effect the deportation of immigrants, asked for and got passed Senate Bill 4, the anti–sanctuary cities law.

The law made it a criminal offense for a local official not to comply with an ICE detainer request, thus making a legal obligation of something under state law that had not been required under federal law.

That changed things on the ground for us because we would always follow the law.

The new law also contained a provision directed at Austin's policy of telling police officers, "Don't ask people about their immigration status on the street unless it's related to a separate crime."

Senate Bill 4 made it illegal for a city to have such a policy.

Our council was concerned about where and how the new state law would be implemented and what impact it might have on our limited public safety resources. So in response, our city council passed an ordinance directed at our law enforcement personnel that said, Okay, we can't stop you from asking about immigration status, and you're free to do it if you are so moved. But we want to keep track of our resources, our officers' time, and how it's spent, and we want data to learn under what circumstances our police officers would ask that question.

This new city ordinance required officers to help us keep track of the variables by requiring a report to be filled out by an officer who chose to ask an immigrant about their immigration status.

Maybe it was because our officers didn't see a need to ask to do their job to keep our community safe, maybe they wanted to preserve the valuable trust relationship they had with all parts of our community, or maybe because it would be a hassle to ask such a question and fill out all the paperwork, but as far as I know, none of our officers asked questions about immigration status.

The new law also contained a provision, passed by the legislature and signed by the governor, that said local officials who advocated policies counter to Senate Bill 4 could be jailed or removed from office. Those officials included mayors.

Come get me, I thought.

I made my opposition to the new law very publicly known as an advocate for my community's values. In the back of my mind, I kind of hoped I would be the first mayor arrested or removed from office for that criminal act. The right of free speech is so much a part of what I treasure about my country that I knew I could write a compelling letter from jail.

My wife Diane said she'd visit me in jail, but before that could happen, the federal Fifth Circuit Court of Appeals in New Orleans invalidated as unconstitutional the provision that would have jailed me and other elected officials for advocating against the new state law, even as the court upheld other provisions making it illegal for cities to refuse detainer requests and to adopt policies stopping officers from asking about immigration status.

I'll say it again: We have a lot of undocumented immigrants in our community. They are hard workers. They are part of our community. They didn't elect me because they couldn't vote, but they are residents of our community, and my goal and the city council's goal was to improve the quality of life of *everyone* in our city, to keep all parts of our city and all of our residents safe and healthy, and for our police to find the real criminals in everybody's neighborhood.

When President Trump talked about building his wall, I used to say that my job as mayor was to build bridges.

I tried to do everything I could to deal with the blanket of fear in the immigrant community. I wanted to make sure that residents, including immigrants, knew their rights under our Constitution. Those who had entered our country legally but whose permission had lapsed were told that ICE agents could not force entry into their homes without a warrant. If uniformed agents without warrants were pounding on their door, yelling, "I know you're in there," those inside didn't have to open the door. But if they opened it, then ICE could come in.

What a frightening thing it would be for a family to be huddled together, holding each other and trying not to panic with an ICE agent outside trying to get in.

A council member was talking to a teacher who had gotten a call from a second-grade student apologizing because she would be late for school since she couldn't leave her house as ICE agents were at her door. This child was whispering on the phone, and the teacher could hear the pounding and the yelling in the background.

Parents would take their children to school not knowing if they'd be able to pick them up at the end of the day or if they'd first be picked up themselves and put on a bus or plane heading south. If that happened, who would pick up their kids? The families all had contingency plans. They had to build systems of support, and it added to the family's fear.

The whole thing was and is very scary.

We have 10 million to 15 million undocumented workers in this country, and Trump says he wants to deport them all, which would be an ethical, moral, and economic disaster. Already, we are having trouble finding enough workers to build our homes, sustain our economy, and do jobs like picking vegetables that others aren't ready to do.

For the longest period of time, we were actively inviting undocumented immigrants to cross the border and to help us because it was good for our economy. We rarely went after the companies they were working for. It was no secret they were hiring lots of undocumented workers.

In my mind, we were tacitly inviting these workers into our country to help our economy, and now that they're here, we bear a moral responsibility for their well-being. It's like the scene in the Humphrey Bogart movie *Casablanca*: are we surprised that our communities contain so many undocumented workers?

We invited them here.

And now that they're here, who's responsible for that?

In Trump's second term, he is once again threatening cities and nonprofit organizations in those cities with the loss of funding if they don't support and act beyond what the law requires to assist his draconian immigration policies.

This time, I'm not as confident that the courts will stand guard over the rule of law. I hope so. In the meantime, just as we did in the first Trump administration, cities and communities need to band together to preserve public health and safety.

16

LIES ARE EVERYWHERE

Over the last decade, we've seen change happen with something so fundamental that most people never realize what has happened: too often, our reality is no longer real.

Our politics, government, and public life increasingly are flooded with disinformation. The staying power of lies is amazing; it's worse than a bedbug or termite infestation.

Disinformation played a role in Austin's handling of public safety, COVID, and homelessness during my time as mayor, as was evident in earlier chapters.

Our leaders need to have a strategy to combat disinformation, or the country risks being consumed by it. I'll share what I saw and what I learned, but I was never able to execute a plan to effectively combat the damage done by misinformation and disinformation.

The substantive issues associated with the city council's denial of the proposed police contract in 2020 were immediately overtaken by the false talking point that I and the council had "defunded" and didn't support its police force.

A host of problems—real and imaginary—were explained through the prism of a decision to drastically cut funding to the Austin Police. Some, especially Republicans, were sharply critical, condemning it by saying it recklessly endangered the public, or worse. There were defenders, who rightly noted that changes in police budgets do not correlate to whether crime rates rise or fall. They supported the budget cut, saying it was a tool to make this desired cultural change in criminal justice.

In the end, PolitiFact, the fact-checking website, noted that crime in Austin was in keeping with national trends and that it was impossible to conclude that budget cuts had resulted in increased crime, as Republicans falsely claimed.

There was only one thing wrong with that reporting: *We hadn't defunded the police.* The underlying premise was wrong, but it had become so widely accepted at that point that its continued assertion happened automatically.

Dangerous disinformation that occurred during the COVID crisis resulted in people needlessly getting sick and dying. Donald Trump was president, and he did everything he could to minimize COVID's deadly nature as a way of denying responsibility for what would become so many deaths.

Let's focus on his disinformation. The virus hit the country in March, and in July, he told the public that in 99 percent of the cases, the coronavirus "was totally harmless." That, of course, was a lie. He said that children were "almost immune to this disease." That too wasn't true. Trump undermined public health guidance on masks, he refused to model mask-wearing despite CDC recommendations, and his behavior discouraged mask compliance.

Instead, he ridiculously promoted hydroxychloroquine as a cure. Not only wasn't it an effective medication, but hydroxychloroquine was a drug that could cause heart problems for those who had underlying conditions. Trump dangerously questioned whether disinfectants could treat COVID patients.

Other Republicans tossed out myths and falsehoods as true. They fought against people getting the Pfizer and Moderna vaccines, which saved so many lives. They said that if you took the vaccine, you could get COVID. Not true. Robert Kennedy Jr., some QAnon supporters, and Trump advisor Roger Stone all suggested that there was a microchip in the vaccine, and if you got vaccinated, the deep state could track your movements. This too was utterly ridiculous, but too many people believed it. (RFK Jr. is now head of the federal health department.)

Trump didn't want to be blamed for the destruction brought on by the virus, so he pretended it didn't exist. In Austin, we did the opposite. We did everything we could to inform our residents about the dangers of the disease, as previously discussed. Austin is a healthy city because its people want to take care of themselves and each other, and during the COVID crisis, city officials gave them factual information so they would know how to do it.

We focused so thoroughly and so relentlessly on that principle that most of the time our information was able to cut through the disinformation. For almost a year, I conducted a live, daily, 7 p.m. Facebook video stream that was watched by many in the community and used by the media for sourcing information.

Major U.S. cities are much safer today than they were twenty years ago and generally getting safer still. Yet this doesn't stop disinformation from President Trump and many other politicians describing cities as havens for crime that need intervention.

In 2019 when I and the Austin council passed an ordinance that lifted the ban on public camping, Governor Greg Abbott tweeted a video that showed a man who appeared to be attacking drivers in cars. Abbott claimed that this was proof that the city's new ordinance decriminalizing homelessness was sending Austin out of control. The video, it turned out, had been recorded a year before. Not only that, but the man, obviously dealing with personal demons, was not homeless.

When I pointed out these deliberate errors, Abbott doubled down on his post.

Austin is and was a safe city—one of the safest of its size in the country. A single mendacious tweet doesn't change that, but Abbott's post was part of a torrent of public and social media statements from prominent Republicans and their supporters, all wrongfully implying that Austin's efforts to address and raise awareness of homelessness made our city less safe.

The local police union, always lobbying for a pay raise, got in on the act, continually questioning the city's safety despite the clear and objective evidence frequently cited by our police chief that Austin was still among the safest large cities in the country.

The union's constant disinformation campaign began when I and the council didn't approve the proposed 2018 police contract, as discussed in the earlier Chapter 13 on policing. It was at the council meeting when that action was taken that many officers became convinced that they didn't have the support of their elected leaders.

Why didn't the officers know what was really happening at the meeting and with that contract?

I believe it was because the police labor union leaders wanted it that way.

The union executed a negative campaign against the council in hopes that it would turn the community against it to force the council to accede to the union contract demands.

It didn't work. Because the Austin Police union is politically tone deaf, Austin citizens vote against nearly all the propositions it puts forward and supports. The union heads were good at one thing: painting the city council and me in a negative light with a false narrative.

In my private conversations with many Austin Police officers, I found that almost all of them welcome oversight and want accountability enforced. They have a real desire for there to be a greater focus on mental health challenges using experts on the streets. The police don't want to be the ones responsible for meeting the challenge of poverty or homelessness. They want to spend more time dealing with real crime.

Policy differences between the city council and the police union on public safety funding, training, tactics, and culture do not mean that the police and their work aren't supported and valued. And yet these policy differences were weaponized by the police union to create that very false impression.

What resulted was low morale among the officers who wrongly believed the elected officials and even the community did not support them.

In almost everything I and the council worked on or talked about, even beyond public safety and policing, COVID, and homelessness, we faced disinformation campaigns. There is not a single aspect of government where disinformation isn't a growing challenge.

President Trump's first presidency was fact-checked, and it was determined that he told 33,000 lies in those four years. When the Republican Party saw how effective this was, vocal Republican members of the Senate and House began to follow his example. Despite its undemocratic underpinning, disinformation—lies—has been remarkably effective for Trump, who was elected to a second term in significant measure on the strength of false assertions.

When I first ran for office in 2014, I didn't think much about the dangers of disinformation. I got my first taste of it in that campaign, when an opponent accused me of having represented the ultra-conservative Koch brothers in my legal practice. For many left-of-center voters, such an accusation was as grave as if I had represented the devil himself.

During my campaign, I made it clear that I had *not* represented the Koch brothers, and in this case, the simple truth was enough to put the issue to rest. I was fortunate that I could put more resources behind the truth than my opponent could put behind the lie.

As the 2010s evolved, the simple truth became less of a defense. At the time, most candidates and elected officials weren't thinking about disinformation as a problem, at least not below the national level of politics and policy. We would encounter a few persistent myths as we developed and drove our agenda because people will always believe outlandish things if they are said often enough. ("They're eating the dogs, they're eating the cats," Trump claimed about Haitian immigrants in Springfield, Ohio.)

A lie can evolve from an inaccurate statement (misinformation) to an inaccurate statement intended to deceive (disinformation).

What do you call it when one shares an outlandish story or piece of information as fact without knowing whether it's true or not? The way I see it, the reckless disregard for the truth is more malice than mistake and therefore also qualifies as disinformation—a lie. Most of the discourse around conspiracy theories falls into this category.

Our society would be much better off if the reckless propagation of outlandish claims was called out and condemned. There should be no safe harbor for someone who weaponizes a falsehood by stating, as Donald Trump often does, that the falsehood is something that *some say* or is just *something that he's heard.* I continue to be shocked at the lack of blowback from his use of this device.

As mayor, I thought I was prepared for the myths and outright lies propagated by politicians and the media, for whom politics has become a zero-sum game. To far-right Republicans, it is power, not governance, that's important. With winning as the goal, they have shown a willingness to lie about anything.

I wasn't ready for the scale or the relentlessness of the disinformation—the lies—I had to face from those adversaries.

Social media is an important carrier for this kind of nonsense, but its starting point is often murky. Did it evolve out of a conspiracy theory chat group, or was it part of a planned disinformation campaign backed by a state actor? Or was it the work of someone with an overactive imagination and a Twitter (now X) account?

Sometimes, as used by President Trump, Texas Governor Greg Abbott, Lieutenant Governor Dan Patrick, and Attorney General Ken Paxton, disinformation is a tool used to build a political brand and to organize and fundraise in a political base.

I was least prepared for the misinformation and disinformation that came from the mouths of people who I liked and respected. I just assumed they would know better. Why did this happen? Because misinformation and disinformation that appear online take hold and then spread like wildfire.

It was difficult for me to recognize that not all those pushing misinformation were malicious. Some were repeating lies out of ignorance. I would get a more positive response from these people when I spoke to them as my friends.

I recognize that liberals tend to dismiss any information they find suspect because they have seen how badly and often Republican leadership lies. It's an understandable response but also dangerous.

Donald Trump Jr. shared a video after the Hamas attack on Israel in October 2023 and claimed it depicted Hamas committing atrocities. The video was dismissed by some on the political left as having been taken years before and in a different context. The apple never falls far from the tree, they said. The messenger, Trump Jr., like his father, has never demonstrated any great regard for telling the truth.

But the video was genuine.

It does no one any good to dismiss the truth because we dislike the messenger or the message.

If you can't agree with someone based on their facts, see if you can agree with them on their values. As mayor of Austin, I spent way too much time correcting people's facts and not enough time listening for the experiences and values they reflected. It's one of my regrets about my time in office. I could and should have heard those pieces of misinformation and disinformation for what they often were—ordinary people worried about whether a sudden change in their environment had made them less safe.

If I had had greater empathy for their need not only to be safe but to feel safe, I would have been a more effective advocate and leader. If someone is safe but is being repeatedly told that they're not, they will come to believe they aren't safe. Once they believe that, it's difficult to convince them otherwise. The greater the effort to establish the truth about safety, the more the effort is perceived as discounting and minimizing the people themselves.

Lies become self-realizing. A community that doesn't believe it is safe will tend to become unsafe over time.

After the camping ban was lifted, Governor Abbott ridiculously suggested he would send in the State Department of Public Safety (DPS) to help law enforcement gain control of Austin. It was political theater, and of course, I declined all such suggestions. One reason I did so was that the Austin Police were required and trained to avoid practices that disproportionately arrested and incarcerated community members of color, and there were certain crimes, like smoking marijuana, that our local force didn't enforce because the benefit of enforcement was outweighed by the community burden it created. State police officers were under no such constraints.

There's harm even in the innocent reinforcement of misinformation. After I left office, my successor, Kirk Watson, invited in the DPS officers, not because the city was unsafe and needed help, he said, but because everyone should "feel" safe. By saying this, Watson empowered and reinforced the belief that Austin was not safe. By inviting in the DPS, the new mayor was inadvertently sending the message to the community that maybe they shouldn't feel safe, even though most should and most did.

Governor Abbott's use of the DPS foreshadowed the similar plays with the National Guard and the Marines by President Trump in his second term, first in Los Angeles and then in Washington, D.C. Some see sending such forces as proving the lie that cities are not safe or cannot manage their own affairs. Such action validates the disinformation.

Before I ran for mayor, my law firm clients included both those seeking protection of their civil rights as well as many of the more successful business and real estate owners in Austin and around the state. I am a proud progressive Democrat, but also proud that, when I ran for mayor, both the first time and for reelection, I had the support of most Republicans. Mayors in Austin run in nonpartisan elections where candidates are not aligned with parties. After all, potholes are not a partisan issue.

When I left office, after having unsuccessfully responded to the many partisan attacks and misinformation directed toward me and our city initiatives, my approval rating among Republicans was only about 10 percent. I didn't think anyone could ever get a number that low! I knew this change was happening, knew it was significantly based on misinformation and disinformation, but I didn't know what to do to turn it around.

Austin's local nonpartisan elections are more clearly going to turn on national political issues in the future, and that's unfortunate.

I am extremely nervous about the developing and newly employed means and delivery of lies. Future advances in algorithms, I fear, will more efficiently target those most susceptible to believing lies. Purveyors of misinformation/disinformation will get even better at identifying early those ultimately susceptible and engage their initial interest in matters seemingly far afield from the grounds on which future political battles will be fought. With the use of AI, there seems to be an ever-increasing speed and scale at which low-credibility content goes viral.

We cannot merely bemoan and tremble at the lie machines around us.

We must engage.

My time on the front lines of political and partisan policy divides has convinced me that people will trust and believe those they think are on their team. They will take as true whatever purported fact those they think are on their side present.

I spent a lot of time presenting in a non-confrontational way objective truth to some on "the other side." I thought that if I could better convey the facts, I could succeed in changing minds. But it rarely worked. I thought I might not be messaging well, and so I tried to communicate differently. I tried to find areas of agreement first and then move to the disputed issues of fact. Too many times, none of this worked.

I thought that if I could convince them of my facts, if I could get them to trust what I was saying was true, then they would join my team.

But I had it backward. I needed to convince them first to join my team, and then they would trust my facts and what I was saying.

Said differently, people believe whatever facts those they trust espouse. No matter how outrageous others might think the disinformation presented might be, if it comes from someone trustworthy, people are more likely to believe it.

Candidate Donald Trump created quite a stir when he said, "I could stand in the middle of Fifth Avenue and shoot somebody, and I wouldn't lose voters."

The statement drew a lot of criticism and became one of many examples used by his opponents to demonstrate that he shouldn't be elected. But what if he had merely said: "My supporters trust me completely." More reasonable? Maybe even truthful?

Trump wasn't actually suggesting he would shoot someone or that it was okay to shoot someone. But what he understood better than his opponents was that his supporters would give him the benefit of any doubt they might have and would believe that whatever the reason for the shooting, it was justified.

In President Trump's second term, he is creating great disruption and imposing burdens unanticipated by many of his supporters, and most of those supporters are willing to accept these actions and impacts, which they wouldn't accept from someone else, because they trust him.

Some of the smartest business people I know support President Trump because they trust him. These are people who are watching the administration implement policies, like tariffs, that they do not support. They are watching soft diplomacy and the public research they do support being shuttered. They lament the market and international instability, which is greater now than in living memory. But when asked if they are ready now to end their support for Trump, many say that we just need to give him a chance. That we need to see how this plays out. They are saying that they trust Trump.

After his first year in office, many Democrats are hoping that Trump will eventually lose much of his support when his policies inevitably result in more and more people suffering long lines at VA clinics, poor social security service, increased inflation and health care costs, and international turmoil.

I question whether this would really happen to the extent that Democrats may wish. I believe many of Trump's supporters will accept these tough conditions as being the necessary sacrifice to make the country in his vision because they trust the man to have the right vision. They will liken their hardship under a Trump administration to the heroic sacrifices Americans made during World War II.

People believe those they trust. It's not about the objectiveness of facts or the way facts are messaged or presented. My experience as mayor is that people who supported and trusted me were willing to accept the truths I asserted and presented.

The Republican Party understands this. The Democratic Party does not. Working-class white males supported Republican candidates because they believed those candidates were on their side. This is despite the fact that Democratic policies far better protect their welfare.

The corollary is also true. People will not believe the facts presented and asserted by those they do not trust. Once they choose their team, it is very difficult if not impossible for them to give any weight to even the objective truths on which the other team relies.

This is the dilemma for Democrats.

Defeating disinformation and misinformation requires earning people's trust by first getting them on your team.

17

FEAR

You don't have to have been mayor of a major city to know that there are public figures who wield fear as a weapon. Some do it convinced of the righteousness of their cause. The motive of others is baser. I confess I was surprised by how frequently, intensely, and blatantly various leaders stoked fear as a means to their own short-term ends. It was so breathtakingly obvious that it caught me off guard.

You could not, for instance, find a clearer example than Donald Trump and his MAGA senators, congressmen, and state leaders, including Senator Ted Cruz, Governor Greg Abbott, and Lieutenant Governor Dan Patrick, in their dire condemnation of immigrants. From the earliest days of his campaign, then-candidate Trump characterized undocumented migrants as rapists and murderers, conjuring up the specter of a vast, nameless horde of criminals streaming across the

Southern border. Abbott and Patrick would later talk about immigrants crossing the border as "an invasion."

"Homes are being invaded," said Abbott.

Patrick repeated this hyperbole and the mischaracterizations that demonize immigrants because they so effectively strike fear in the hearts of those who feel threatened.

Said Representative Veronica Escobar, a Democrat from El Paso, "There are no invaders here—only people."

She warned Patrick, "If people die again, blood will be on your hands."

Two years earlier, a twenty-one-year-old gunman killed twenty-three people and injured twenty-two others in a Walmart in El Paso, complaining in his manifesto of a "Hispanic invasion."

Trump was not the first presidential candidate to employ this tactic. Anyone old enough remembers the noted bigot Pat Buchanan, who was remarkable in his willingness to make his xenophobia explicit and obvious. Previous candidates had pushed nativist policies by attempting to give their fear-mongering a patina of credibility, framing them as lofty-sounding concerns about American culture or worries about jobs.

"These people are coming to kill you," Trump said.

What poisonous nonsense. Migrants are just people, with all the virtues and vices inherent in us all. It's worth noting that crime rates among undocumented migrants are lower than they are among citizens. The data is clear: If we want to create stable, orderly communities full of industrious and tax-paying people, we should welcome more migrants. At the very least, they'd bring down our crime rates.

But Trump had no plans to create stable, orderly communities of any kind. This rhetoric about immigrants poisoning the blood of our country was and is about dehumanizing and demonizing a group through outrageous caricatures so he can tell his supporters who to fear.

And here's the rub: fear creates powerful groups of allies. Fear is an even surer way to establish and reinforce a group identity—an "us"—than it is to identify and vilify a "them."

This isn't just a matter of political rhetoric; it has horrifying real-world consequences, because the expectation is that we will prosecute them to the utmost.

When Trump became president, he ordered U.S. Immigration and Customs Enforcement (ICE) to carry out raids in American cities to round up undocumented immigrants for imprisonment or deportation. ICE needed the help of local authorities and expected to get it. If they didn't, Trump threatened those cities with the loss of federal grants, which are vital to virtually every big and medium-sized city in America.

His cruelty went so far as to separate immigrant children from their parents, sending them north without documentation so their parents could never find them again. The cruelty was disgraceful. But that was the point.

Be afraid. Be *very* afraid.

It wasn't clear to me as mayor how much the city of Austin could do to thwart the Trump administration's anti-migrant policies. ICE's primary war against immigrants was with Travis County, which overlays Austin, not with the authorities in Austin itself. In the same election that saw Trump secure the White House, Travis County elected a sheriff, Sally Hernandez, who pledged not to cooperate with ICE to the extent legally allowed—a pledge on which she made good.

Even though Austin wasn't involved in the immigration battle, Governor Greg Abbott, a far-right Republican, his Lieutenant Governor Dan Patrick, and even President Trump attacked us for being a sanctuary city, a term that they used for cities that refused to comply with their inhumane immigration policies.

Several times over the years, Austin passed city resolutions in support of migrants, but it wasn't what they were describing as a sanctuary city because we weren't breaking the law. We wanted to thwart Trump's policies, and we would act—but always within the law.

As part of a small delegation from the United States Conference of Mayors, I traveled to Washington, D.C., and argued with President Trump's first U.S. attorney general, Jeff Sessions, about the definition of a sanctuary city.

The term was deliberately nebulous, an attempt to frighten the authorities of progressive cities into going along with ICE for fear of losing federal dollars. Sessions told me that neither the city of Austin nor Travis County would be considered noncompliant because we hadn't stopped any government agency or employee from providing information to the immigration authorities. We could ignore some requests from the feds, but as a matter of policy, we couldn't direct our governments not to comply with a legal request.

Sessions issued a public statement to this effect. But not long afterward, Ian Prior, a Justice Department spokesman, issued a statement contradicting Sessions. He implied that Austin and Travis County might still be considered noncompliant. It was a sham, but the point was to be intimidating.

The next day, the Republican-dominated Texas state legislature passed a bill allowing local police to ask people about their immigration status. If a sheriff, constable, or police chief refused to communicate with federal officials, they could be subject to a Class A misdemeanor. The bill was intended to make every government apparatus in Texas part of the Trump administration's crackdown.

As I explained earlier in the book, I wasn't buying Trump's demonizing of immigrants. The city of Austin passed an ordinance stating that before a police officer could ask a resident about his immigration status, the officer had to tell him that he was not obligated to answer questions about his immigration status. We also kept track of how much time and resources our police were spending on this effort.

Most of our police never asked a single immigration question, and after we passed that ordinance, those who did stopped doing so.

We had found a real way to preserve a local community's ability to exert local control and set its own safety priorities.

Other cities spent years defending such choices in court, after they were accused of thwarting the Trump administration's priorities. We never were. And because the county sheriff chose to ignore ICE's requests for assistance and work with the Mexican consul general and because we spent public money on lawyers to ensure that undocumented migrants were given due process, Austin suffered only a few of the large-scale ICE raids and interventions that blighted some of the other communities.

The raids themselves, while clearly a priority for Trump and his people, weren't the point. Again, *cruelty* was the point. So was the fear it generated.

This wasn't the only manufactured and largely fictitious issue I had to deal with that was designed to create fear. I told this anecdote once before, but it bears repeating. Governor Abbott or his communications staff, in an effort to scare people, put up a video on Twitter depicting a distressed man having a mental breakdown. The conduct in the video was jarring, and thus captured people's attention, but it was an old video and what was filmed did not happen, as the governor claimed, because of our mismanagement of homelessness.

In fact, the video had been taken several years earlier.

I was bothered by the dishonesty of it, but what most upset me was the ghoulishness of exploiting a severely unwell person for political gain—employing any means to label the homeless as criminals who are a danger to the public.

Is it too much to expect the governor of Texas to demonstrate basic human decency?

It was no surprise that the governor and various other Republicans in the Texas legislature spent most of my years as mayor characterizing Austin as a lawless hellscape in which ordinary people scuttled fearfully from the safety of one locked door to another. If you listened to the Republicans, we lived in a pre-Batman Gotham City, which would have come as a surprise to the people who actually lived in Austin and who spent their time going to live music and sitting in the sun eating tacos and kayaking on the lake and generally building lives for themselves and their families in one of the safest big cities in the country.

But, again, *truth was not the point.* The point was the fear; the governor and his coterie of political dependents, as well as members of the Trump administration, including Trump himself, told his MAGA followers that they should be afraid of the lawless, dangerous people who govern and live in cities like Austin.

This came to a head in the summer of 2020, as discussed earlier, with the false claim that Austin had defunded its police. A howl arose from the governor, the lieutenant governor, and eventually President Trump, outraged that we were actively trying to make our communities less safe and that we did not believe in public order. To listen to them, you'd have thought we'd abandoned the concept of law itself.

The message from our political adversaries was clear: Be afraid of crime because the mayor and city council of Austin had defunded the police, exposing you and the public in general and the police officers and their families in particular to a heightened risk of crime and threat to safety.

Ordinary people should feel afraid, and police officers should feel afraid and betrayed.

Crime did increase in Austin in 2020 and 2021, as it did in every other American mid-sized or big city in those years, but relative to its peer big cities, Austin remained and remains one of the safest cities in America. It has since reverted to the mean.

But those facts—the truth—did not stop Governor Abbott from

pointing to those rising crime rates as a sign of our—and especially *my*—incompetence and untrustworthiness. They used their loudest megaphones. When the crime rate began to fall precipitously in 2022, Abbott and his cohort went silent. In 2024, crime rates were down about 40 percent from 2020, with even fewer officers on our streets. Cue the crickets.

Fear-mongering, scapegoating, demonization, and dehumanization are all proof that fear works.

To this day, Austin battles the perception that it is unsafe. Respected media outlets, which have a duty to fact-check and at least have some capacity to see through the disinformation about the safety of Austin, still too often accuse Austin of having defunded its police department.

All of this is to confirm that we as humans are susceptible to having our fears stoked, conflated, and manipulated in ways that divide us against each other. That fear has predictable effects. We lose trust in each other, and we lose trust in institutions. And it stimulates a desire for protection, for order.

Social psychologist Arie Kruglanski wrote in a 2015 opinion piece in *The Guardian* that "existential anxieties . . . spawn yearnings for order and predictability."[1] John T. Jost, another social psychologist known for his work on political ideology, referenced and expanded on this in a 2017 *Social Cognition* article that "uncertainty and threat" lead some people to seek "tradition and hierarchy" as the remedy, essentially avoiding nebulous fear by placing their fate in the hands of "powerful, prestigious authority figures."[2]

If that sounds like authoritarianism, it should, because that's what

---

1 Arie W. Kruglanski, "Trump and Isis Both Benefit from a Powerful Fuel: Our Fear," *The Guardian*, December 23, 2015, https://www.theguardian.com/commentisfree/2015/dec/23/donald-trump-isis-benefit-from-powerful-fuel-fear.

2 John T. Jost et al., "The Politics of Fear: Is There an Ideological Asymmetry in Existential Motivation?" *Social Cognition* 35, no. 4 (2017): 324–353, https://doi.org/10.1521/soco.2017.35.4.324.

it is. Authoritarianism is a natural political outcome from a prolonged state of widespread, heightened anxiety. As we've seen, that anxiety can come about organically, from worries about changing economic conditions, for example, or it can be engineered by people like Trump who are determined to stoke fear to their own advantage as they seek power.

But the lesson is clear: invoking fear works.

We saw the powerful political effect of fear in the ballot proposition in Austin to reinstate the public camping ban. For some voters, that campaign was about fear of unhoused people, a population that is statistically far more likely to be the victims of crime than perpetrators of it but that includes a small but visible portion of people who are suffering through mental health disorders and whose behavior may be unpredictable and, very rarely, dangerous.

Some voters, I am sure, voted out of a different kind of fear—a more generalized anxiety about a change in their environment that had happened overnight, the day mere public camping was decriminalized, and that represented a less specific, physical threat than an uncomfortable example of apparent disorder.

Democrats have made fear of Republican cultural overreach a load-bearing part of their campaigns for decades—spurred mostly by Republicans who cannot seem to go an election cycle without taking away existing rights, like abortion, or proposing some other reactionary and startlingly regressive social policy. This has allowed Democrats to prevail or at least hold their ground in a number of critical elections, especially and recently the U.S. House and U.S. Senate elections of 2022.

Vote for us because they're dangerously insane has a reasonable track record.

But there are also limitations to the effectiveness of Democrats using fear as a tool. You can see the weakness of that approach in poll after poll that show that Americans aren't clear about what the Democratic Party stands for, even though the Democratic Party is for lots of things that people want. General approval for the Democratic Party, as opposed to some of its individual candidates, is low.

The problem for Democrats is that when your closing argument, cycle after cycle, is "they're crazy, so vote for us," you win elections without voters actually learning who you are or what you care about. There's a price to be paid for consistently using fear over time.

What can we do? Much political fear derives from voters feeling a loss of control over the circumstances of their own lives. One thing we can do is attempt to give people a feeling of agency, to defang that fear.

A small example of this came from Austin's COVID response. The first moments of the pandemic were frightening and disorienting because no one seemed to know what was safe to do and what wasn't. In Austin, we put together a Risk Chart, a color-coded system that outlined personal interactions and activities on a spectrum from low to high risk.

I wanted this chart to give the public some sense of agency and control over outcomes. It worked and was well received. People were extraordinarily grateful to have a tool by which they could make their own decisions about interacting with others with a degree of confidence about how much risk they were taking on.

It's worth remembering that humans are the most adaptable animal on the planet. We're capable of staggering bravery in the face of the unknown, and it seems to me that we face it best when we feel we have some measure of control over the outcome based on how we confront the mystery and the peril.

So how do we find the courageous part of ourselves and others and stare down fear?

We can start by being aware of *when* we are afraid and ask ourselves why. If something we've seen on the news or the internet seems too frightening to be true, maybe it is. If something scary appears in the media, we can ask why it's getting so much attention.

For example, it is statistically inevitable that one undocumented migrant will commit a violent crime. Most migrants are excellent residents. A small number are inclined to violence. But why do we hear so much about the one migrant who commits a violent crime against an American citizen when American citizens commit significantly more violence against each other every day?

We should ask ourselves, *Aren't we being manipulated?*

Over my eight years in office, the use of fear as a tool in political settings seemed to increase in frequency and power. I was surprised at how effective a tool creating fear proved to be and at how much of my time would be centered on addressing it.

My giving warnings to the community about actual hazards created fear, and in this context, fear was helpful because it got people working together and being more careful. Contrast this with the fear created by the Republicans, who use it as a tool to organize, rally, and raise political funding.

I wish I could close this chapter with a perfect solution to combat fear. I could never figure out how to do that. Two of my most significant and meaningful policy initiatives, adopting a comprehensive land development code rewrite and trying to meet the challenge of homelessness, were less successful than they would have been had my opponents not been able to convince a significant part of the community to fear what we were trying to do.

There wasn't a factual basis for the fear, but I was unable to stop its spread.

The fear that Donald Trump has sown nationally and that red state leaders, including those from Texas, also foment has infected us locally as well. We live in an increasingly politically polarized and divided country.

Differences that divide us have become part of what living in a democracy is all about. I'm not someone who believes that finding a compromise solution is always the best outcome. Sometimes we have irreconcilable differences, and one side must prevail. But, despite the absence of compromise, the dispute may still be just a difference of opinion.

What I fear is that differences of opinion will increasingly morph into a fear of those with opposing views. If we come to believe we need to be protected against people with different opinions, does that mean that someday most Americans will seek an authoritarian leader to help them feel safe?

Is it possible that Americans might choose a path that isn't what living in a democracy is all about and that this, for them, will be the better choice? Is it possible that a Donald Trump presidency will lead this country into becoming an autocracy?

Many of us pray it be not so.

Creating fear, as we have seen from the Trump administration, is an effective tool. But, ultimately, to what end? We need politicians—Democrats and Republicans—to step forward and confront him and his authoritarianism. We desperately need political leaders who value the gift of democracy to fight the fear of the unfounded as an even higher purpose than winning any policy-related objective.

This must happen before it's too late.

For those public officials who choose not to do what they know in their hearts to be best for America and who instead acquiesce in the amoral use of fear in exchange for short-term policy and political advantage, there is a special place in hell.

18

WHAT A MAYOR KNOWS

The office of mayor, I've learned, is unlike any other in American government. It is both the closest and the most practical level of politics. The mayor is not insulated by layers of bureaucracy or distant from the people served. The mayor is their neighbor, their emergency contact, the voice of the city, and its conscience. The mayor is the first one blamed and often the first one called—not because the mayor holds all the power but because the mayor is expected to act.

When I think back on how I ended up there—standing behind a city seal at press briefings, streaming videos to the community, banging a gavel at heated council meetings, sitting at my office desk late at night, comfortable doing what I thought was best and not getting too excited when things went well or too discouraged when they did not—it goes all the way back to fighting for my fourth-grade classmates who wanted more to eat, to defending the elderly office worker who lost her job, and to giving it my all as I slid close to second base and was very much out.

I entered city hall wanting to do good but having little understanding of what that meant or what that involved. Over my eight years in office, I increasingly came to the realization that local government is simply neighbors trying their best to help neighbors solve problems too big for any one household to handle alone.

Beginning in my earliest days in office, I came to lean on that belief when we faced storms that shut down power grids and froze all our streets. I held it close when we launched bond packages to fix roads I had complained about for years while stuck in traffic. I found comfort in it when I watched neighbors argue about how new housing would either save them a place in our city or change the character of the city they loved.

It's at the local level where you see it all from up close: the cracks in the national narrative, the fragile trust that holds a city together, the moments when people of wildly different views can still stand shoulder to shoulder because they share the same storm drain, dislike the same graffiti, watch their children play in the same neighborhood park, experience the same pride for their city, and know that there is no level of government or other institution waiting in the wings to take care of us. At the city level, we often disagree, but we also know that at the end of the day, whether we like it or not, we're in this together.

Being a mayor is about proximity. It's about hugely important but relatively small-scale day-to-day victories, immediate hopes, efforts we see up close, and people we know so well making hard compromises and feeling those costs. And it's about getting slapped on the back by people who are more than just numbers and getting yelled at in the grocery store when the potholes aren't filled or the promises don't match the policies.

When you govern a city, politics becomes personal. It's not about abstract ideology but about trash pickup, potholes, flood zones, and whether the lights come back on after a storm. This proximity breeds a kind of accountability that is rare in other levels of government. If you promise something, you'd better deliver—or you're going to hear about it.

That pressure can be intense. But it's also clarifying. In national and state politics, you can posture. In local government, you must perform. There's no hiding behind slogans when the streets flood or when you tell the community they have to boil their water before they drink it. There's no blaming the other side if the rent keeps rising or the congestion never ends.

I learned this lesson early in my mayoral years during our city's infrastructure bond campaigns. I saw it every time we made the case for new roads, new flood improvements, or resilience projects to handle multiple storms that weren't supposed to happen but once every hundred years. The arguments weren't about partisan talking points—they were about whether your kid had water to drink when the taps couldn't be trusted or whether your house stayed dry when the creek rose. That proximity keeps leaders honest.

This accountability offers a great gift: people will believe in government again if you give them a reason to. Not because you hit every benchmark but because you listened, showed up, told the truth, and did the work—even when it was messy, even when you fell short. People appreciate when their neighbors try to help. And they'll tell you, loudly, when you get it wrong. And they should.

If there's one thing that runs through every story in this book—from my earliest days to the last city council vote I presided over—it's this: trust matters more than alignment. You can survive disagreement. You can survive defeat.

What you can't survive, as a city or a country, is when people stop believing that you or anyone else is telling them the truth.

Facts alone rarely win an argument—relationships do. People don't just want to be right; they want to feel seen and heard. And when they don't, they go looking for someone—anyone—who they think understands what they're saying and will tell them what they want to hear, no matter how implausible it may be. You saw this on a national level in the last presidential election.

I saw this play out in my years at city hall. Rumors outpace press releases. Lies travel farther and faster than complicated truths. I saw this in neighborhood meetings as tempers flared over housing density, where I knew the numbers backward and forward but still had to convince people that their stake in the city's future was worth more than my spreadsheet could prove.

Every big plan depended on whether the public trusted that we were listening—and whether we would stick around to hear the second question, the hard one, the angry one that came in the raw voice of someone afraid he'd be left behind again.

During my time as mayor, I witnessed how fragile trust could be. I saw it during the pandemic, when our city had to fight not just a deadly virus but a parallel pandemic of misinformation and lies. In the early days, I remembered lessons from my first trials—keep your evidence clear, repeat it often, keep your tone calm.

I stood behind podiums where I told worried families what we knew and what we didn't yet know, knowing that half the battle was helping people believe we were telling them the truth, even when the answers were scary, and that they had agency and some control over their futures.

I saw how quickly fear could outpace facts. Our efforts to expand testing and vaccination centers got tangled up in the political noise. National voices spun local decisions on public safety into talking points for cable news, and neighbors turned on each other in comment sections that made reasonable disagreement seem like betrayal.

What I came to believe is this: you cannot out-argue a lie with a spreadsheet. You can only outlast it by standing in the room, repeatedly, telling the truth calmly, admitting what you don't know yet, and showing people that your motives are honest, even when your answers are incomplete. People don't trust numbers; they trust people. Really listening is more than being patient and giving people your time. It's paying the necessary focused attention to learn the fears and values that underpin even positions you cannot support. Listening enables you to try to address the "whys," even if you are going to disagree on the "whats."

In the hardest moments, I learned to listen first, argue second. Trust is built in the everyday, not in the emergency. It is built when the small promise is kept so that the bigger promise has a chance to stand when the winds howl. It is built when the rumor is met with a calm explanation instead of a dismissive shrug. It is built when leaders remember that the title means nothing if you won't look your neighbor in the eye and say, *This is what I know, this is what I don't, and I am still here anyway.*

Plans fail when people feel left out of the conversation. Real progress happens when you invite the people most skeptical into the room and give them a real stake in shaping the outcome. It's slower. It's harder. But it's the only way the work holds up when you're gone. People may want their businesses to be efficient. They want their local government to be effective. Sometimes being effective means choosing a path that's purposefully not efficient.

That does not mean people want their local government to be slow, staid, and overly cautious. Such cities die. People are proud of their city when it creates and expands horizons. Cities have a unique ability to be innovative and have always been the laboratories of democracy. In Austin, we repeatedly proved that we could step in where national policy lagged and labored.

Austin was out front in the testing of autonomous vehicles and the birth of rideshare platforms, investing early in solar and wind power, exploring modern ways to address public safety, investing in guaranteed income safety nets, rewriting land use codes that hadn't been touched in decades, and finding ways to build capital improvement projects that Austin residents only a generation earlier could never have imagined. Austin is a creative community that wants its local government to be creative as well. That's why people love our airport—it's where local bands play. Local government is where hope stays practical—and sometimes where democracy premieres when the bigger stage grows unsteady.

Our country stands at an inflection point. President Trump is back in the Oval Office, and he and the silent Republicans are calling the shots. The midterm elections of 2026 loom just ahead, with razor-thin margins in the House and Senate.

The midterm elections this November are shaping up to be among the most contested in modern history. Many races may come down to hundreds of votes. Already, operatives on all sides are gearing up for challenges. There may even be some legitimate challenges. But many will echo the same discredited playbook we saw in 2020: confusion weaponized, coincidence twisted into conspiracy, local officials harassed into paralysis while the machinery of democracy is jammed on live TV.

Will there be tampering with election results even before votes are gathered? What does it mean if the president is able to nationalize elections? Do vote tallies change if ICE announces it will have a presence at voting locations ostensibly to look for "illegal aliens"?

What keeps me up at night isn't just that attempts by Trump to steal the November election will happen. It's that this time the courts may be more willing to entertain them. Where once the judiciary absorbed chaos and reaffirmed norms, today it feels more brittle, more partisan, more willing to indulge manufactured doubt.

Conspiracy can become procedure if the door cracks open wide enough. What happens if close elections are frozen in litigation for weeks or months? What happens if state legislatures refuse to certify winners? What happens if cable news and social media amplify every rumor until no one knows what to believe anymore? If the president, citing "unrest" or "fraud"—real or invented—calls for delays or suspensions of certifications for new office holders or tries to order new elections all in the name of "order" or "security," who holds the line?

What happens if multiple House and Senate races drag on through January, if new delegations cannot be seated, if no clear majority is recognized—where does that leave the country?

If the president, once again Donald Trump, uses the same language he did years ago but now with new levers—warning of unrest, demanding order, suggesting a "pause" on swearing in new members of Congress until the "fraud" is sorted out—how does that end? It will come, if it comes, drip by drip: deadlines delayed, norms bent, court decisions that sound reasonable if you don't look too closely at what they quietly enable.

What happens if the machinery of democracy is turned inward against itself? Not through tanks in the streets but through procedural sleight-of-hand, confusion, and the endless chipping away of the expectation that the peaceful transfer of power is nonnegotiable?

The Constitution doesn't enforce itself. Norms don't defend themselves. They live or die by what people are willing to tolerate.

I don't say this to conjure ghosts or to lean on cheap drama. I say it because after years inside rooms where trust was the real currency, I know how quickly trust can vanish. I say it because I spent nights in my office during the pandemic, watching rumor outrun fact, watching fear turn neighbor against neighbor if no one ultimate authority could or did step up to say, *Here is what is true; here is what is not.*

It isn't just the election that worries me. While all this unfolds, other storms gather. The currents that run underneath are just as strong. Disinformation is more sophisticated now, turbocharged by AI tools that can mimic real voices, real faces, real evidence. The lies will come faster than we can fact-check them. If we're not careful, the only "truth" left standing will be the one that confirms what we already want to believe. And once we reach that point, what happens in a courtroom or a statehouse won't be enough to stitch the fabric back together.

Other pressing challenges can only be met by a clear-headed country. Climate migration is already reshaping cities, including mine. AI is rewriting how we work, what we trust, and who decides truth from falsehood—and no one seems to be providing oversight to protect the public. Housing affordability remains a crisis for working families, the backbone of any healthy city. Our national deficit grows while faith in the dollar's supremacy flickers, and the world takes note. Allies look for new arrangements and new friends. Rivals like China test old assumptions. The United States marks its 250th birthday—a milestone that should unite us in celebration. Instead, it may be happening at a time that exposes how fragile our union has become.

With such scenarios, the temptation is to despair. But the lesson of my years as mayor—watching neighbors rebuild after storms, volunteer at food banks, bring food and water to those without homes, and show up for each other without asking permission—is that despair and resignation are not the final words.

Love of thy neighbor and democracy are.

In the midst of all this, we may find the promise for ourselves and for the world in our cities, showcased for the world's eyes as the World Cup comes to America. Stadiums packed, streets alive, languages mingling, cultures crossing. It's a chance to show who we still are—or who we are no longer. Will we meet that moment united, proud, and generous? Or fractured, suspicious, and in a world-televised moment, fighting each other over who gets to claim patriotism the most while our trust in each other continues to drain away?

This doesn't mean cities are immune to disinformation. We're not. But we have tools that Washington can't buy: presence, proximity, the simple human obligation to knock on a door and explain yourself when the rumor mill gets going.

If the worst happens at the national level, cities may become not just the front line but the fallback—the lifeboats that carry democratic culture across the storm. Mayors—more than any other public servants—have the power to restore faith not just in government but in the idea that we still belong to and care for one another.

If the United States is more self-centered, cities will continue to build the blossoming of new partnerships abroad—relationships with sister cities all over the world, direct trade, climate pacts, cultural exchanges, and knowledge sharing. When Washington, D.C., wavers, mayors can be the last diplomats standing for their people. Some of the best information I got as the 2020 pandemic was just about to arrive didn't come from our federal government; it came from mayors across the world—friends with whom I shared a network and cell phone numbers. From them, I learned firsthand what was really happening.

As we face what 2026 may bring—close elections, courts bending under pressure, rumors becoming headlines before facts can catch up—I hold tight to my faith in my neighbors and my city. We need leaders who won't flinch when misinformation or bald-faced lies strike. We need neighbors who won't let the loudest voices drown out the honest and sincere ones. We need local governments ready to stand up when national systems fall down.

Because when the courts are jammed and the talking heads spin half-truths for ratings, it's the mayor's office that still answers the phone. It's the city council that still decides if the library stays open, if the bridges are sanded, if the emergency shelter has heat when the grid goes down. It's local election officials—underpaid, sometimes under threat—who count the ballots that really decide whether we trust the results.

I didn't learn these lessons from books. As a new mayor, I lamented there was no guide to being mayor with the answers in the back. I learned from the people who showed up when our city was hurting. From the neighbor who knocked on doors in a flood. From the small business owner who fed strangers during a shutdown. From the volunteers who staffed our shelters, who marched for justice, who testified late into the night on how to make our city more livable for everyone.

Leadership, I discovered, isn't about certainty—it's about steadiness. It's about refusing to turn away when the conversation gets uncomfortable. It's about admitting what you got wrong and doing better the next day.

Equity is a practice, not a promise. Belonging is an invitation, not a decree. Trust is fragile, but it's renewable if we do the work together.

So, I ask, *What do we do now?*

We protect our cities. We protect our local independent journalism, our civic education, our public spaces, our shared truths. We resist division. We accept complexity. We expect nuance. We reject fatalism. We show up. We tell the truth. We act like the future is worth the fight—because it is.

Pete Buttigieg, the former transportation secretary and former South Bend mayor, often says that freedom is not only measured by what we're protected from but what we're entitled to. We celebrate the freedom to have opportunity, a good job, and a safe community for our children. Freedom is not owned by one political party or another. And government's job is to make us all freer, sometimes by getting out of the way and sometimes by providing the services and protections necessary to live the lives of our choosing as neighbors helping each other out.

In the months ahead, we may see close races drag on longer than they should. We may see losing candidates refuse to concede, courts split on what counts as credible evidence, legislatures tempted to twist process into power. We may see calls to delay what should be certain, to cloud what should be clear. If that comes, our national story will depend on who holds the line.

National leaders must do their part—and they will take courage from watching local leaders do theirs. When cities show the country that trust can survive the strain, that truth can outrun rumor if enough people keep repeating it, that neighbors can still choose each other over chaos—then the democratic promise we have argued over for 250 years has a fighting chance to last.

And that's why my last word is not just for Congress or the courts or the national press—it's for the people closest to the work. The mayors. The council members. The city managers, city staff, clerks, volunteers, and neighborhood leaders who never get a national spotlight but who hold more of our daily lives together than most people realize.

To you I say, keep showing up. Keep telling the truth when it's unpopular. Keep explaining the complicated thing when a lie would be simpler. Keep knocking on doors when social media says no one wants to listen. Keep the water running, the traffic moving, the parks open, and each other safe and healthy. Keep the facts flowing faster than the rumor mill. Keep each other honest. Keep each other standing when the storms come.

And to neighbors everywhere, keep believing that this block, this street, this school, this park, this city is yours to steward. Keep choosing to belong to each other. Keep remembering that the person across the fence may vote differently, pray differently, see the world differently—but they still count on the same power grid staying up, the same school staying open, the same truth getting told.

When we lost power and our roads were impassable and our city services could not reach those in need, the duty and responsibility—the privilege—of taking care of one another came down to us, to our neighbors, to the other tenants in our buildings, to the people we passed walking along our streets. This was not a failure of government. It is what communities do when the need is great.

When we do that—when we act like neighbors before we act like partisans—we remember that democracy is not a machine that runs itself but a fragile trust passed down through hands that sometimes may not join and yet stay in the room together anyway.

I know the storms ahead will test all of this. They already are. And maybe that's the real point: the promise was never that we would agree on everything or that the future would be easy. The promise was that we would keep choosing to do the work anyway.

I wrote this book to leave behind more than just stories about one city or one mayor. I wrote it to remind myself—and maybe remind you—that the job was never about having all the answers. It was about staying long enough to hear the questions no one wants to ask and are rarely answered. It was about remembering that trust matters more than any temporary win.

A city, at its best, is a promise we keep to one another—that no matter what storms come, we stand together, we show up, and we do the work side by side.

So if you take one thing from these pages, let it be this: the real work of democracy happens close up. It happens in city halls and town hall meetings and living rooms and neighborhood parks. It happens when we keep showing up for each other, especially when we're tired, angry, or afraid.

And when the history of this moment is written—when people look back and wonder if we let the promise slip away—I hope they see that cities held the line. That neighbors showed up for each other. That mayors, council members, and ordinary people did the unglamorous work of telling the truth, showing up in the storm, picking up the pieces when bigger systems stumbled.

That is what I know. That is what I still believe.

No matter how loud the rumor, how close the margin, how fierce the storm—the promise holds if we hold it for each other.

What a mayor knows is this: we do not get to pick our neighbors, but we get to choose how we stand beside them.

When we do, the lights stay on. The city stays standing. And the future—fragile, unfinished, still ours to fight for—stays possible.

That is the promise.

The privilege of being mayor, the best job I ever had, is the gift of being able to help deliver that promise.

APPENDIX

REMARKS BY CONGRESSMAN GREG CASAR

Austin City Council Member (2015 to 2021)
Delivered December 17, 2022,
on Congress Avenue, Austin, Texas

Today, my task is to give a speech appreciating Mayor Steve Adler. The mayor who could run a seventeen-hour-long meeting, while none of us ever figured out when he went to the bathroom.

Mayor Steve Adler: [one of] the first in his family to go to college, the civil rights lawyer, the hardest worker I have ever met, our progressive champion through so much hardship, and my mentor and friend.

Mayor Adler has permanently changed the politics of this city for the better. He has done this in so many ways that I could never lay them out in one speech. Thanks to the mayor, we are international leaders on the climate crisis. We transformed our electric utility from one reliant on fossil fuels to a new Austin Energy whose generation is overwhelmingly clean and renewable. Thanks to his leadership, Austin will finally have everything from sidewalks to bike trails to true mass transit. Our community won transportation investments twenty times greater under Mayor Adler than during the previous ten years combined.

Thanks to Mayor Adler, the live music industry finally has dedicated funding to save it, and workforce development has more support from the city than ever before. Closest to my heart, affordable housing funding increased tenfold under Mayor Adler. Thanks to him, Austinites can finally start to come off the streets and into homes, and working-class people can come back and live in the city that they built.

He did all of this while Trump was sending ICE to raid our communities. The mayor was our standard bearer as Governor Abbott attacked our city constantly. He fought off Republican attempts to rewrite our city budget into a right-wing playbook. He held us together through serial bombings, the winter storms, and the pandemic. He was unshakable and encouraged us to be brave, steady, and committed too.

But this is only the public legacy of our mayor. Those are the things everyone will know when they go back and read the newspaper articles and the history books. They will shape our city for generations to come.

But to me, this is not as important as what the mayor will almost never be thanked for.

What I love about Steve is how he fought for and cared for the people who will never make it in the newspaper, who do not make campaign contributions, and who would likely never be at any political events. This includes people who cannot vote or who may never vote. To me, this is what makes Steve a good mayor.

Because of you, Steve, there are folks working construction sites and cleaning buildings and hotels that have better wages and health care, who will not go bankrupt when they get sick or hurt.

Because of you, there are Austin women who can get abortions despite Texas's ban because you listened to the movement and made sure we could help hundreds of Austinites travel out of state for the care they desperately need.

Because of you, there are thousands of people who did not get evicted or foreclosed upon these last three years, because you could talk to tenants and landlords together in a way I never could, and your eviction moratorium saved lives.

In each of these cases, let me be clear: the constituents we are talking about are primarily working-class Black and brown people. Not the people with the greatest power, or the biggest influence. Not the people who are going on the internet or to the newspapers to review the mayor. Not the people in the room, but you fought for the forgotten and the everyday people and the poor in the halls of power.

I was there in the room as we were advised not to speak up for victims shot by police, but you said that we needed to respect the dead and compensate the families who are suffering.

You never asked what the benefit was to you, but you made sure we got lawyers for those families who could be separated by Trump. There will be teachers, social workers, industry leaders, scientists, future council members, and mayors who got to grow up in Austin because you made sure their parents did not get deported.

I watched as you explained to powerful elected officials what racism was, and you did so kindly and powerfully. I was there as you comforted trans kids and their families. I was on those 4 a.m. phone calls about what to do during COVID.

There are many of us who lost people during this pandemic, but there are vastly more of us who do not even know that we need to thank you because we have loved ones who are alive because of your steady leadership.

On the topic of homelessness, which politicians and political advisors want to avoid, you were the champion. There will be people who sleep in a bed instead of the streets tonight because of you.

Steve, you were attacked, derided, and lied about constantly because you stood for those who are poor and left behind. For this reason, many people will never know what it is you did, or who it is that you truly are. The truth is, no one but you and Diane will ever truly know.

But there is one thing I do know: Mayor, we are going to miss you.

ACKNOWLEDGMENTS

Being mayor was a group effort.

None of this would have happened for me without Diane and our daughters. Diane and I did this together, as we have always done our community service. And in the moments in this job of great doubt, and there were some, I took that last measure of calm and confidence from knowing that I had my girls' love and support and that they were always with me.

Many of the achievements I'm most proud our city realized during my two terms as mayor were initiated by or had the fingerprints of my colleagues on the council, including Pio Renteria (a longtime east Austin community activist who was frequently our moral compass), Delia Garza and Vanessa Fuentes (both mayors pro tem, who gave first voice to Latinas and southeast Austin), Natasha Harper-Madison (the truest council representative the East Austin Black community has ever had), Chito Vela (who mainstreamed radical change), and Paige Ellis (a tireless active transportation advocate and environmentalist). Even council colleagues whose priorities sometimes did not align with mine on important issues were champions or advocates on other issues that we worked on together, like Kathie Tovo (homelessness), Ann Kitchen (mobility), Leslie Pool (environment), Sheri Gallo (fiscal responsibility), Don Zimmerman (accountability), Ora Houston (resource equity), Alison Alter (cybersecurity), and Ellen Troxclair (residential property tax relief).

The city council members with whom I served were great colleagues, and we took turns leading. I want to especially recognize Greg Casar, my closest partner on the council and now the chair of the House Congressional Progressive Caucus. He is a gifted community organizer and he pulled the council further left than it would have been without his presence. It was, however, his willingness to compromise and work with me that often enabled us to find cutting-edge and innovative solutions that appealed to a larger constituency and could get the votes to move forward.

Much of the credit for our successes belongs to my chiefs of staff Lesley Varghese and John-Michael Cortez, who were inspiring and effective leaders of an office in which some extremely smart and dedicated public servants worked to improve the lives of our residents. I will always be in debt to those that brought their passion, innovation, talent, and caring to our work: Barbara Shack, Jim Wick, Michael McGill, Janine Clark, Sly Majid, Amy Everhart, Brandi Clark Burton, Anita Price, Frank Rodriguez, Kazique Prince, Ashley Fisher, Lizzie Lewis, Stephanie Trinh, Sara Hartley, Jason Stanford, Yasmine Smith, Gloria Chin, Ryan Poppe, Vanessa Sarria, Morgan Finlayson, Jakob Lucas, Meg Parker, Nancy Cardenas, Zachary Price, and Charles Greene-Cramer.

Our office also profited from some very successful private sector professionals who took leave to come into or assist in the mayor's office, bringing special expertise for little or no pay. Their time, focus, and effort were gifts to the community: James Russell, Ashton Cumberbatch,

Kirk Rudy, Sherri Greenberg, Joene Grissom, Laura Hernandez, Kerry Tate, Josh Baer, Steven Tomlinson, Josh Jones-Dilworth, and Eugene Sepulveda. Among many other contributions, the latter two joined me for dinners, sometimes as often as bi-weekly, to help me think through what was going on in the city, my office, and my life.

I want to recognize and thank, on behalf of my family, the quiet and mostly unseen work of the members of the executive protection unit of the Austin Police Department, who made sure I was able to focus and safely serve. Because one or more of them was always with me, I spent more time with these guys than anyone else over my eight years of public service: the detail leader, Paul Kaderli, as well as Chris Hanratty, Geoff Sumner, Issa Kafena, Louie Carmona, Wes Martin, West Williams, and Ryan Rawlins.

Thanks to Frank Spring, a beautiful writer and trusted advisor, who helped me communicate while I was mayor and who provided the initial crafting assistance for this book and helped me see the effort over time that would be required.

Thanks to Peter Golenbock, a prolific and best-selling author, who joined to teach me how to take a manuscript and turn it into a book that could present the policy explanations and nuances the wonk in me wanted to share and in a way that might entertain and be enjoyed by more than just my family and friends.

Finally, much appreciation to the people of Austin who entrusted me with the office of mayor and gifted me an incredibly wonderful opportunity and experience. To this day, there are few moments as gratifying as being somewhere in town and having someone I have never met reach out to shake my hand.

ABOUT THE AUTHOR

Photo by Lindsey Thorne

STEVE ADLER served as the fifty-second mayor of Austin, Texas, from 2015 to 2023, leading one of the nation's fastest-growing cities through explosive change and extraordinary challenge—a serial bombing, the COVID-19 pandemic, historic protests over police violence, and growth that transformed Austin into a major technology hub.

As mayor, Adler navigated the tensions of governing a rapidly growing progressive city within a conservative state, expanding affordable housing initiatives, reforming homelessness policy, and implementing police accountability measures while managing infrastructure investment and explosive population growth.

Before his election as mayor, Adler practiced law for more than three decades, specializing in eminent domain and civil rights litigation, representing clients before both the United States Supreme Court and the Texas Supreme Court. A graduate of Princeton University and the University of Texas School of Law, Adler now teaches at the LBJ School of Public Affairs at the University of Texas, Huston-Tillotson University, and St. Edward's University. He lives in Austin with his wife Diane.